D1567262

Making Ecopreneurs

Corporate Social Responsibility Series

Series Editors:
Professor Güler Aras, Yildiz Technical University, Istanbul, Turkey
Professor David Crowther, DeMontfort University, Leicester, UK

Presenting applied research from an academic perspective on all aspects of corporate social responsibility, this global interdisciplinary series includes books for all those with an interest in ethics and governance, corporate behaviour and citizenship, regulation, protest, globalization, responsible marketing, social reporting and sustainability.

Titles in this series

Creating Food Futures
Trade, Ethics and the Environment
Cathy Rozel Farnworth, Janice Jiggins and Emyr Vaughan Thomas
ISBN: 978-0-7546-4907-6

Spirituality and Corporate Social Responsibility
Interpenetrating Worlds
David Bubna-Litic
ISBN: 978-0-7546-4763-8

Global Perspectives on Corporate Governance and CSR
Güler Aras and David Crowther
ISBN: 978-0-566-08830-8

The Gower Handbook of Corporate Governance and Social Responsibility
Güler Aras and David Crowther
ISBN: 978-0-566-08817-9

Corruption in International Business
Sharon Eicher
ISBN: 978-0-7546-7137-4

Wealth, Welfare and the Global Free Market
I. Ozer Ertuna
ISBN: 978-0-566-08905-3

Making Ecopreneurs

Developing Sustainable Entrepreneurship

Second Edition

Edited by

MICHAEL SCHAPER
Adjunct Professor, Curtin University Business School,
Western Australia

GOWER

Gower Applied Business Research
Our programme provides leaders, practitioners, scholars and researchers with thought provoking, cutting edge books that combine conceptual insights, interdisciplinary rigour and practical relevance in key areas of business and management.

Published by
Gower Publishing Limited
Wey Court East
Union Road
Farnham
Surrey, GU9 7PT
England

Ashgate Publishing Company
Suite 420
101 Cherry Street
Burlington,
VT 05401-4405
USA

www.gowerpublishing.com

British Library Cataloguing in Publication Data
Making ecopreneurs : developing sustainable
   entrepreneurship. -- 2nd ed. -- (Corporate social
   responsibility series)
   1. Entrepreneurship. 2. Sustainable development. 3. Social
   responsibility of business--Case studies.
   I. Series II. Schaper, Michael, professor.
   658.4'083-dc22

   ISBN: 978-0-566-08875-9 (hbk)
         978-1-4094-0123-0 (ebk)

Library of Congress Cataloging-in-Publication Data
Making ecopreneurs : developing sustainable entrepreneurship / [edited] by Michael Schaper.
      p. cm. -- (Corporate social responsibility)
   Rev. ed. of: Making ecopreneurs : developing sustainable entrepreneurship. 2005
   Includes index.
   ISBN 978-0-566-08875-9 (hbk.) -- ISBN 978-1-4094-0123-0 (ebook)
   1. Sustainable development. 2. Entrepreneurship. 3. Environmental ethics. I. Schaper, Michael, professor.
   HC79.E5M34 2010
   658.4'083--dc22

                                                                                2010001401

Printed and bound in Great Britain by
MPG Books Group, UK

Contents

List of Figures

List of Tables

List of Contributors

Anne de Bruin is Professor of Economics in the School of Economics and Finance (Albany) at Massey University, New Zealand. Her research interests are entrepreneurship, sustainable employment and regional development. In entrepreneurship, she is particularly interested in new conceptualizations of entrepreneurship, entrepreneurship in the creative industries and women entrepreneurs. She has numerous refereed articles published, including recent articles in *Entrepreneurship Theory* & Practice. She is currently working on two co-edited books: on women's entrepreneurship in association with the Diana International Project, and on entrepreneurship in the creative industries. Contact: A.M.DeBruin@massey.ac.nz

Chris Cocklin is Deputy Vice-Chancellor (Research and Innovation) at James Cook University, Australia. His interests in business and the environment include corporate environmental strategy, the role of the finance sector in promoting good governance in relation to the environment and sustainability, and the challenges for SMEs in responding to environment and sustainability agendas. Professor Cocklin played a key role in establishing a partnership between Monash University and BT Investments in the area of socially responsible investment. Contact: chris.cocklin@jcu.edu.au

Jürgen Freimann is Professor of Management Science, with a focus on corporate sustainability management, and head of the corporate sustainability management research group within the Department of Economics and Management, University of Kassel, Germany. He is also the author of numerous publications (written in both German and English) in the fields of general management, research methodology and sustainability management. Contact: freimann@wirtschaft.uni-kassel.de

Karen Greig received her BA in Business Studies, and her postgraduate certificate in education and MSc in Business from Manchester Metropolitan University. Karen teaches on a range of business and environment related subjects at Manchester Metropolitan University Business School. Prior to entering academia, she worked for 20 years in software design and development. Her current research focus is environmental disclosure and green entrepreneurs. Contact: k.greig@mmu.ac.uk

David Holloway is a senior lecturer in accounting in the Murdoch Business School at Murdoch University in Western Australia. He teaches across both undergraduate and postgraduate units in accounting and corporate governance. His research interests focus on internal and corporate governance, leadership and organizational decision-making from a critical theory perspective. Contact: d.holloway@murdoch.edu.au

Robert Isaak is Guest Professor of Entrepreneurship and International Management at the University of Mannheim, Germany and Henry George Professor of International Management at the Lubin School of Business, Pace University, New York. He is the author of ten books, including *Green Logic: Ecopreneurship, Theory and Ethics* (Greenleaf, 1998) and, most recently, *The Globalization Gap* (FT Press, 2004). Dr Isaak has consulted for global enterprises, including Siemens, Technicon, Prudential Intercultural and Global Intercultural, and has taught at the University of Heidelberg, CERAM European Graduate School of Management at Sophia Antipolis, Franklin College in Lugano and The John Hopkins School of International Studies in Bologna. Contact: risaak@gmail.com

Kumba Jallow, formerly known as Leigh Holland, is a principal lecturer in the Department of Accounting and Finance at De Montfort University, Leicester, UK. She teaches on a range of undergraduate and postgraduate courses in accounting and environmental management. Her research interests include corporate social responsibility and CSR reporting in large organizations, environmental management and ecological footprinting in smaller businesses, and community development. She also leads the Accounting for Sustainability research group and edits the *Journal of Applied Accounting Research.* Contact: lhacc@dmu.ac.uk

Jill A. Kammermeyer PhD has professional experience in business and academia in both North America and Europe. She has served on numerous non-profit boards and is currently on the board of Sustainable Harvest International. Her research interests include entrepreneurship, sustainability, quantitative models of decision-making and ethical issues in decision-making. Contact: kammerhoch@islc.net

Gabrielle Kruks-Wisner is a PhD candidate in Political Science at the Massachusetts Institute of Technology, Cambridge, Massachusetts, USA. She received her Bachelor's degree from Swarthmore College, Pennsylvania and her Masters in City Planning from the Department of Urban Studies and

Planning at MIT. She has worked with a number of development and human rights NGOs, carrying out field research in Nicaragua, Mexico, Mozambique and India. Her research interests lie in the political economy of development, with a particular focus on state–civil society relations, local governance, and the provision of public goods and services. Contact: gkw@mit.edu

Kate Lewis PhD is a senior lecturer in the School of Management and a Research Associate of the New Zealand Centre for Small and Medium Enterprise Research at the Wellington campus of Massey University, New Zealand. Her research interests include green entrepreneurs and environmental management practices in small and medium-sized enterprises. Contact: k.v.lewis@massey. ac.nz

Dr Lassi Linnanen is Professor of Environmental Economics and Management at Lappeenranta University of Technology's Laboratory of Environmental Technology and Management in Finland. Before joining academia in 2000, he was CEO and co-founder of Gaia Group Ltd, a leading Finnish energy and environmental management consultancy. His main research interests include corporate responsibility strategies, greenhouse gas-reduction technology commercialization and system innovations for sustainable development. Contact: Lassi.Linnanen@lut.fi

Sandra Marxen studied economic geography at the University of Osnabruck, Germany, obtaining her degree. She worked as a research assistant with the research group on corporate sustainability management at the University of Kassel.

Jim Macbeth is Dean of the School of Social Sciences and Humanities at Murdoch University in Western Australia. Jim has been undertaking research in tourism social sciences since the mid-1990s and has published numerous reports and papers from tourism projects over that time. His particular interests are the ways in which tourism development can contribute to regional sustainable development on the one hand, and the experience of travellers in the 'outback' or on the ocean, on the other. Contact: j.macbeth@murdoch.edu.au

Yamini Narayanan is a lecturer in Politics and Development Studies at La Trobe University, Melbourne. Her research interests include religion and sustainability, gender and development, and sustainable tourism. Contact: y.narayanan@latrobe.edu.au

Margaret J. Naumes PhD is a senior lecturer in Management at the University of New Hampshire, USA. She has lectured and led workshops on case writing throughout the USA and in Europe and Asia. Her research interests include social entrepreneurship (particularly among female managers) and cross-cultural studies of managerial values. Contact: margaret.naumes@unh.edu

Anastasia O'Rourke is the co-founder of Big Room Inc, a VC-backed firm that is applying for a new ".eco" top-level domain on the Internet (www.doteco. info). She has a PhD from Yale University, with a dissertation on the growth of cleantech in venture capital markets and has written several reports on cleantech venture capital for the Cleantech Venture Network (USA), Silicon Valley Bank (USA), Cleantech Ventures (Australia) and The Carbon Trust (UK). Previously she has worked at INSEAD France, the Institute for Sustainable Futures at the University of Technology, Sydney, and the EcoDesign Foundation, Sydney. Anastasia has an MSc from the International Institute for Industrial Environmental Economics at Lund University, Sweden and a BA with first-class Honours and University Medal from Sydney University, Australia. Contact: anastasia.orourke@aya.yale.edu; website: www.bigroom.ca

Bradley D. Parrish PhD was, until recently, a lecturer in Environmental Social Science at the Sustainability Research Institute, School of Earth and Environment, University of Leeds, UK where he is now a Visiting Research Fellow. His research and work on the policy and implementation of environment and development programmes has spanned four continents, including North America, Europe, East Africa and Asia-Pacific regions. Over the past six years he has co-designed and delivered courses on sustainability entrepreneurship and organizational change management for sustainability, and has been invited to deliver workshops to educators, practitioners and policy-makers on entrepreneurial approaches to sustainable development. In July 2007 he co-organized the First World Symposium on Sustainability Entrepreneurship and recently co-founded the Onesa Institute International, which works to translate these advances in research and theory into practical applications. Contact: b.parrish@see.leeds.ac.uk Website: www.onesa.org

Astad Pastakia has a Fellowship in Management from the Indian Institute of Management, Ahmedabad, and is a freelance consultant in the field of environment and natural resource management. His paper 'Grassroots Ecopreneurs: Change Agents for a Sustainable Society', was adjudged Outstanding Paper in the *Journal of Organizational Change Management* (1998). He has edited the book *Locked Horns: Conflicts and their Resolution in Community*

Based Natural Resource Management (Books for Change, 2008) and is author (with two others) of *Farmer-led Participatory Research: Cases from Western India* (Books for Change, 2002). Contact: astadp@gmail.com

Holger Petersen is Senior Education Manager for MBA Sustainability Management at the Centre for Sustainability Management (CSM), Leuphana University, Lüneburg, Germany. Between 2003 and 2008 he worked at the leading green bank in Germany, the UmweltBank AG in Nürnberg, Germany as an investment consultant, specializing in ecological funds and stocks. Between 1999 and 2002 he worked as a research assistant to Professor Stefan Schaltegger at the University of Lüneburg. His PhD was on the subject of ecopreneurship and strategic management. Together with Stefan Schaltegger, Holger has written course books on corporate environmental management. At the University of Lüneburg he was an initiator of the first MBA programme on sustainability management and ecopreneurship. Contact: holpetersen@uni.leuphana.de

Stefan Schaltegger is Professor of Management and Business Economics at Leuphana University of Lüneburg, Germany, head of MBA Sustainability Management and head of the Centre for Sustainability Management (CSM). He received the environmental award of the German Association of Environmentally Oriented Companies in 2007. His research areas include corporate environmental management, environmental accounting, value-based environmental management, sustainable finance and sustainable entrepreneurship. Contact: schaltegger@uni.leuphana.de

Michael Schaper is full-time Deputy Chairperson of the Australian Competition and Consumer Commission and is also an Adjunct Professor with the Curtin Business School, Curtin University of Technology in Western Australia. He has a wide background in business, academia and public policy. Previously he was Dean of Murdoch University Business School and, prior to this, served as Small Business Commissioner for the Australian Capital Territory. A former president of the Small Enterprise Association of Australia and New Zealand, Michael has been a member of the board of directors of the International Council for Small Business. Between 2003 and 2005 he held the foundation professorial chair in Entrepreneurship and Small Business within the University of Newcastle, Australia. Before his academic career, Michael worked for several years as a professional small business adviser in Australia, ran his own business and was involved in a numerous other start-up projects. He also spent several years working as a ministerial adviser at the state and federal level. Contact: michael.schaper@gmail.com

Hildegard Schick worked as research assistant with the research group on corporate environmental management at the University of Kassel, Germany, from 2000 to 2004. Prior to this, her work experience was in further education and vocational training. She is now a teacher. Contact: HilleSchick@yahoo.de

Elya Tagar is Director of Global HIV Financing with the Clinton Health Access Initiative (CHAI), based in New York. He was previously Country Director for CHAI in the Democratic Republic of the Congo, and Regional Manager in West Africa, based out of Dakar, Senegal. Elya's interest focuses on the role of the private sector in sustainable development. His was formerly a Senior Associate with McKinsey and Company in New York and his experience includes work with the UN Global Compact in New York, with Social Accountability International in New York and Vietnam, and with the Sustainable Agriculture Network in Latin America. The research on which his chapter is based was carried out while Elya was employed at the Monash Environment Institute in Melbourne, Australia, and is related to his role as the chair of the BP-based Business and the Environment (BATE) network. Contact: elya.tagar@clintonfoundation.org or elya.tagar@gmail.com

David Taylor received his BSc in Business from Manchester Metropolitan University, his postgraduate certificate in education from Bolton University and his MSc in Human Resource Management from Salford University. David works on enterprise initiatives in the Manchester Metropolitan University Business School and is particularly interested in employability and the promotion of self-employment as a career option for graduates. David has published in the areas of transition in Eastern Europe, green entrepreneurs, entrepreneurial networks and enterprise education. His main research interest is the role of personal networks in the learning and decision-making processes of the entrepreneur and the role of enterprise education in the creation of graduate employability. David has worked for over ten years in small businesses in the advertising industry. Contact: d.w.taylor@mmu.ac.uk

Fiona Tilley joined the School of Earth and Environment at the University of Leeds, UK in 2002 and left in 2009. She was a member of the Sustainability Research Institute within the School. She was the programme manager for the BA in Environment and Business and taught on a range of environmental social science subjects. Her most recent research has been in the field of sustainability entrepreneurship on which she has published widely. In July 2007 she co-hosted the First World Symposium on Sustainability Entrepreneurship. For further information on this and other projects and publications in this area go to www.onesa.org or email Fiona at fiona.tilley@virgin.net.

Liz Walley joined what is now Manchester Metropolitan University Business School (MMUBS) in 1992 and is a member of the Strategy, Entrepreneurship and International Business Division. Over recent years she has championed the 'greening of the curriculum' within the Business School, introducing and developing various undergraduate and postgraduate units in business and sustainability. Prior to MMU, her 15 years' work experience was in consultancy, banking and industry. Liz's first degree was in Economics and Statistics from York University, and she later gained an MBA from Manchester Business School. She has published in the areas of environmental management and transition in Eastern Europe. Liz's current research focus is organizational greening and, specifically, the role of environmental champions and green entrepreneurs. Contact: l.walley@mmu.ac.uk

Introduction
Michael Schaper

This second edition of *Making Ecopreneurs* provides readers with a better understanding of the entrepreneurial perspective in the sustainability debate. It has been revised and updated to reflect changes in this fast-evolving field, and draws on the work of many different businesspeople, writers and researchers from around the world.

The business case for sustainable development and the greening of industry is based on many different arguments, but one area that has been frequently overlooked is the entrepreneurial perspective. The shift to more sustainable, 'green' business practices poses not only challenges, but also many potential opportunities for the business operators and firms that are prepared to be innovative, adopt different business models, take some risks, and approach this area as a viable commercial prospect rather than a threat.

This book gives readers a snapshot of the current level of understanding of this topic. It seeks to analyse and explain the behaviour and world-view of ecopreneurs, to pass on the lessons and advice that they can give other prospective business venturers, and assess the macro-level frameworks that can help or hinder green entrepreneurship.

This book is accordingly divided into three broad segments: concepts, context and conditions, and case studies.

Part One examines in some detail the conceptual models and classification frameworks used in this field of study. In the very first chapter, I attempt to provide readers with an overview of the field, by helping to define what is really meant by the term 'ecopreneur', the characteristics of entrepreneurs and entrepreneurial firms, and the typical features of ecopreneurship. I then give a brief history of research work in the field to date and an agenda for future development of the area. A similar approach is taken by Bradley Parrish and Fiona Tilley, who chart the emergence of the field in greater detail. One of the early theorists in the area, Robert Isaak, then examines the different types of green entrepreneurs that exist and the micro- and macro-level policy structures which might facilitate the

growth of more green entrepreneurs in future. The next two chapters – one by
Liz Walley, David Taylor and Karen Greig, and the other by Stefan Schaltegger –
attempt to examine green entrepreneurship at a broad level. The authors suggest
models which can be used to help define, categorize and explain the notion of
ecopreneurship in a generic sense. This work will, it is hoped, help pave the
way for future development of conceptual models that can be used to describe,
understand and analyse the behaviour of green entrepreneurs. Anne de Bruin
and Kate Lewis then delve into another frequently overlooked area – that of
microbusinesses, the very smallest enterprises that actually make up the bulk of
the world's new and small business ventures – and suggest a descriptive model
of their behaviour in regard to sustainability and environmental performance.
Finally, Lassi Linnanen provides some personal reflections on environmental
entrepreneurship in Finland, based on a combination of both personal experience
and research. From this background he also suggests a framework that helps
explain different types of ecopreneurial activity.

In Part Two the conditions and frameworks in which ecopreneurship works
are analysed in detail. In this section, we look at the factors that promote and
hinder environmental entrepreneurship, as well as some of the characteristics
that typify actual ecopreneurs and their firms. Astad Pastakia looks at some
of the preconditions needed to foster ecopreneurship in a developing country
(in this case, India) and explains how these can be analysed and assessed. This
chapter will be of particular interest to regulators and policy-makers seeking
to compare and promote greener, more entrepreneurial firms in different
countries and regions. Next, Jürgen Freimann, Sandra Marxen and Hildegaard
Schick discuss, on the basis of their own research in Germany, how new
entrepreneurs who are currently in the process of creating and launching new
business ventures can be encouraged to adopt a more sustainable perspective.
Anastasia O'Rourke then critically analyses the role of the venture capital
industry in promoting – and sometimes inhibiting – the creation and growth of
green firms in developed economies. In the next chapter Elya Tagar and Chris
Cocklin look at the effectiveness of networking and the development of industry
clusters as a tool to promote sustainability. David Holloway then examines the
importance of internal decision-making processes within the firm as a tool to
promote ecopreneurship. Finally, Holger Petersen reports on a survey into
strategic marketing tools and competitive strategies used by entrepreneurial
green firms in Germany, Switzerland and Austria.

Part Three of the book concludes with a number of case studies that highlight
environmental entrepreneurship in action. These have been drawn from a wide

variety of different countries and business models, and help show just how varied green entrepreneurship can be. The first chapter, by Jim MacBeth and Yamini Narayanan, examines a small Australian outback tourism venture. The next two cases, one by Gabrielle Kruks-Wisner and the other by Margaret J. Naumes and Jill A. Kammermeyer, look at ecopreneurship in the non-profit sector. Both of these cases show how social entrepreneurs can establish and grow sustainable conservation projects that deliver environmental, social and financial returns for local communities. Finally, a North American firm focusing on energy and carbon offsets is examined by Bradley Parrish, and Kumba Jallow looks at the creation of a recycling micro-business venture in the United Kingdom.

As this collection shows, ecopreneurship is an exciting area to be involved in. At its best, entrepreneurship is about harnessing the enthusiasm, initiative and creative energy of individuals. When this dynamism is applied to developing business solutions that help move enterprise into more sustainable pathways, then the results have the potential to be truly fascinating – and rewarding. I hope you enjoy reading this book.

Finally, a brief note of thanks. The preparation of any book also relies on many other people apart from the editor and individual contributors. During the preparation of both this and the first edition of *Making Ecopreneurs*, I have been grateful for the practical help provided by Walter Wehrmeyer (editor of the journal *Greener Management International*, who originally commissioned a special edition on this topic, out of which the current book has grown), Rene van Berkel (United Nations Industrial Development Organization), Joel Mendelson (Coastal Business Centre, Western Australia) and my research assistants, Rhoda Kiptanui and Anne Croft, for their help in this project.

PART ONE
Concepts

1

Understanding the Green Entrepreneur

Michael Schaper

ABSTRACT

This introductory chapter provides an overview of the phenomenon of 'environmental entrepreneurship'. It examines the key characteristics of entrepreneurs and entrepreneurial firms, and the link with sustainability and environmental responsibility. Ecopreneurship is a relatively new field of academic inquiry and study, and, although some work on the phenomena began in the 1970s, it was not until the 1990s that the topic began to receive much attention. Today there are still many areas in which more understanding of ecopreneurship and individual green entrepreneurs is needed. Current issues that require greater investigation include the development of an accurate and widely acceptable definition of the concept; profiling and identifying 'typical' characteristics of green entrepreneurs and the industries they occur in; identifying the factors that act as barriers and triggers to environmental entrepreneurship; the development of a body of research-based case studies and quantitative studies; and understanding policies which can be used to encourage a greater level of ecopreneurship. Difficulties in researching and understanding ecopreneurs include the problem of developing effective operational definitions of the concept, the choice between emphasizing qualitative or quantitative research approaches, and the fact that most studies only examine business ventures already in action, thus omitting both nascent green entrepreneurs and terminated ventures.

Introduction

What role do entrepreneurial individuals and firms have to play in the adoption of more sustainable business practices?

As the first decade of the twenty-first century draws to a close, increasing concern about the environment is providing one of the biggest new global markets – a phenomenon that has been referred to as a 'cleantech boom' (Warren 2007), and which some suggest may ultimately be more enduring than the dot.com boom that preceded it. This development has been driven by the recognition that business has a key role to play in combating issues like climate change, since the traditional response of many environmentalists and governments (namely, to encourage behavioural and attitudinal change amongst the general population) is not enough in itself to ultimately produce desired environmental outcomes. Market-based solutions are a critical component in the drive to sustainability, and in turn have led to a marked growth in the number of new, supposedly green, firms.

This marks a new phase for researchers and policy-makers seeking to understand the nature of 'green' business practices. Traditionally, environmental business management has focused on how and why existing firms can become greener. It has spent a substantial amount of time and effort examining the tools that can be used to make firms more sustainable and environmentally responsible; attempting to classify and categorize the responses of existing firms to the environmental and sustainability agendas; and identifying the barriers and triggers that can be used to make firms 'go green'.

However, there is now a growing recognition of the equal importance of issues such as: the links between sustainability and innovation; the role of small and medium-sized enterprises; the importance of sustainability in strategic business development; the emergent significance of green consumer demands on firms; sustainable practices in particular industries; and how firms can utilize the opportunities that market-based environmental policies (such as 'cap and trade' limits on water usage, or greenhouse gas emissions) provide.

The emerging consensus suggests that green perspectives can often provide the foundation for the creation and growth of viable, commercially successful business ventures. Individuals and organizations that take the time to understand sustainability issues, study the emergent trends and develop a feasible business idea can create successful niches for themselves. Indeed, this has often been a foundation stone of the business case for sustainable development: green businesses are successful ones.

Yet, curiously, until now much of this argument has overlooked one critical element – the entrepreneur. This person is the linchpin in the creation, development and growth of a successful business venture, and ultimately also serves as a role model from which new ideas are subsequently disseminated into the wider business community. New business opportunities bring both risks and rewards. So-called 'ecopreneurial' solutions can provide long-term, high-level rewards for successful proponents, but by their nature they are somewhat speculative and risky – there is no guarantee of success, or even of sufficient market demand – and they require entrepreneurs willing to take on such risks. It is now time to pay more attention to the role that entrepreneurs can play in the move towards a more sustainable economic and commercial system.

This introductory chapter provides an overview of the phenomenon of 'environmental entrepreneurship'. It begins by explaining the key characteristics of entrepreneurs and entrepreneurial firms, before examining the link with sustainability and environmental responsibility. It then gives a brief history of research work in the field to date, before examining the current understanding of what really is meant by the term 'ecopreneur' and its typical features. It concludes by outlining some of the areas in which further knowledge about ecopreneurship is still required, and some of the problems involved in researching this topic.

What is an Entrepreneur?

As has sometimes been remarked, an entrepreneur is easy to recognize and hard to define. In general, entrepreneurs are individuals who conceive new business opportunities and take on the risks required to convert those ideas into reality. They are people who are able to identify new commercial ventures (which often involves a willingness to 'look outside the box' and examine issues in fundamentally different ways to more conventional approaches), incubate ideas and champion their adoption, assemble the resources needed to bring the idea to commercial reality (such as money, people and technologies) and, finally, launch and grow the business venture.

Like a number of other management concepts, entrepreneurship is easy to conceptualize but hard to explain. Developing a precise form of words which clearly states what entrepreneurship is has led to numerous semantic and philosophical arguments, although in a practical sense most people know entrepreneurship when they see it in action, even if they cannot define such behaviour. For example, the person who takes a new business idea, pours their energy and enthusiasm into making that vision a reality and then oversees the venture as it grows and develops is clearly an entrepreneur; on the other hand, a manager who simply takes a firm and ensures that it is run efficiently and effectively, day in and day out, demonstrates no entrepreneurial disposition.

In other words, entrepreneurship arises when enterprising individuals identify an unsolved problem, or an unmet need or want, which they then proceed to satisfy. In the process, they transform the existing status quo into a future opportunity and turn ideas into a commercial reality.

Entrepreneurs seek to bring about change and new opportunities, both for themselves and for the communities they belong to. They are often agents of what one of the early researchers in the field, Schumpeter (1934), labelled 'creative destruction': old ways of doing things are transformed, or overtaken, when enterprising individuals wreak change in business systems. In this way, entrepreneurs often play an important role as the engine of change in a market-based economy, since they are responsible for introducing innovation, adaptation and new ideas. Economies – and societies, for that matter – do not change simply because of an inevitable set of circumstances or trends; they can only transmute when there are people who individually set new directions, suggest new ways of doing and then successfully become role models.

Enterprising individuals can be found in all sectors of society, and today there are three broad recognizable types of entrepreneur. Traditionally, the concept of entrepreneurship has been closely aligned to that of small business management: the classic archetypical entrepreneur is often regarded as an individual who starts his or her own small business, which may eventually grow into a much larger and more successful corporation. But entrepreneurs can also be found within existing large corporations, where they help create new business divisions, products and changes to internal operations, and are known as corporate entrepreneurs or intrapreneurs (Pinchot 1985). Finally, there are also many social entrepreneurs working within non-profit organizations, who attempt to bring about innovations to resolve community problems (Ashoka Foundation 2003).

Whatever the milieu, successful entrepreneurship requires more than merely energy and money. It does not arise out of blind faith, enthusiasm or luck. These attributes are always welcome, but desire can only succeed when it is allied with organizational and business-building skills. For an idea to be successful, the entrepreneur must also undertake a cohesive process of planning, idea development, marshalling resources, sourcing finance, careful research, adopting creative and innovative techniques, and calculated risk-taking.

Entrepreneurship is not confined to any one particular industry, country or group of people. Enterprising behaviour can be found in all societies and in all types of economic circumstances. Indeed, whilst the term usually refers just to an individual, it is also possible to find whole organizations that can also be classified as entrepreneurial in the way they do business and seek to grow.

Sustainability, Greening and Entrepreneurship

The adoption of environmentally responsible business practices can conceivably open up an additional range of opportunities for entrepreneurs. The move to a sustainable business framework provides numerous niches which enterprising individuals and firms can successfully identify and service. These include the development of new products and services, improving the efficiency of existing firms, new methods of marketing; reconfiguring existing business models and practices and so forth.

But green entrepreneurship is not only important because it provides new opportunities for the nimble first-movers who identify and exploit such opportunities. Ecopreneurship matters because it also has the potential to be a major force in the overall transition to a more sustainable business paradigm. In a market-based economy, entrepreneurs play a critical role in the eventual adoption of green business practices by the wider business community, because of the leading role which they provide to other firms. In many market-based economies, entrepreneurs are often lauded as exemplars and heroes: their success helps give guidance and motivation to other practising and aspiring businesspeople. By demonstrating the economic benefits which come from being greener, ecopreneurs act as a 'pull' factor that entices other firms to proactively go green, as opposed to the 'push' factors of government regulation, risk minimization factors and stakeholder or lobby group pressure.

The Evolution of Environmental Entrepreneurship

As management disciplines, both entrepreneurship and environmental business management are comparatively new concepts. Although there is now a relatively large body of established research into the phenomenon of entrepreneurship, the field itself has only been widely recognized as a meaningful discipline since about the 1980s. Before this, study of the topic was largely confined to a small number of institutions and researchers. Today, however, most business schools and most members of the business community are familiar with the concept and accept the importance of fostering enterprising behaviour within a commercial context.

The greening of management is also a relatively new phenomenon, albeit less well known, less researched and less understood than entrepreneurship. To date, most written material in the field of greener management has dealt with the greening of existing business organizations. However, a number of authors have argued that greening and sustainability could also provide the basis for substantial new business opportunities. In the early 1970s *Harvard Business Review* published a pioneering article arguing that the 'ecology movement' could provide profitable new markets for business expansion, rather than simply being a drain on economic activity (Quinn 1971). By the late 1980s this theme had started to become more prominent.

Elkington and Burke (1989), for example, argued that innovative business solutions could be used not only to improve the environment, but also to provide the basis for new business prospects overlooked by mainstream firms. In the early 1990s a more explicit examination of environmental entrepreneurship began to emerge, with authors such as Bennett (1991), Berle (1991), and Blue (1990), who began to employ the terms 'environmental entrepreneur', 'green entrepreneur', 'eco-entrepreneur' and its derivation 'ecopreneur'. After a hiatus during the mid-1990s the concept has been examined more recently by Anderson and Leal (1997), Isaak (1998), Andersen (1998), Keogh and Polonsky (1998), Hostager, Neil, Decker and Lorentz (1998), Adeoti (2000), Larson (2000) and Kyrö (2001), amongst others. A more recent addition has been the work of Walley and Taylor (2002), Schaltegger (2002), Pastakia (2002), Seelos and Mair (2005), Cohen and Winn (2007), Dean and McMullen (2007), Dixon and Clifford (2007) and others (for more details, see Schaper 2002a).[1]

As these papers – plus the current book – indicate, there is now a small but growing body of written literature on the topic of ecopreneurship. This interest has also begun to spillover into the broader entrepreneurship discipline (Schaper 2002b), with the role of environmental issues and sustainability now slowly starting to be incorporated into some conventional texts on entrepreneurship (for examples, see Kuratko and Hodgetts 2002; Kao, Kao and Kao 2002).

---

1   These papers, all published in a special edition of the journal *Greener Management International* (Number 38, Summer 2002), are amongst those included in the current book.

Apart from written publications, there have also been a number of recent initiatives designed to foster and promote ecopreneurship. Within academia, a number of tertiary institutions have now introduced units in environmental entrepreneurship, and at least one European university has endowed a chair in sustainable entrepreneurship. For practising entrepreneurs in business, a number of micro-finance and business funding schemes have been introduced to provide start-up and growth capital for green enterprises. There are now also specialist business incubator centres for new firms with a sustainability orientation, schemes to make entrepreneur advisory services greener, and a new focus by many non-profit organizations on fostering entrepreneurial business ventures that meet key sustainability criteria.

Current Understandings about Ecopreneurship

The end result of this work is that there is an emerging recognition today that green entrepreneurs exist, that they have the potential to play a substantial role in the development of a more sustainable economic and commercial system, and that there are certain steps which can be taken to facilitate their work.

Different writers have also used differing terms to describe this phenomenon. Some of the more common phrases currently in parlance include 'ecopreneurship', 'eco-entrepreneurship', 'green entrepreneurship' and 'environmental entrepreneurship'. In this chapter, and throughout much of the rest of the book, readers will note that the terms have been used interchangeably. Likewise, the concepts of 'sustainable development' and 'environmental responsibility', although not strictly synonymous, have also been employed as substitutes for each other.

Clearly there are some characteristics shared by all ecopreneurial activity. First, it is entrepreneurial in some way, shape or form. All green entrepreneurs undertake business ventures which involve a measure of risk, whose outcomes are never predictable and for which the possibility of failure is always present. And, like other entrepreneurs, they must also identify a feasible business opportunity, research it, harness resources to turn the idea into reality, develop and execute a plan for business development, and oversee its growth.

A second feature common to all ecopreneurs is that their commercial activities have an overall positive effect on the natural environment and the move towards a more sustainable future. It may be that all of their business is structured and operated in such a way that every component has a neutral or positive impact on the environment; but just as plausibly, it might be that some aspects are green, whereas others are still 'brown'. Indeed, since we live in an imperfect world, few business ventures are likely to be able to remain 100 per cent pure; there will almost always be some waste, pollutant or dirty resource use. On balance, however, the environmental entrepreneur creates and operates a project whose net environmental impact is positive.

A third factor that appears to be common to many environmental entrepreneurs is their intentionality. Their personal belief system – their set of values and aspirations – usually sees protection of the natural environment, and a desire to move on to a more sustainable future pathway, as important goals in themselves. Yet, as this book shows, this desire does not need to be paramount. Ecopreneurs vary dramatically in the significance they place on this goal. For some business venturers, such altruistic goals are more important than financial return or commercial viability; for others, it assumes equal ranking with traditional measures of economic and commercial success; and, for others still, it is only a secondary factor after business feasibility. But by including an aspect of intentionality, we can separate green entrepreneurs from 'accidental ecopreneurs' – business venturers whose firms operate in an environmentally friendly manner, but do so more as an unanticipated by-product of other business processes than because of a deliberate focus on this issue.

Beyond this, however, it becomes much harder to identify and define environmental entrepreneurship. Ecopreneurs do not fit a mould – they come in many different forms and engage in a wide variety of business activities – and thus far it has not been possible to identify a 'typical' profile. Only the entrepreneur's behaviour – their goals, what they actually do in their business and the outcomes they produce – can safely be used to set them apart.

Like mainstream entrepreneurship, it is also clear that green entrepreneurship cannot simply be conjured into existence on the whim of policy-makers. To come into being, successful ecopreneurship requires the presence of numerous favourable circumstances: an enterprising individual or small group of lead individuals, who take charge of the business venture project; the existence of a suitable market niche; access to suitable human resources; sufficient capital to fund start-up and venture growth; and access to appropriate business support and advice, either from the private sector or the public arena. Even this is not enough. The outcome of any entrepreneurial venture is never guaranteed. Business ventures do not automatically survive and flourish in the presence of a set mixture of ingredients. Circumstances, opportunities and the whim of the external market also play a role.

An Agenda for Future Development of this Area

With these comments in mind, it is clear that there is still much more that needs to be understood about ecopreneurship, from both a research and a practical perspective. Some of the important issues that remained to be examined can be broadly grouped into five categories, as discussed below.

WHAT CONSTITUTES A GREEN ENTREPRENEUR?

It has been suggested above that, up to this point, it has been difficult to establish a profile of the 'green' or environmentally responsible entrepreneur. However, this does not mean that the issue should not be investigated in more detail. How does one profile a 'green entrepreneur' – are there characteristics that set them apart from other entrepreneurs? Are particular groups of people, or industries, more likely to generate ecopreneurial ventures than others? Are women, for example, more likely to start a green venture than men? Are particular age cohorts more ecopreneurially inclined than others? Certain cultures? Do the models that various authors put forward in this book, which attempt to describe, classify and categorize ecopreneurs, have any practical utility?

A secondary issue is to compare green entrepreneurs with their more conventional counterparts. Do ecopreneurs tend to create business ventures that are more (or less) profitable than mainstream or 'dirty' ventures within the same industry? Are there differences in management styles, strategic orientation, growth patterns, and survival and failure rates?

For that matter, what is the most appropriate way to measure the performance and success of ecopreneurs? Should the major criteria be sustainability-based ones (such as social and environmental indicators), conventional existing measures of firm performance (such as financial indicators, market share and growth), or the 'added value' (benefit) which they provide to the broader society?

WHAT ARE THE BARRIERS AND TRIGGERS TO ENVIRONMENTAL ENTREPRENEURSHIP?

What factors serve as either a barrier or trigger to their activities? What are the forces and process that give rise to green entrepreneurship? How do individuals and firms identify opportunities, filter them and ultimately select a project to embark upon? A better understanding of these steps in the entrepreneurial process will also help us develop a better understanding of the practical measures that can be taken to foster eco-entrepreneurship in both nascent and existing firms.

LEARNING FROM EXAMPLES

Another rich source of knowledge which is yet to be comprehensively examined is the experiences, reflections and perspectives of those 'already in the game'. Ecopreneurs who have already started their own businesses have a body of experience which needs to be listened to. This store of knowledge is often overlooked, but it is firsthand and accumulated at the expense of much personal effort. What are the stories and experiences of past and present ecopreneurs (both successful and otherwise)? What lessons can be learnt from them, and how can this information be effectively disseminated to other current and would-be ecopreneurs?

SECTORAL AND INDUSTRY-SPECIFIC CONTEXT

Do some industries or markets lend themselves more easily to ecopreneurial ventures? It may well be that different commercial sectors are more – or less – receptive to green entrepreneurship than others. An obvious example is the emergence of regional and potentially global trading markets in greenhouse gas emissions, which is already acting as a spur to the formation of new business ventures involved in measuring, monitoring and verifying the trading process. In some nations, markets have also begun to emerge in areas such as water-usage rights, or in the breeding and conservation of native wildlife species. Some established industries (such as tourism) also seem disposed to encourage eco-friendly ventures. However, other industry sectors have remained resistant to the adoption of new, innovative sustainable business practices. What industries are these, and why are some sectors more inclined than others to give birth to ecopreneurial firms?

POLICIES TO FOSTER ECOPRENEURSHIP

Legislation, government regulation and industry support agencies all have a role in shaping the way in which business conducts its activities. The regulatory framework that governments impose on business operators can have a substantial effect on their ultimate ability to succeed in the marketplace (Warren 2007). So, too, can the financial inducements (such as government subsidies and tax concessions) that are made available to green entrepreneurs. Their impact and effectiveness needs to be comprehensively evaluated and assessed. Other stakeholders, such as lobby groups, NGOs, venture capitalists, industry associations and local communities can also influence the context in which ecopreneurs operate. How can the activities of these bodies be encouraged to foster environmental entrepreneurs? What policy frameworks can promote a greener perspective in both existing and nascent entrepreneurs? What strategies have already been shown to work, and what other prospective tools might also be helpful?

The Research Challenge in Ecopreneurship

Before embarking on these voyages of inquiry, it must be borne in mind that conducting research into this field is often problematic. The discipline of entrepreneurship has some features which can, on occasion, make it difficult to critically study and analyse.

As has been discussed, ecopreneurship is an extremely complicated phenomenon to define, which makes it difficult to identify and measure green entrepreneurship. And what is the correct unit of analysis – the individual entrepreneur or the business venture that he or she operates? An extra complication is also introduced by the existence of social entrepreneurs who undertake enterprising activities in the non-profit field. Many of these have an avowed green perspective; should they be evaluated in the same way as their private-sector counterparts?

There is also a broader ontological issue that is often overlooked in entrepreneurship research. Is entrepreneurship a relatively universal phenomenon that lends itself to quantitative analysis, in the hope that such study can uncover relatively broad-ranging laws that govern the entrepreneurial process? Or, alternatively, is each venture unique in its own way, driven by an individual whose motivations, background, abilities and activities are different to those of the next person? If so, only qualitative research can shed light on what they do and how they do it, and it may be well-nigh impossible to generalize such findings into the broader business community.

Finally, most entrepreneurship research tends to concentrate on business ventures in action. It overlooks the role of the entrepreneur prior to start-up (so-called 'nascent' entrepreneurs), because such individuals can be hard to identify and locate before the business is registered and trading. It is often not possible to evaluate nascent ecopreneurs during the critical formative period

– the point at which their motivations for starting the business, identifying and evaluating green business opportunities, and developing a business model are usually cemented. At the other end of the entrepreneurial timeframe, research also tends to suffer from 'survivor bias' – it is easier to track and analyse firms that grow and succeed, rather than those that fail. This can lead to skewed results, in which the stories and accomplishments of the winners have greater significance than those of the losers – even though the latter may be more important in identifying barriers to successful business venture formation.

Conclusion

Like its mainstream cousin of entrepreneurship, ecopreneurship can be a complex issue to fully understand and manage. It takes many forms, flourishes under many different conditions and can often emerge under the most unlikely and least predictable circumstances. It is also difficult to accurately measure and research.

Despite these limitations, it is an increasingly important area of business activity. Understanding this phenomenon, and utilizing it to build a more sustainable future, is the common focus of the many various authors in this book, each of whom bring their own unique perspective to the study of this issue. Hopefully, this will provide a springboard from which others will also become motivated to work in this fascinating new field of business.

References

Adeoti, J.O. (2000) 'Small Enterprise Promotion and Sustainable Development: An Attempt at Integration', *Journal of Developmental Entrepreneurship*, Vol. 5, No. 1, pp. 57–71.

Andersen, A.R. (1998) 'Cultivating the Garden of Eden: Environmental Entrepreneuring', *Journal of Organizational Change Management*, Vol. 11, No. 2, pp. 135–144.

Anderson, T.L. and D.R. Leal (1997) *Enviro-Capitalists: Doing Good While Doing Well*, Rowman & Littlefield, Boston, MA.

Ashoka Foundation (2003) *What is a Social Entrepreneur?*, at: www.ashoka.org/fellows/social_entrepreneur.cfm (accessed 15 November 2005).

Bennett, S.J. (1991) *Ecopreneuring: The Complete Guide to Small Business Opportunities from the Environmental Revolution*, Wiley, New York.

Berle, G. (1991) *The Green Entrepreneur: Business Opportunities That Can Save the Earth and Make You Money* Liberty Hall Press, Blue Ridge Summit, PA.

Beveridge, R. and Guy, S. (2005) 'The Rise of the Eco-preneur and the Messy World of Environmental Innovation', *Local Environment*, Vol. 10, No. 6 (December), pp. 665–676.

Blue, J. (1990) *Ecopreneuring: Managing for Results*, Scott Foresman, London.

Cohen, B. and Winn, M.I. (2007) 'Market Imperfections, Opportunity and Sustainable Entrepreneurship', *Journal of Business Venturing*, Vol. 22 No. 1 (January), pp. 29-49.

Dean, T.J. and McMullen, J.S. (2007) 'Toward a Theory of Sustainable Entrepreneurship: Reducing Environmental Degradation through Entrepreneurial Action', *Journal of Business Venturing*, Vol. 22, No. 1 (January), pp. 50–76.

Dixon, S.E.A. and Clifford, A. (2007) 'Ecopreneurship – A New Approach to Managing the Triple Bottom Line', *Journal of Organizational Change Management*, Vol. 20, No. 3, pp. 326–345.

Elkington, J. and Burke, T. (1989) *The Green Capitalists*, Victor Gollancz, London.

Hostager, T.J., Neil, T.C., Decker, R.L. and Lorentz, R.D. (1998) 'Seeing Environmental Opportunities: Effects of Intrapreneurial Ability, Efficacy, Motivation and Desirability', *Journal of Organizational Change Management*, Vol. 11, No. 1, pp. 11–25.

Isaak, R. (1998) *Green Logic: Ecopreneurship, Theory and Ethics*, Greenleaf, Sheffield.

Kao, R.W.Y., Kao, K.R. and Kao, R.R (2002) *Entrepreneurism: A Philosophy and a Sensible Alternative for the Market Economy*, Imperial College Press, London.

Keogh, P.D. and Polonsky, M.J. (1998) 'Environmental Commitment: A Basis for Environmental Entrepreneurship?', *Journal of Organizational Change Management*, Vol. 11, No. 1, pp. 38–49.

Kuratko, D.F. and Hodgetts, R.M. (1998) *Entrepreneurship: A Contemporary Approach* (5th edn), Dryden Press, Fort Worth, TX.

Kyrö, P. (2001) 'To Grow or Not to Grow? Entrepreneurship and Sustainable Development', *International Journal of Sustainable Development and World Ecology*, Vol. 8, No. 1, pp. 15-28.

Larson, A.L. (2000) 'Sustainable Innovation through an Entrepreneurship Lens', *Business Strategy and the Environment*, No. 9, pp. 304–317.

Pastakia, A. (2002) 'Assessing Ecopreneurship in the Context of a Developing Country: The Case of India', *Greener Management International*, No. 38 (Summer), pp. 93–108.

Pinchot, G. (1985) *Intrapreneuring*, Harper & Row, New York.

Quinn, J.B. (1971) 'Next Big Industry: Environmental Improvement', *Harvard Business Review*, Vol. 49, No. 5 (September–October), pp. 120–131.

Schaltegger, S. (2002) 'A Framework for Ecopreneurship: Leading Bioneers and Environmental Managers to Ecopreneurship', *Greener Management International*, No. 38 (Summer), pp. 45–58.

Schaper, M. (2002a) 'The Essence of Ecopreneurship', *Greener Management International*, No. 8 (Summer), pp. 26–30.

Schaper, M. (2002b) 'The Challenge of Environmental Responsibility and Sustainable Development: Implications for SME and Entrepreneurship Academics' in U. Füglistaller, H.J. Pleitner, T. Volery and W. Weber (eds) *Radical Changes in the World – Will SMEs Soar or Crash?*, University of St Gallen KMU-HSG, St Gallen, Switzerland, pp. 541–553.

Schumpeter, J.A. (1934) *The Theory of Economic Development*, Cambridge, MA, Harvard University Press.

Seelos, C. and Mair, J. (2005) 'Social Entrepreneurship – The Contribution of Individual Intrapreneurs to Sustainable Development', IESE Business School Working Paper No. 553.

Walley, E.E. and Taylor, D. (2002) 'Opportunists, Champions, Mavericks…? A Typology of Green Entrepreneurs', *Greener Management International*, No. 38 (Summer), pp. 31–43.

Warren, M. (2007) 'Looking to Clean up in the Coming Cleantech Boom', *The Australian*, Vol. 5 (November), p. 40.

2

Sustainability Entrepreneurship: Charting a Field in Emergence

Bradley D. Parrish and Fiona Tilley

ABSTRACT

Chapter 1 provided an overview of the phenomenon of 'environmental entrepreneurship'. This chapter will extend our understanding of entrepreneurship by introducing the concept of sustainability entrepreneurship to the lexicon. Ecopreneurship is a relatively young field of academic inquiry and study, while sustainability entrepreneurship can best be described as an emergent discipline. The latter brings with it a necessary and important distinction between standard economic entrepreneurship and the newer forms of social and environmental entrepreneurship. It helps practitioners and academics alike to recognize the different contributions each makes to sustainable development. It may not be possible to fully resolve the difficulties posed in identifying operational definitions of each concept; however, it is possible to become more precise in describing the terms of references and the qualities each form of entrepreneurship possesses.

Introduction

This chapter will explore the emergence of sustainability entrepreneurship and how we conceptualize this phenomenon. We do this first by defining the concept and positioning it against other forms of entrepreneurship, namely social, environmental, and economic. We then consider why these other forms of entrepreneurship are not, on their own, sufficient to achieve sustainability. Finally, we examine how sustainability entrepreneurship goes beyond the principles of efficiency, effectiveness and equity to include extended time-horizons and recognition of critical limits in order to contribute a more holistic and integrated form of entrepreneurship that is sustainable in all senses of the word.

What is Sustainability Entrepreneurship?

Put at its simplest, sustainability entrepreneurship links our knowledge about entrepreneurship to our knowledge about sustainable development. The emerging field is therefore interdisciplinary by nature and draws on a number of established fields that also tend to be interdisciplinary. The focus of entrepreneurship research is on the activities of individual entrepreneurs or small entrepreneurial teams, and the impacts they have on the wider socioeconomic system. The focus of sustainable development research is on the development and sustainability of whole societies and ecosystems. However, this in and of itself is not sufficient in defining the concept of sustainability entrepreneurship because sustainable development and entrepreneurship are highly complex and contested terms of reference. It is therefore necessary to begin by defining what we mean by these underpinning terms before we can begin to answer the question 'What is sustainability entrepreneurship?'.

Sustainable Development

By far the most prolific interpretation of sustainable development is in terms of three distinct but interrelated spheres: economy, society and environment. This trichotomy of sustainability has been used extensively and is widely accepted by businesses, governments, NGOs and academia. However, more recently, the limitations and arbitrary foundations of this model (Giddings, Hopwood and O'Brien 2002; Thin 2002) have led researchers to move towards a model of sustainable development in which human development and its sustainability are viewed as a joint product of the interactions between an ecosystem, consisting of a web of complex relationships between biotic and abiotic elements, and a social system, consisting of humans and the artefacts of human interaction such as technology, organizations and institutions (Westley et al. 2002). The range of perspectives in the literature on sustainable development can usefully be charted on the basis of how authors view the relationship between these two systems (summarized in Figure 2.1).

The most significant division is between a 'humans-*and*-ecosystems' perspective and a 'humans-*in*-ecosystems' perspective (Davidson-Hunt and Berkes 2003). The former includes the self-correcting markets perspective that sees the concept of sustainable development as redundant and possibly harmful (for example, Beckerman 2003) and the technocratic interventionist perspective that posits a need for technological and technocratic interventions to correct

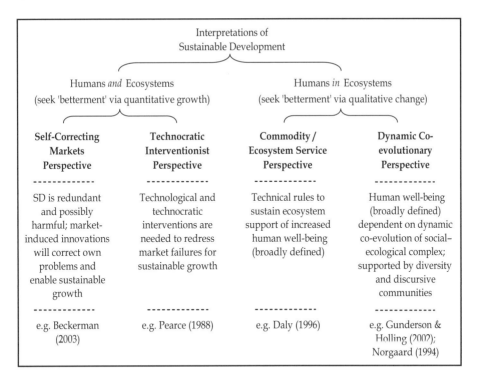

Figure 2.1   Interpretation of sustainable development

for market failures (for example, Pearce 1988). The 'humans-*in*-ecosystems' perspective, in contrast, recognizes the essentially dependent and embedded nature of the social system within the ecological system. This includes both the commodity perspective and the co-evolutionary perspective (see Holling, Berkes and Folke 1998). The former views ecosystems in terms of stocks and flows that provide critical resources and services to humans and human society (for example, Daly 1996), while the latter sees sustainable development being supported by diversity and discursive social–ecological communities (Gunderson and Holling 2002; Norgaard 1994).

As will be evident in our discussion below, these various interpretations of sustainable development are reflected in the differing views of how to conceptualize the emerging phenomenon of sustainability entrepreneurship. In our work we embrace the 'humans-*in*-ecosystems' perspective, in that we take the view that sustainable development provides a vision of the future that couples the long-term survival of humans with a qualitative improvement in the experience of life on earth. In this way we see the social system as being contained within the ecosystem and development as encompassing a much broader spectrum than just economic activity (see Parrish 2007). This makes sustainable development both a goal and a process, as it represents both a vision of the future worthy of human aspiration and an unending process of adapting human activities to correspond with that aspired future.

Entrepreneurship

Like the concept of sustainable development, entrepreneurship is equally as contested and complex in theory and practice. Interest in entrepreneurship as a phenomenon rests in the perceived contributions entrepreneurs make to public policy goals such as economic growth, increased productivity, job creation, technological innovation, deregulation and privatization, and structural adjustments or realignments (Gibb 1996; Shane 1996). Although the effects of entrepreneurship are rarely contested, a common observation about the field of entrepreneurship research is that it lacks consensus about its object of study (Cornelius, Landström and Persson 2006; Schildt, Zahra and Sillanpää 2006). Bull and Willard lamented that 'the term has been used for more than two centuries, but we continue to extend, reinterpret, and revise the definition' (1993, p. 185).

The close relationship between entrepreneurship studies and the fields of economics and strategic management is credited with imbuing our understanding of the concept of entrepreneurship with assumptions that no longer appear appropriate, or that are appropriate for only a small subsection of cases (McMullen and Shepherd 2006). Mitchell et al. explain that 'the highly economic orientation of strategy research led many studies to equate entrepreneurial motive with the desire for profit' and suggest that more needs to be known about how 'individuals with personal motivations other than profit maximization perceive opportunity, apply decision logics, etc.' (2007, p. 15). With the recognition that entrepreneurship is a fully social process, from the formation of entrepreneurial intentions to the creation of opportunities, its realization through various modes of organizing, and the new value that is created, there is growing appreciation of just how much entrepreneurship is a product of its times, as entrepreneurs continue to both 'reproduce and challenge the existing social order (Aldrich 2005, p. 451).

From this perspective, it should be no surprise to Bull and Willard that 'the term has been used for more than two centuries, but we continue to extend, reinterpret, and revise the definition' (1993, p. 185). It is this process of periodic reinterpretation that enables entrepreneurship to contribute to society in new and significant ways. Entrepreneurship may have gained prominence on the basis of its promise to fulfil public policy goals such as economic growth and increased productivity, but with rising social and ecological challenges to sustained human well-being, the stage is set for entrepreneurship to contribute to new and more pressing concerns. As Sarasvathy (2004) argues, entrepreneurship provides a means 'to create the society we want to live in from the society we have to live in'.

At the same time, entrepreneurship researchers (for example, Venkataraman 1997) are seeking to escape the narrow confines of conventional business and economic applications of the concept to explore how the general concept of entrepreneurship may be usefully applied in wider contexts. The important precursors to sustainability entrepreneurship are the allied concepts of social and environmental entrepreneurship. Before moving on to explore sustainability entrepreneurship in more detail, it is necessary to review these allied fields and their respective contributions.

Social Entrepreneurship

While the practice of social entrepreneurship is not considered to be a new phenomenon, social entrepreneurship as a field of research only crystallized in the late 1990s (Dees 1998; Leadbetter 1997) and has, in a short period of time, bourgeoned in both academia and the popular press (see, for example, Bornstein 2003; Nicholls 2006). In this time social entrepreneurship has become a catch-all for any entrepreneurial activity not driven (strictly) by a profit motive. Perrini and Vurro have suggested that the concept 'is a composite phenomenon and can initially be explained by the strengthening requests from various stakeholders to the nonprofit sector to enhance its economic efficiency and effectiveness, as well as to the for-profit sector to encourage the adoption of socially responsible behaviour' (2006, p. 58). Mair and Marti (2006) have identified three general clusters to the literature. The first and by far the most dominant interpretation is the introduction of business principles to non-profit organizations (see, for example, Dees, Economy and Emerson 2002). A second use of the term applies to socially responsible commercial businesses with cross-sector partnerships (see, for example, Sagawa and Segal 2000; Waddock 1988). A third use of the term applies more generally to innovative pursuits that catalyse social transformations and provide solutions to social problems (see, for example, Perrini and Vurro 2006; Robinson 2006), including environmental problems (see, for example, Clifford and Dixon 2006; Seelos, Ganly and Mair. 2006).

The emphasis on *social* purpose as the distinguishing characteristic of social entrepreneurship led to the field focusing predominantly on entrepreneurial non-profit management (for example, Thompson 2002) and community ventures (for example, Haugh 2007; Haugh and Pardy 1999). Much of this literature is concerned with exploring the differences between conventional and social entrepreneurship. For example Mair and Martí (2006) investigated the applicability of the concepts and definitions of entrepreneurship to initiatives with a social mission as their core purpose. Austin, Stevenson and Wei-Skillern (2006) conducted a more systematic examination of the similarities and differences between 'commercial' and 'social' entrepreneurship using Sahlman's (1996) framework for analysing entrepreneurial management. They concluded that instead of the 'deal' that is at the heart of a commercial venture, a 'core social value proposition (SVP)' is at the heart of a social venture due to 'the centrality of the social purpose' (2006, p. 16).

Weerawardena and Mort (2006) conducted a grounded theory study of nine social entrepreneurial non-profit organizations to identify the unique characteristic of social entrepreneurs and the contexts in which they operate. They developed a model of social entrepreneurship as a problem of 'constrained optimization' in which efforts to sustain the organization and environmental dynamics both act to constrain the entrepreneur's ability to create social value. Both Weerawardena and Mort (2006) and Austin, Stevenson and Wei-Skillern (2006) emphasized the dangers of goal displacement whereby organizational maintenance takes priority over the social mission. This concern perhaps reflects the positioning of social entrepreneurship within the paradigm of non-profit management. However, there is also a growing interest within the field in 'social purpose business ventures' as for-profit businesses that exist for a primarily social purpose (Choi and Kiesner 2007; Wallace 1999). For example, Hockerts (2006) examined three areas of opportunity for such ventures – activism, self-help and philanthropy – and, for each area, identified where economic value propositions and social value propositions might converge to create 'blended value' opportunities.

Paredo and McLean (2006) attempted a reconciliation of these disparate views of social entrepreneurship by developing a pair-wise spectrum of social goals and commercial goals to show how the two combine to produce a range of organization types. At one extreme are non-profit organizations and at the other extreme are commercial businesses that engage in 'cause-branding'. Another stream of the literature focuses more explicitly on the role of social entrepreneurship in solving social problems and catalysing social transformations. With this perspective, the precise legal form (that is, for-profit or non-profit) becomes less important as the function of social entrepreneurs as society's change agents is brought to the fore. For example Seelos, Ganly and Mair (2006) sought to find a link between social entrepreneurship and progress towards the UN General Assembly's Millennium Development Goals. Perrini and Vurro (2006) examined the process by which social entrepreneurs 'manage social change', including the identification of social problems, how these problems are paired with economic opportunities, and how the entrepreneurs organize in efforts to bring about transformative change.

Two of the field's cross-cutting themes – innovative solutions to social problems and catalysing social transformation – have also been the targets of critique. For example, Thompson, Alvy and Lees (2000), among others, questioned whether social entrepreneurship represents a shift to the private sector of social services that should rightfully be provided by governments as public goods. Cho focused on social entrepreneurship's 'juxtaposition of "social" objectives and the instruments of private enterprise' (2006, p. 36). He questioned whether social entrepreneurship is 'a substitute for, rather than a complement to, concerted public action' (2006, p. 51) and suggested that, by focusing on the symptoms of social pathologies, it may actual prevent more profound social transformations from addressing the root causes of those problems. As a field of research, Hockerts (2006) criticized the broad scope of the field by suggesting contributions to knowledge may get lost in a 'quagmire of definitions'. By contrast, other authors seem to relish the field's diverse scope of subject matter (Mair and Martí 2006).

Environmental Entrepreneurship

Schaper (2002) identified three general types of entrepreneurship in existence today: classic entrepreneurship as individuals who start their own businesses, intrapreneurship as entrepreneurs operating within large organizations and social entrepreneurship as entrepreneurs working within non-profit organizations. To these he suggested a fourth type was emerging: environmental entrepreneurship. Use of the terms 'environmental entrepreneurship', 'eco-entrepreneurship' and 'ecopreneurship' emerged in the early 1990s as the idea that growing demand for environmental quality might represent new business opportunities and also might help to redress some of the environmental damage caused by industry (Bennett 1991; Berle 1991; Blue 1990). This early literature largely dealt with opportunities for existing small businesses, but when the term re-emerged in the late 1990s it was grounded more explicitly in a view of entrepreneurship as innovation (Isaak 1999; Schaper 2005). Although some authors dealt with issues of corporate venturing, or intrapreneurship (Azzone and Noci 1998; Krueger Jr 1998; Post and Altman 1994), the vast majority of authors focused on innovative new ventures. The three themes that dominated this literature were: development of typologies to distinguish varieties of environmental entrepreneurship; identifying the push and pull factors that constrain and promote environmental entrepreneurship; and exploring how environmental entrepreneurs might catalyse larger transformations in the economy.

For example, Isaak (2002) made the distinction between what he called 'green businesses' and 'green-green businesses'. The former is a conventional business that has subsequently 'discovered the cost and innovation and marketing advantages, if not the ethical arguments, for "greening" their existing operations' (Isaak 2002, p. 82). This idea corresponds to what is termed in this study as environmentally responsible business. According to Isaak, a 'green-green business … is one that is designed to be green in its processes and products from scratch, as a start-up, and, furthermore, is intended to transform socially the industrial sector in which it is located towards a model of sustainable development' (Isaak 2002, p. 82).

As with Isaak's typology, the values and motives of entrepreneurs is a key dimension of all of the suggested typologies. For example, Linnanen distinguished between a desire to change the world and a desire to make money, and suggested that a 'virtuous cycle of ecopreneurship' can result when entrepreneurs are driven by both motives (2002, p. 79). Similarly, Pastakia distinguished between 'commercial ecopreneurs' and 'social ecopreneurs', depending on whether an individual is driven primarily to maximize personal gains or to promote an 'eco-friendly idea/product/technology' (1998, p. 159). In a study of environmental influences at business incubators, Schick, Marxen and Freiman (2002) distinguished between 'eco-dedicated', 'eco-open', and 'eco-reluctant' start-ups.

Other authors also added an external dimension to their typologies. For example, Schaltegger (2002) identified five types of environmental entrepreneurs based on the priority of the environment as a business goal and the market effects of the business. He suggested that 'companies contribute most to the overall environmental progress of an economy and society if their business deals with environmental solutions and environmentally superior products and if their innovations substantially influence the mass market' (2002, p. 48). Walley and Taylor (2002) based their typology on Giddens's framework that links structure and action. They developed a framework with two dimensions. One described an entrepreneur's motives on a spectrum from 'economically oriented' to 'sustainability oriented' and the other described the social structural influences on a spectrum from 'soft structures' (for example, personal networks) to 'hard structures' (for example, economic) structures (Walley and Taylor 2002, p. 39). They argued that entrepreneurs from any of the resulting categories can contribute to a sustainable society, even if they are 'opportunistically green' or 'accidentally green'. Pastakia (2002) constructed a framework to explore the internal drivers, such as personal values and competitive advantage of eco-friendly products, and external drivers, such as the power of stakeholders and the power of legislative and regulative policies, of environmental entrepreneurship.

In an interesting inversion from the rest of the field's interest on the impacts of environmental entrepreneurs on society, Bryant and Bryant (1998) used four historical case studies to explore how changes in social values influence changes in entrepreneurial behaviour. Anderson (1998) provided theoretical support for both approaches by using the concept of 'value' to link the traditions of environmentalism and entrepreneurship. He argued that even though environmentalism emerged as a 'reaction to the excesses of industrial modernity', both environmentalism and entrepreneurship are 'embedded in the "subjective 'rationality'" of society, and this 'is why entrepreneurship is most likely to sustain environmentalism than any other form of imposed change' (1998, pp. 135, 136, 139).

Most of the empirical work in the field consists of illustrative case studies used as examples of typological categories. However, Volery (2002) conducted a single case study of 'commercialised conservation' from which he found support for the importance of the founder in shaping company values, and concluded that even though it may not be the main driver, the financial 'bottom line' is still the most urgent bottom line. Beveridge and Guy (2005) suggested that the literature on environmental entrepreneurship has usefully demonstrated that an entrepreneur's motivations and values, and the contextual conditions that influence their ability to instigate change in society, are critical explanatory factors. However, they caution that 'the literature is in danger of narrowing our focus to make innovation appear like a linear process in which motivated individuals with "positive" environmental attitudes flourish or flounder as a result of external structural forces.' They proposed that more attention needed to be devoted to 'processes and practices of emergence, negotiation and innovation' (2005, p. 672).

Sustainability Entrepreneurship

The concept of sustainability entrepreneurship or, more precisely, sustainability-driven entrepreneurship, as a unique phenomenon worthy of academic inquiry is still in its infancy.[1] In fact, both academics and practitioners are just beginning to grapple with what sustainability entrepreneurship means, what it might look like and how relevant it is likely to become. Just as conventional entrepreneurship research is conducted in support of the normative goal of economic growth (Gibb 1996; Shane 1996), so, too, sustainability entrepreneurship research is conducted in support of the normative goal of sustainable development (cf. Jacobs 1995).

   In an effort to demonstrate the limits of relying on concepts such as eco-efficiency for achieving sustainable development, and to demonstrate the importance of distinguishing between the types of entrepreneurship discussed above, Young and Tilley (2006) developed a model of sustainability entrepreneurship based in part on Dyllick's and Hockerts' (2002) model of corporate sustainability and McDonough's and Braungart's (2002) model for sustainable design processes. Young and Tilley used this model to make four arguments. First, they suggested that there is a current trend for entrepreneurs to cluster around one of three existing philosophies, as either economic (conventional), social or environmental entrepreneurs. These three forms of entrepreneurship can each make a contribution to sustainable development; however, individually or in aggregate they perpetuate the compartmentalization and trade-offs of outcomes and therefore do not represent sustainability in its full sense (Tilley and Parrish 2006). This is because economic, social and environmental entrepreneurship represents the primacy of one purpose over the other two and therefore fails to provide an integrative, holistic approach. It is the process of sustainability entrepreneurship that creates enterprises that can be contributory and restorative in their interaction with human

---

1   At the First World Symposium on Sustainable Entrepreneurship held 15–17 July 2007 at the University of Leeds, the delegates discussed 'sustainability entrepreneurship' as being a more precise description of the topic domain. For that reason and for consistency we refer to the work of all authors in this field using that term, even though most authors discussed here have used the term 'sustainable entrepreneurship' in their works.

and ecological systems. We are interested in sustainability entrepreneurship because it gives primacy to sustainable development in full and therefore, unlike the other forms of entrepreneurship, provides a means of holistically balancing multiple ends and generating a 'virtuous circle' of positive benefit streams to the entrepreneur, to other people and to non-human nature (Parrish forthcoming).

Second, Young and Tilley (2006) showed how the sustainability agenda is interpreted from each of these single-purpose vantage-points. For example, when viewed through the lens of the efficiency concerns of economic enterprises, environmental and social issues become interpreted as eco-efficiency and socio-efficiency. Third, they argued that even if an entrepreneur were to fulfil the principles of efficiency, effectiveness and equity, this is still insufficient to achieve sustainability entrepreneurship. This is because efficiency alone cannot counter the increasing demands of economic growth, effectiveness does not address the inherent harm of a product or service, and equity issues require the resolution of contested ownership of responsibility for intended and unintended outcomes. Finally, they argued that the additional elements of a long-term time-horizon and appreciation for the non-negotiable critical limits of the social–ecological system are necessary components for the realization of sustainable development and that these elements are not addressed through the combined effects of social, environmental and economic entrepreneurship.

Dean and McMullen (2007) and Cohen and Winn (2007) offer a different approach to the subject. These authors use economic theories of entrepreneurship to demonstrate some of the sources of opportunities for entrepreneurs to profit by contributing to sustainable development. Both sets of authors use the neoclassical economic theory of market failures to show how market inefficiencies, externalities, imperfect information, flawed pricing mechanisms, government interventions and monopoly power result in environmental degradation and therefore produce market conditions in which entrepreneurs can earn entrepreneurial rents by reducing environmental harm. Both sets of authors acknowledge that the concept of sustainable development is broader than the issues addressed by this framework. However, Dean and McMullen do define sustainability entrepreneurship strictly in terms of correcting 'market failures that detract from sustainability' (2007, p. 58). Cohen and Winn allow for a broader interpretation by suggesting that sustainability entrepreneurship is about the economic, psychological, social and environmental consequences of future goods and services (2007, p. 35).

Both sets of authors present a similar picture, in which sustainability entrepreneurs are attracted by the prospects of earning entrepreneurial rents from market failures to redress some of the environmental harm that results from those failures. However, the authors each reach different conclusions from this analysis. Dean and McMullen argue that their theoretical discussion of sustainability entrepreneurship demonstrates 'that market systems and the institutions that define them evolve over time in a manner that can resolve social ills' (2007, p. 72), thereby positioning sustainability entrepreneurship within ecological modernization theory (see Hajer 1995). Cohen and Winn, on the other hand, envisage a broader role of sustainability entrepreneurs as agents of Schumpeterian 'creative destruction of unsustainable practices and their replacement with sustainable technologies, business models and resulting lifestyles' (2007, p. 46). Because of this, they also suggest that the 'dependent variables' or performance indicators for studying sustainability entrepreneurship need to be multifaceted to account for these entrepreneurs' 'triple bottom line' impacts.

Cohen, Smith and Mitchell (2008) follow up on this last suggestion by exploring a range of possible 'dependent variables' for the value created by sustainability entrepreneurship. They suggest a list of indicators for the value created from economic, environmental, and social processes, activities, and impacts, as well as overlaps between each sphere such as eco-efficiency for the overlap between economic and environmental spheres, socio-efficiency for the overlap between economic and social spheres, stewardship for the overlap between environmental and social spheres, and sustainability for the overlap of all three. They seem to depart from Cohen and Winn (2007) by developing the argument that entrepreneurs can be motivated by concerns other than capturing entrepreneurial rents. In fact, they argue that the 'primary value creation strategies and focal positioning' of enterprises will be different, depending on which value sphere the entrepreneurial motives place them, with sustainability entrepreneurs being motivated by all three value spheres (Cohen, Smith and Mitchell, 2008). They provide results from a review of empirical articles that suggest the most active overlapping domains are between economic and social spheres, with the environmental and sustainability spheres almost completely neglected.

Finally, three empirical studies by three sets of researchers were conducted during roughly the same period. An in-depth, qualitative study by Parrish (2008) of leading sustainability entrepreneurs from Europe, North America, East Africa and Asia-Pacific regions provides an insider's look at the critical drivers of success. This research identified five unique principles of problem-solving used to guide the process of enterprise design that have allowed sustainability entrepreneurs to successfully capitalize on market opportunities in the service of ecosystems and communities. This innovative approach to enterprise design suggests the emergence of a new organizing logic that eschews the dichotomy between 'opportunistic' business and 'altruistic' charity in favour of a new logic based on the co-production of multiple benefit streams through the perpetuation of human and natural resource quality. Thus, far from being a middling compromise between business and charity, the organizational forms being pioneered by sustainability entrepreneurs represent innovative organizational solutions that resolve the shortcomings inherent in conventional organizing logics.

Schlange has also contributed both conceptual and empirical work on the topic. In a conceptual paper he developed a model of stakeholder identification that addresses the unique motives of sustainability entrepreneurs (Schlange 2007). This model was based on a concept of sustainability entrepreneurship similar to Young's and Tilley's model, in which the importance of long-term time-horizons is recognized and sustainability entrepreneurship is viewed holistically as operating above and beyond the sum of economic, social and environmental goals. In a related empirical study, semi-structured interviews were conducted with the founders of ten enterprises in eastern Switzerland that scored high against a set of environmental, social–ethical, and economic sustainability criteria (Schlange 2006). Schlange found that sustainability entrepreneurs are motivated by a desire to catalyse regional development and, in so doing, instil their values into the regional economy and broader social system. In practice these entrepreneurs were notable for their ability to simultaneously meet competing objectives in the environmental, social–ethical and economic realms. This suggests that sustainability entrepreneurs not only exhibit values and motivations that are distinct from those of other types of entrepreneur, but also that they exhibit distinct capabilities.

Clifford and Dixon (2006; Dixon and Clifford 2007) conducted a qualitative study of the launch and early-stage development of a single UK-based enterprise that operates on earned income and seeks to reduce solid waste and the use of virgin materials in the furniture industry while providing opportunities for disadvantaged members of society. Although these authors do not use the term 'sustainability entrepreneurship', this case study is congruent with the meaning of the concept as defined in this chapter. A key finding of their study was that this enterprise was able to succeed because it developed a symbiotic business model within an embedded network of other organizations which included larger, conventional companies and 'social franchises'. This illustrates why the social contexts within which entrepreneurs and enterprises operate are as important to consider as the entrepreneur's own activities.

Each of the authors discussed in this section have contributed to expanding the concept of entrepreneurship to explore how entrepreneurship might contribute to sustainable development. However, some of the conceptions of sustainability entrepreneurship are more restricted by conventional economic assumptions of entrepreneurial motives than others. As the primacy of the profit motive is relaxed, the potential contribution of entrepreneurial ventures to sustainable development increases and the possibility-space of sustainability entrepreneurship as a concept expands. Figure 2.2 represents how the concepts of sustainability entrepreneurship posited by different authors expand this possibility-space to greater or lesser degrees. For example, the concepts posited by Dean and McMullen (2007) and Cohen and Winn (2007) provide only limited possibilities beyond that of conventional entrepreneurship, while the perspectives of Parrish (2008), Young and Tilley (2006), Schlange (2007), Clifford and Dixon (2006) and, to a lesser degree, Cohen, Smith and Mitchell (2008) posit greatly expanded possibilities for the potential contribution of sustainability entrepreneurship.

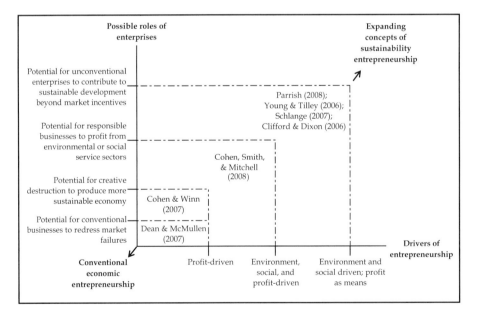

Figure 2.2   Possibility-space for sustainability

Concluding Thoughts

From this review of the entrepreneurship literature we can see the importance of distinguishing between at least three types of entrepreneurship based on entrepreneurial motives or purpose: 'responsible entrepreneurs', who are conventional, profit-seeking entrepreneurs but are motivated to try to reduce their negative environmental and social impacts out of a sense of duty (cf. Fuller and Tian 2006); 'opportunistic entrepreneurs', who may directly contribute to environmental and social improvements but, because they are primarily motivated by profit-seeking, will only do so for as long as market incentives exist (cf. Cohen and Winn 2007; Dean and McMullen 2007; Walley and Taylor 2002); and 'sustainability-driven entrepreneurs' whose fundamental purpose for starting an enterprise is to contribute to improved social and ecological well-being, as well as to satisfy their own quality-of-life interests, and who earn market-based income as a means of achieving these ends (cf. Parrish 2008; Schlange 2006; Young and Tilley 2006). The first two types continue to rely on the dominant organizing paradigm to engage with their social and ecological environments, while the last type has rejected this paradigm in favour of a newly emergent organizing logic that resolves the shortcomings of conventional organizing logics to incorporate principles of sustainable development in enterprise designs. From this we can conclude that social and environmental entrepreneurship may contribute to sustainable development in important but partial ways, and therefore, individually and in aggregate, do not offer a full solution. Sustainability entrepreneurship is an outgrowth of the forms of entrepreneurship that have come before, and we do not intend to suggest that it usurps social, economic or environmental entrepreneurship. What we are proposing, and what the initial findings of recent empirical research suggest, is that sustainability entrepreneurship leads to a new organizational form that is uniquely suited to contribute to sustainable development in ways that other forms of entrepreneurship are not. This is a very emergent field of inquiry that is in need of greater empirical research so that the possible contributions which this form of entrepreneurship can make to sustainable development can be more fully understood, and so that these contributions can be more precisely positioned alongside those of social and environmental entrepreneurship.

References

Aldrich, H.E. (2005) 'Entrepreneurship' in N.J. Smelser and R. Swedberg (eds) *The Handbook of Economic Sociology* (2nd edn), Princeton University Press, Princeton, NJ and Oxford, pp. 451–477.

Anderson, A.R. (1998) 'Cultivating the Garden of Eden: Environmental Entrepreneuring', *Journal of Organizational Change Management*, Vol. 11, No. 2, pp. 135–144.

Austin, J, Stevenson, H. and Wei-Skillern, J. (2006) 'Social and Commercial Entrepreneurship: Same, Different, or Both?', *Entrepreneurship Theory and Practice*, Vol. 30, No.1, pp. 1–22.

Azzone, G. and Noci, G. (1998) 'Seeing Ecology and "Green" Innovations as a Source of Change', *Journal of Organizational Change Management*, Vol.11, No. 2, pp. 94–111.

Beckerman, W. (2003) *A Poverty of Reason: Sustainable Development and Economic Growth. Oakland*, The Independent Institute, Oakland, CA.

Bennett, S.J. (1991) *Ecopreneuring: The Complete Guide to Small Business Opportunities from the Environmental Revolution*, John Wiley and Sons, New York.

Berle, G. (1991) *The Green Entrepreneur: Business Opportunities that Can Save the Earth and Make You Money*, Liberty Hall Press, Blue Ridge Summit, PA.

Beveridge, R. and Guy, S. (2005) 'The Rise of the Eco-preneur and the Messy World of Environmental Innovation', *Local Environment*, Vol. 10, No. 6, pp. 665–676.

Blue, R.J. (1990) *Ecopreneuring: Managing for Results*, Scott Foresman, London.

Bornstein, D. (2003) *How to Change the World : Social Entrepreneurs and the Power of New Ideas*, Oxford University Press, Oxford.

Bryant, T.A. and Bryant, J.E. (1998) 'Wetlands and Entrepreneurs: Mapping the Fuzzy Zone between Ecystem Preservation and Entrepreneurial Opportunity', *Journal of Organizational Change Management*, Vol. 11, No. 2, pp. 112–134.

Bull, I. and Willard, G.E. (1993) 'Towards a Theory of Entrepreneurship', *Journal of Business Venturing*, Vol. 8, pp. 183–195.

Cho, A.H. (2006) 'Politics, Values and Social Entrepreneurship: A Critical Appraisal' in J. Mair, J. Robinson and K. Hockerts (eds) *Social Entrepreneurship*, Palgrave Macmillan, New York, pp. 34–56.

Choi, D.Y. and Kiesner, F. (2007) 'Homeboy Industries: An Incubator of Hope and Businesses', *Entrepreneurship Theory and Practice*, Vol. 31, No. 5, pp. 769–786.

Clifford, A. and Dixon, S.E.A. (2006) 'Green-Works: A Model for Combining Social and Ecological Entrepreneurship' in J. Mair, J. Robinson and K. Hockerts (eds) *Social Entrepreneurship*, Palgrave Macmillan, New York, pp. 214–234.

Cohen, B., Smith, B. and Mitchell, R. (2008) 'Toward a Sustainable Conceptualization of Dependent Variables in Entrepreneurship Research' *Business Strategy and the Environment*, Vol. 17, No. 2, pp. 107–119..

Cohen, B. and Winn, M.I. (2007) 'Market Imperfections, Opportunity and Sustainable Entrepreneurship', *Journal of Business Venturing*, Vol. 22, No. 1, pp. 29–49.

Cornelius, B., Landström, H. and Persson, O. (2006) 'Entrepreneurial Studies: The Dynamic Research Front of a Developing Social Science', *Entrepreneurship Theory and Practice*, Vol. 30, No. 3, pp. 375–398.

Daly, H.E. (1996) *Beyond Growth: The Economics of Sustainable Development*, Beacon Press, Boston, MA.

Davidson-Hunt, I.J. and Berkes, F. (2003) 'Nature and Society through the Lens of Resilience: Toward a Human-in-Ecosystem Perspective' in F. Berkes, J. Colding and C. Folke (eds) *Navigating Social-Ecological Systems*, Cambridge University Press, Cambridge.

Dean, T.J. and McMullen, J.S. (2007) 'Toward a Theory of Sustainable Entrepreneurship: Reducing Environmental Degradation through Entrepreneurial Action', *Journal of Business Venturing*, Vol. 22, No. 1, pp. 50–76.

Dees, J.G. (1998) *The Meaning of 'Social Entrepreneurship*, Ewing Marion Kauffman Foundation and Stanford University, Stanford, CA.

Dees, J.G., Economy, P. and Emerson, J. (2002) *Enterprising Nonprofits: A Toolkit for Social Entrepreneurs*, John Wiley and Sons, New York.

Dixon, S.E.A. and Clifford, A. (2007) 'Ecopreneurship – A New Approach to Managing the Triple Bottom Line', *Journal of Organizational Change Management*, Vol. 20, No. 3, pp. 326–345.

Dyllick, T. and Hockerts, K. (2002) 'Beyond the Business Case for Corporate Sustainability', *Business Strategy and the Environment*, Vol. 11, No. 2, pp. 130–141.

Fuller, T. and Tian, Y. (2006) 'Social and Symbolic Capital and Responsible Entrepreneurship: An Empirical Investigation of SME Narratives', *Journal of Business Ethics*, Vol. 67, pp. 287–304.

Gibb, A.A. (1996) 'Entrepreneurship and Small Business Management: Can We Afford to Neglect Them in the Twenty-First Century Business School?', *British Journal of Management*, Vol. 7, No. 4, pp. 309–322.

Giddings, B., Hopwood, B. and O'Brien, G. (2002) 'Environment, Economy and Society: Fitting Them Together into Sustainable Development', *Sustainable Development*, Vol. 10, pp. 187–196.

Gunderson, L.H. and Holling, C.S. (2002) *Panarchy: Understanding Transformations in Human and Natural Systems*, Island Press, Washington, DC.

Hajer, M.A. (1995) *The Politics of Environmental Discourse: Ecological Modernization and the Policy Process*, Oxford University Press, Oxford.

Haugh, H. (2007) 'Community-Led Social Venture Creation', *Entrepreneurship Theory and Practice*, Vol. 31, No. 2, pp. 161–182.

Haugh, H.M. and Pardy, W. (1999) 'Community Entrepreneurship in North East Scotland', *International Journal of Entrepreneurial Behaviour and Research*, Vol. 5, No. 4, pp. 163–172.

Hockerts, K. (2006) 'Entrepreneurial Opportunity in Social Purpose Business Ventures' in J. Mair, J. Robinson and K. Hockerts (eds) *Social Entrepreneurship*, Palgrave Macmillan, New York, pp. 142–154.

Holling, C.S., Berkes, F. and Folke. C. (1998) 'Science, Sustainability and Resource Management' in F. Berkes, C. Folke, and J. Colding (eds) *Linking Social and Ecological Systems: Managing Practices and Social Mechanisms for Building Resilience*, Cambridge University Press, Cambridge, pp. 342–362.

Isaak, R.A. (1999) *Green Logic: Ecopreneurship, Theory, and Ethics*, Kumarian Press, Hartford, CT.

Isaak, R. (2002) 'The Making of the Ecopreneur', *Greener Management International*, Vol. 38 (Summer), pp. 81–91.

Jacobs, M. (1995) 'Sustainable Development, Capital Substitution and Economic Humility: A Response to Beckerman', *Environmental Values*, Vol. 4, No. 1, pp. 57–68.

Krueger Jr, N. (1998) 'Encouraging the Identification of Environmental Opportunities', *Journal of Organizational Change Management*, Vol. 11, No. 2, pp. 174–183.

Leadbetter, C. (1997) *The Rise of the Social Entrepreneur*, Demos, London.

Linnanen, L. (2002) 'An Insider's Experience with Environmental Entrepreneurship', *Greener Management International*, Vol. 38, pp. 71–80.

McDonough, W. and Braungart, M. (2002) 'Design for the Triple Top Line: New Tools for Sustainable Commerce', *Corporate Environmental Strategy*, Vol. 9, No. 3, pp. 251–258.

McMullen, J.S. and Shepherd, D.A. (2006) 'Entrepreneurial Action and the Role of Uncertainty in the Theory of the Entrepreneur', *Academy of Management Review*, Vol. 31, No. 1, pp. 132–152.

Mair, J. and, Martí, I. (2006) 'Social Entrepreneurship Research: A Source of Explanation, Prediction, and Delight', *Journal of World Business*, Vol. 41, pp. 36–44.

Mitchell, R.K., Busenitz, L.W., Bird, B., Gaglio, C.M., McMullen, J.S., Morse, E.A. and Smith, J.B. (2007) 'The Central Question in Entrepreneurial Cognition Research 2007', *Entrepreneurship Theory and Practice*, Vol. 31, No. 1, pp. 1–27.

Nicholls, A. (ed) (2006) *Social Entrepreneurship: New Models of Sustainable Social Change*, Oxford University Press, Oxford.

Norgaard, R.B. (1994) *Development Betrayed, The End of Progress and a Coevolutionary Revisioning of the Future*, Routledge, New York.

Paredo, A.M. and McLean, M. (2006) 'Social Entrepreneurship: A Critical Review of the Concept', *Journal of World Business*, Vol. 41, pp. 56–65.

Parrish, B.D. (2007) 'Designing the Sustainable Enterprise', *Futures*, Vol. 39, No.7, pp. 846–860.

Parrish, B.D. (2008) 'Sustainability Entrepreneurship: Design Principles, Processes, and Paradigms', PhD thesis, University of Leeds, UK.

Parrish, B.D. (forthcoming) 'Sustainability-driven Entrepreneurship: Principles of Organization Design', *Journal of Business Venturing*.

Pastakia, A. (1998) 'Grassroots Ecopreneurs: Change Agents for a Sustainable Society', *Journal of Organizational Change Management*, Vol. 11, No. 2, pp. 157–173.

Pastakia, A. (2002) 'Assessing Ecopreneurship in the Context of a Developing Country', *Greener Management International*, Vol. 38, pp. 93–108.

Pearce, D. (1988) 'Economics, Equity and Sustainable Development', *Futures*, Vol. 20, No. 6, pp. 598–605.

Perrini, F. and Vurro, C. (2006) 'Social Entrepreneurship: Innovation and Social Change Across Theory and Practice' in J. Mair, J. Robinson and K. Hockerts (eds) *Social Entrepreneurship*, Palgrave Macmillan, New York, pp. 57–85.

Post, J.E. and Altman, B.W. (1994) 'Managing the Environmental Change Process: Barriers and Opportunities', *Journal of Organizational Change Management*, Vol. 7, No. 4, pp. 64–81.

Robinson, J. (2006) 'Navigating Social and Institutional Barriers to Markets: How Social Entrepreneurs Identify and Evaluate Opportunities' in J. Mair, J. Robinson and K. Hockerts (eds) *Social Entrepreneurship*, Palgrave Macmillan, New York, pp. 95–120.

Sagawa, S. and Segal, E. (2000) 'Common Interest, Common Good: Creating Value through Business and Social Sector Partnerships', *California Management Review*, Vol. 42, No. 2, pp. 105–122.

Sahlman, W.A. (1996) 'Some Thoughts on Business Plans' in W.A. Sahlman, H.H. Stevenson, M.J. Roberts, and A.V. Bhide (eds) *The Entrepreneurial Venture*, Harvard Business School Press, Boston, MA, pp. 138–176.

Sarasvathy, S.D. (2004) 'The Questions We Ask and the Questions We Care About: Reformulating Some Problems in Entrepreneurship Research', *Journal of Business Venturing*, Vol. 19, pp. 707–717.

Schaltegger, S. (2002) 'A Framework for Ecopreneurship', *Greener Management International*, Vol. 38, pp. 45–58.

Schaper, M. (2002) 'The Essence of Ecopreneurship', *Greener Management International*, Vol. 38 (Summer), pp. 26–30.

Schaper, M. (2005) *Making Ecopreneurs: Developing Sustainable Entrepreneurship*, Ashgate Publishing, Burlington VT.

Schick, H., Marxen, S. and Freiman, J. (2002) 'Sustainability Issues for Start-up Entrepreneurs' *Greener Management International*, Vol. 38, pp. 59–70.

Schildt, H.A., Zahra, S.A. and Sillanpää, A. (2006) 'Scholarly Communities in Entrepreneurship Research: A Co-Citation Analysis', *Entrepreneurship Theory and Practice* Vol. 30, No. 3, pp. 399–415.

Schlange, L.E. (2006) 'What Drives Sustainable Entrepreneurs?', paper presented at the Applied Business and Entrepreneurship Association International Conference, Kona, HI, USA, 16–20 November.

Schlange, L.E. (2007) 'Stakeholder Perception in Sustainable Entrepreneurship: The Role of Managerial and Organizational Cognition', paper presented at the First World Symposium on Sustainable Entrepreneurship as part of the Corporate Responsibility Research Conference, University of Leeds, Leeds, UK, 15–17 July.

Seelos, C., Ganly, K. and Mair, J. (2006) 'Social Entrepreneurs Directly Contribute to Global Development Goals' in J. Mair, J. Robinson and K. Hockerts (eds) *Social Entrepreneurship*, Palgrave Macmillan, New York, pp. 235–275.

Shane, S. (1996) 'Explaining Variation in Rates of Entrepreneurship in the United States: 1899–1988', *Journal of Management*, Vol. 22, No. 5, pp. 747–781.

Thin, N. (2002) *Social Progress and Sustainable Development*, Kumarian Press, Bloomfield CT.

Thompson, J. (2002) 'The World of the Social Entrepreneur', *International Journal of Public Sector Management*, Vol. 15, No. 5, pp. 412–431.

Thompson, J., Alvy, G. and Lees, A. (2000) 'Social Entrepreneurship – A New Look at the People and the Potential', *Management Decision*, Vol. 38, No. 5, pp. 328–338.

Tilley, F. and Parrish, B.D. (2006) 'From Poles to Wholes: Facilitating an Integrated Approach to Sustainable Entrepreneurship', *World Review of Entrepreneurship, Management and Sustainable Development*, Vol. 2, No. 4, pp. 281–294.

Venkataraman, S. (1997) 'The Distinctive Domain of Entrepreneurship Research: An Editor's Perspective' in J. Katz and R. Brockhaus (eds) *Advances in Entrepreneurship, Firm Emergence, and Growth*, JAI Press, Greenwich CT, pp. 119–138.

Volery, T. (2002) 'An Entrepreneur Commercialises Conservation', *Greener Management International*, Vol. 38, pp. 109–116.

Waddock, S.A. (1988) 'Building Successful Partnerships', *Sloan Management Review*, Vol. 29, No. 4, pp. 17–23.

Wallace, S.L. (1999) 'Social Entrepreneurship: The Role of Social Purpose Enterprises in Facilitating Community Economic Development', *Journal of Developmental Entrepreneurship*, Vol. 4, pp. 153–174.

Walley, E.E. and Taylor, D.W. (2002) 'Opportunists, Champions, Mavericks….?', *Greener Management International*, Vol. 38, pp. 31–43.

Weerawardena J. and Mort, G.S. (2006) 'Investigating Social Entrepreneurship: A Multidimensional Model', *Journal of World Business*, Vol. 41, pp. 21–35.

Westley, F., Carpenter, S.R., Brock, W.A., Holling, C.S. and Gunderson, L.H. (2002) 'Why Systems of People and Nature are not just Social and Ecological Systems' in L.H. Gunderson, and C.S. Holling (eds) *Panarchy: Understanding Transformations in Human and Natural Systems*, Island Press, Washington, DC, pp. 103–119.

Young, W. and Tilley, F. (2006) 'Can Businesses Move Beyond Efficiency? The Shift Toward Effectiveness and Equity in the Corporate Sustainability Debate', *Business Strategy and the Environment*, Vol. 15, No. 6, pp. 402–415.

3

The Making of the Ecopreneur

Robert Isaak

ABSTRACT

This chapter contrasts 'green businesses' (moving an existing firm towards environmental responsibility) with 'green-green businesses' (a business designed in process and product to be green as a start-up). The ideal type of 'ecopreneur' is defined as one who creates green-green businesses in order to radically transform the economic sector in which he or she operates. Ecopreneurship is an existential form of business behaviour committed to sustainability. Ecopreneurs are counter-cultural or social entrepreneurs who want to make a social statement, not just money. They benefit not only from free advertising, given their advocacy of a public good, but also from a strong sense of individual and team motivation since their objective taps into social and political, as well as economic, needs. The classic examples of Ben & Jerry's, The Body Shop and the Honey Bee Network are deliberately selected here as perhaps the most 'ideal typical' illustrations of ecopreneurship as a form of human behaviour latent in all entrepreneurs who want to get the most wide-ranging benefit from their natural 'free-rider' instincts.

Practical suggestions for businesspeople who want to try the ecopreneurial strategy in the private sector are suggested, including green brainstorming, reduction of costs, the stimulation of innovation through green design and networking, and attracting the interest of overwhelmed consumers through green marketing and the funding of the public sector in an emerging 'attention economy'.

Concrete steps which governments and public officials can take to promote ecopreneurship include competitions for the most imaginative green business plans, changing tax regimes to promote resource conservation, building ecopreneurship into standards for public-sector managers and targeting the creation of high-tech development centres to build serial ecopreneurship and attract 'blended value' venture capital.

The Making of the Ecopreneur

'GREEN-GREEN BUSINESS' AS IDEAL TYPE

Environmentally responsible businesses come in two basic varieties: 'green businesses' and 'green-green businesses'. A typical 'green business' did not start out that way, but once it was established, managers discovered the cost and innovation and marketing advantages, if not the ethical arguments, for 'greening' their existing enterprise. The efforts of the 3M Company are but one example: since its 'Pollution Prevention Pays' or '3Ps' programme was launched in 1975, the company has saved over $750 million as a result of reformulating products and processes and recycling.

In contrast, a 'green-green business' is one that is designed to be green in processes and products from scratch, as a start-up, and, furthermore, is intended to socially transform the industrial sector in which it is located towards a model of sustainable development (Isaak 1998). Since this kind of business is what sociologist Max Weber called 'an ideal type', there is no perfect example in reality, but Ben & Jerry's and The Body Shop come close. Both of these companies were started by counter-culture entrepreneurs who not only wanted their businesses to be environmentally responsible, but also wanted to make a social statement, not just make money. The success of their marketing efforts and growth was as much a result of savvy social consciousness in business design, production and marketing as of a preoccupation with 'the bottom line'. Ultimately, these ecopreneurs realized that business is a people-to-people exchange of goods and services and that there was a growing niche for products that symbolized loyalty to the principle of sustaining the planet, its resources and its biodiversity for future generations. Often they came to this realization by accident.

Of course, Ben Cohen, Jerry Greenfield and Anita Roddick were not perfect, flawless ecopreneurs. Once again, 'ecopreneur' is a Weberian ideal type that refers to an individual who seeks to transform a sector of the economy towards sustainability by starting up a business in that sector with a green design, green processes and a lifelong commitment to sustainability in everything that is said and done.

> *To become an ecopreneur is an existentialist commitment in which the entrepreneur knows he or she will never reach the ideal, but that very ideal of sustainability gives meaning to everything the ecopreneur does upon the earth. (Isaak 1998, p. 113)*

Knowing full well that most entrepreneurs spend seven days a week in the early years to found a company that can survive, the ecopreneur figures that he or she will be better motivated and sleep well at night if whatever is done in the business is undertaken on the terms of a mission of social consciousness and political transformation in order to make the earth a more sustainable place, as well as to make money. The ecopreneur knows what to live for and that everywhere on earth is 'home'. My book, *Green Logic: Ecopreneurship, Theory and Ethics* (1998) shows how this kind of thinking and commitment differs from 'globalization', for example, where no place on earth is considered 'home' since one is always moving on to some other place, chasing 'future freedom' and global market share. Mobility is all, and roots are left behind, if not cut off. Often the globalized manager leaves a mess – environmental waste, a corporate headquarters in organizational chaos and a disintegrated family where he or she is rarely to be seen. Their freedom is a 'freedom from'!

In contrast, the ecopreneur accepts the same 'free-rider' motivations that stimulate any entrepreneur and transforms them into a 'freedom to' – the freedom to create a new, environmentally responsible community, however small that community may be. In other words, whereas all entrepreneurs make their living by risking other people's money and resources, aiming to get things as cheaply as possible in order to enable their businesses to survive a bit longer (the 'free-rider' motivation), the ecopreneur, often through accidental experimentation, saves money in an environmentally responsible way and gets 'free advertising' by being identified with a worthy social cause from the media. At one point, for example, Ben and Jerry promoted 'Peace Pops' in order to promote their idea that 1 per cent of the US military budget should go to 'peace'. There is a more subtle form of 'free-rider' motive involved here: by using their social imaginations to further their view of community responsibility in a free-flowing, hedonistic climate, Ben and Jerry used 'the business system' to have a good time. Jerry's motto was 'If it's not fun, why do it?'. Meanwhile, Ben's philanthropic logo of motivation was 'business has a responsibility to give back to the community from which it draws its support'. By the time they sold their business to someone else, Ben and Jerry had been so successful with their socially-laced advertising that their original ice-cream factory, a converted former petrol station, became the number one tourist site in Vermont.

Of course, if anything, Anita Roddick was even a greater expert at social or political marketing. From travelling the world as a hippy she had learned that there were at least 12 ingredients which women in developing countries such as Fiji used to keep their skin 'as smooth as silk'. Back in England, she became upset that she could not buy cosmetics by weight or bulk like other groceries and had to pay so much just for the packaging.

In her book *Body and Soul* (1991, p. 9), she opens with a statement which shows why she was determined to transform the sector of the industry in which she would set up shop: 'I hate the beauty business. It is a monster industry selling unattainable dreams. It lies. It cheats. It exploits women. Its major product lines are packaging and garbage.'

So, using the name of a mechanics garage she had seen in California on her travels, 'The Body Shop', she started a business on the cheap where women could bring their own containers to fill with the natural cosmetics they needed. A local funeral parlour nearby objected, fearing a loss of customers if a 'Body Shop' was located so close. Roddick's counter-culture husband had just left to fulfill a lifelong dream of riding a horse from Buenos Aires to New York. So she called the local newspaper anonymously and said that there was this poor woman, whose husband had just left to ride from Buenos Aires to New York on a horse, trying to feed her two children by starting a local business and that mafia undertakers were threatening to close her down. She got a full-page spread on the first page of the paper and her brilliant marketing campaign for The Body Shop was underway. Soon she was arguing for 'trade not aid', paying Indians in the Brazilian rainforests to process and sell her the oil from nuts rather than chopping down trees – oil which she used in her creams and advertised as such. She was astute at political marketing. Her 'green business' was an existential odyssey that took her all over the world, combining her financial needs, her political and social needs, her desire for foreign adventure and, ultimately, her effort to move the cosmetics industry towards sustainability.

The fact that both The Body Shop and Ben & Jerry's became more preoccupied with corporate structure, compensation and legal issues than with the environment once their companies became established beyond a certain size does not detract from their 'ecopreneurial' beginnings. It merely suggests that ecopreneurs may be well advised to move on to start up other 'green-green' companies rather than hanging on to one that enters an older, established 'maintenance' phase, which demands a trustee manager role more than an entrepreneurial one. For sustainable development, the world needs 'serial ecopreneurs' just as Silicon Valley needed serial new economy entrepreneurs in order to flourish.

Nor are ecopreneurs from developed countries the only ones involved in this existential odyssey of sustainability. In 1993 Professor Anil Gupta of the Indian Institute of Management set up a non-profit governmental organization (NGO) called the Society for Research and Initiatives for Sustainable Technologies and Institutions (SRISTI) to 'strengthen the capacity of grassroots inventors, innovators and ecopreneurs engaged in conserving biodiversity and developing eco-friendly solutions to local problems'. The key instrument of this NGO is the *Honey Bee Newsletter*, published in six languages and dealing with examples of local ecopreneurship and ways of preventing the intellectual property rights of local inventors in developing countries from being exploited by multinational corporations based in wealthy countries. Recently, the focus has been on women's indigenous knowledge, given its traditional neglect in India.

The Honey Bee philosophy is aimed at remedying one of the negative free-rider effects of entrepreneurial capitalism: the temptation of large corporations from developed economies to take or buy out the innovative technologies of indigenous people in developing counties, without giving them sufficient credit for their intellectual discoveries or payment for their ideas and inventions. Such protection and support is critical in order to motivate ecopreneurship in the first place: why bother to innovate and create a green business if the inevitable consequence is to have everything extracted and exploited? The metaphor of the honey bee indicates the cross-fertilization of ideas and initiatives that aim to stimulate, reward and protect the creativity of grassroots ecopreneurs. Stemming from this rich Indian tradition, Astad Pastakia (1998, p. 158) distinguishes between two kinds of ecopreneurs – commercial ecopreneurs and social ecopreneurs. These are discussed below.

COMMERCIAL VERSUS SOCIAL ECOPRENEURS

Pastakia surveyed ecopreneurs in the agricultural sector in order to describe their role as change agents for a sustainable society at the grassroots level. He defines *commercial ecopreneurs* (or ecopreneurial corporations) as those who seek to maximize personal (or organizational) gains by identifying green business opportunities (that is, eco-friendly products and processes) and transforming them into viable business ventures. In contrast, *social ecopreneurs* (or social ecopreneurial organizations) are those who seek to promote eco-friendly ideas, products or technologies through either market or non-market routes. Given the deep spirituality in many areas of India, the idealist notion of social ecopreneurship is of particular importance since it defines an existential choice that is not dependent on material rewards, but leads to spiritual fulfilment and, surprisingly often, to worldly success in the long term. One of Pastakia's examples of social ecopreneurship is Dr G.L. Atara, who applied the ancient science of *ayurveda* to plants (for example, *Vrukshayurveda*) – a process which dramatically increased the productivity of crops while eliminating the use of chemicals, so sharply reducing costs. Rejecting offers from private industrialists who wanted to purchase this technology from him, Atara tapped the energies of the Swadhyay spiritual movement and supplied the technology to these volunteers on a no-profit/no-loss basis. He was determined to make his liquid fertilizer available to local farmers on a non-exploitative basis and succeeded.

Far away in the Austrian Alps, organic farmer Sepp Holzer uses similar strategies of avoiding industrial farming, which he claims to be hugely destructive in the developing countries, creating chronic dependency. Holzer grows exotic plants and lemons the natural way and gives tours April through October at €130 a ticket.

In Nepal, 17 per cent of the total forest land in 73 districts is managed by Forest User Groups, local independent corporate bodies who receive 100 per cent of timber sales provided that they spend it on village development and forest regeneration: this local decentralization mitigates against the deforestation caused by the centralized policies of the Nepali national government and large multinational agribusiness concerns.

MUST COMMERCIAL ECOPRENEURSHIP BE COUNTER-CULTURAL?

Clearly, the spiritual traditions of Asian cultures and particular individuals are unique and suggest that the universe of potential 'social ecopreneurs' may be limited. Yet all cultures have traditions and subcultures of idealism based on harmony with the earth that can be tapped for the development of social ecopreneurial organizations.

A more pressing question may be: must commercial ecopreneurship be 'counter-cultural'? In the classic examples we have cited – from Ben & Jerry's to The Body Shop to the Honey Bee Network – there has been a 'counter-cultural spirit' in the sense of a political agenda to change, if not transform, the 'mainstream culture' towards more harmony and sustainability. Like wines of the top vintage, these examples may not be 'true' of all ecopreneurs, but they have been highlighted in this chapter because they are 'ideal typical.'

While the 'ideal type' of ecopreneurship – that of 'green-green businesses' or start-ups – *does* imply a deliberate (albeit sometimes accidental) strategy to transform the sector in which one operates towards sustainability, it is also possible to have incremental ecopreneurial efforts that aim towards cost-reduction by means of efficiencies which reduce resource use and thereby contribute to sustainability.

The language aimed at this broad audience whose primary objective is to save money is perhaps best stated in *Factor Four: Doubling Wealth, Halving Resource Use* (1997). Here Ernst von Weizsäcker, Amory Lovins and L. Hunter Lovins argue that resource productivity can and should grow fourfold: the amount of wealth extracted from one unit of natural resources could be quadrupled, and we could live twice as well while using half as much. The book provides many practical business applications that support this technological argument. However, the call to cut consumption or resource use is too often translated by mainstream politicians and economists as a potential reduction in economic growth. Von Weizsäcker, Lovins and Lovins clearly demonstrate the opposite – that the creativity of ecopreneurial thinking can lead to increased productivity and economic growth – but their sophisticated argument too often falls upon deaf ears. From hyper-cars (hybrids) to cyber-trains, from cooling engines to superwindows, they give concrete examples of how to do what they suggest.

Contemporary examples of commercial ecopreneurship abound. Dean Kamen (who invented the Segway human transporter) is producing a non-polluting, easily transportable Stirling engine that can produce clean water from polluted sources and generate small amounts of electricity cheaply: this could radically further sustainable development for the 2 billion people in the world who have no access to fresh water.

Seaweed farms on the edge of the Red Sea grow 'sea asparagus' (or *salicornia*) with delicious tips, and seeds that can be ground into high-protein meal or pressed into quality cooking oil. The process supports flora and fauna from the sea and helped to generate $10 million worth of fish, shrimp and sea asparagus in 2001 (with ten times this amount projected as possible in the next five years). One of the fish harvested, the *tilapia*, is a light-fleshed edible fish whose skin can also be made into leather goods (US Water News 2002).

On a smaller scale, the Milesnick Ranch outside Belgrade, Montana transformed a situation in which some 1,500 fly fishers tromped through their land in order to fish in the creeks there into an ecopreneurial opportunity. The

Milesnicks limited the number to 500–600 fishers a year, who pay a fee (and treat the land with more respect), generating 40 per cent of the ranch's profits (Kumlien 2002).

Earth Sanctuaries Ltd has demonstrated that conservation can also be targeted as a primary business. Breeding endangered animals, the private reserves are open to paying visitors that support the enterprise – not to mention the shares listed on the Australian stock exchange as of 2000.

And Yvon Chouinard created a new kind of piton for mountain-climbing, accidentally leading him to start the Great Pacific Iron Works, which, in turn, became Patagonia – an outdoor clothing manufacturer which is a model of corporate responsibility. Since 1985 10 per cent of the profits (or 1 per cent of sales, whichever is greater) is passed to over 1,000 grassroots environmental groups. The Patagonia Environmental Internship Program allows employees to take up to two months' paid leave to work for a non-profit environmental organization of their choice. And the Patagonia Land Trust, a non-profit organization founded in 2000, has protected more than a quarter of a million acres of grasslands, forests and coastal areas in the Patagonia region of South America.

Nevertheless, there is a feeling that few people will take the time to digest the message of ecopreneurial discovery and success in this fast-moving society where competitive models are picked up through fashion and frequency of exposure rather than by thorough analysis and efficiency of means. Green marketing, for example, is often assumed to be pushing products that may be more inconvenient (such as electric cars) or more expensive (such as solar energy) and is, for these reasons, ignored. In the United States, after a decade of designing eco-friendly products, many companies have unfortunately concluded that 'green' sales pitches do not sell (Fowler 2002). So, given a globalized economy in which people are inclined to take short-cuts to economic growth and take minimal time in making consumption decisions, the question becomes: what can be done practically in the private sector to further ecopreneurship and what strategies can the public sector adopt to complement and support such efforts to create a sustainable society?

Private Sector Initiatives that can Promote Ecopreneurship

Merely 'greening' business as usual appears to have had only a marginal effect in moving society towards sustainability. It has been shown that companies usually begin with basic compliance with environmental regulations and only then move to environmental management to reduce emissions beyond compliance (Fischer and Schot 1993). Only after that do they strive to set proactive goals for sociopolitical and environmental purposes. Yet, the World Resources Institute (2002) estimated that less than 20 per cent of North American and European companies can be described as proactive in their commitment to improve environmental performance in alignment with sustainable development objectives (for example, to ensure that today's wealth and lifestyles are not being achieved at the expense of future generations). Making society sustainable requires a jump-start process of spreading 'green-green businesses' – incentives to make all future businesses environmentally friendly from the initial, start-up phase.

There are a number of a number of private-sector incentives that can foster green start-ups:

1. *Create your own world of value by setting limits.* Entrepreneurs are often motivated to set up their own businesses so that they have more control over their own lives and can create a small world of their own: by doing this on a green platform, they build the future interests of their children and grandchildren into the initial design and are involved day and night in bringing into being a small world within a world of which they can be proud.

   As ecopreneur Paul Hawken puts it, businesses are like cults that create their own values: 'Great value-added propositions in this world start not from liberty and license but from need and want and hunger. Breakthroughs come from limits.' Hawken believes that the post-boom era is an ideal time to found a small, green business since 'nothing kills a good idea faster than money' (cited in Whitford 2002, p. 43). Indeed, the time may be ripe for what Jed Emerson (2000) has called 'blended value' investing which looks beyond the financial to the social and environmental values of all investments to have them symbolize the personal values of the investor.

2. *Undertake green strategic innovation.* Innovation can be made more fruitful with limits, just as tennis is more satisfying with a net. In an ambiguous world economy, one needs a limit, a focus: the sustainability criterion limits the parameters and makes business

strategy more focused. Knowledge about existing environmental laws among small firms, for example, is generally limited and needs to be made more transparent (Schaper 2002, p. 527).

3. *Add distinction by understatement through green marketing.* A company becomes competitive by offering the best product, process or service at the lowest viable price. But an 'environmental' aspect can be 'value added' – subtly drawing the consumer in with a green design or context. The company philosophy should be one of taken-for-granted sustainability, as if everyone in the world naturally did the right, 'green' thing. This makes for an atmosphere of civilized grace that will shine through implicitly in everything the firm undertakes. The green theme should be revealed in advertising, but in the background like the underpainting on a canvas. This subtle marketing applies to existing large companies that decide to 'green' themselves as well as to small start-ups. Green marketing should be holistic, expanding on the basic transaction concept by minimizing a transaction's negative impact on the natural environment.

4. *Use green brainstorming to reduce cost.* Once a week the company could sponsor a 'green brainstorming' session over a meal provided by the company aimed at finding new, innovative ways of reducing costs. Modelled somewhat on Japanese-style 'quality control circles', these events should be social events in which the working staff have the floor and the managers are quiet or maybe even not present in order to inspire unrestrained, free-flowing exchanges in which even the most ridiculous ideas are given their chance.

5. *Use green networking in the community to generate free publicity.* The new company should network in an understated way with environmentally friendly interest groups, community groups and schools in the area – focusing on those particularly who are most likely to provide future customers or employees. By 'doing good' in this targeted way, the company can be expected to 'do well' in generating free publicity from the local press for its community activism. Anonymous articles can be contributed to the press to point out the obvious in case anyone misses it. (This strategy worked not only for Anita Roddick, but also for Benjamin Franklin – one of the most pragmatic of entrepreneurs, he used anonymous editorials to push for public changes he wanted in the newspaper he published.)

6.   *Use social ecopreneurship as an extraordinary motivator.* In cynical times of world economic crisis, both young and old workers seek work with existential meaning that goes beyond a wage, task or market networking scheme. A sense of social significance is an important motivator for many employees who harbour a need for idealism, for serving some cause beyond mere self-interest or corporate interest. By giving people a stake in an organization dedicated to being green in process, product and consciousness, it is easier for them to give their all, to forget the clock, to transcend their normal levels of productivity and contribution. Indeed, there may be social ecopreneurial capacities latent in all of us just waiting to be given an opportunity to bring this sense of sustainable community to worldly fruition. And if a private firm is sufficiently farsighted as to profit from this, so be it.

Public Strategies to Foster Ecopreneurship

The difficulty for public officials, whether at the regional, national or international level, is that in the 'attention economy' they are always playing catch-up with the latest crisis or public concern, limiting their perception of choice. Von Wiezäcker, Lovins and Lovins argue that such a perception is more a matter of creative imagination than of necessity, and that public officials should steer public perceptions towards green job creation:

> We need a rational economic incentive that allows us to employ more people and fewer resources, solving two critical problems at the same time. Businesses should sack the unproductive kilowatt hours, tonnes and litres rather than their workforce. This would happen much faster if we taxed labour less and resource use correspondingly more. (von Wiezäcker, Lovins and Lovins 1997, p. xxiv)

Clearly, businesses alone cannot bring about sustainability without tax and other government incentives to make it more attractive. Some of these public policy strategies to encourage ecopreneurship might be:

*   *Change tax incentives to reward the creation of green jobs and punish resource use.* Job creation is the number one priority in most countries in the twenty-first century. Morally, there is no justification for using public resources to fund or encourage jobs that work against

sustainability. Logically, grassroots seed-money should go to green start-ups, not just any start-ups. And heavier taxes on resource use would encourage brainstorming to cut costs in terms of resources and stimulate the evolution of ecopreneurship. Such public incentives stimulate the creation of 'green alliances' to help companies comply with laws and address green problems before their market positions are undermined by rigid and costly government mandates.

Build creativity and ecopreneurship incentives into standards for public-sector management. Creativity and entrepreneurship can be built into public-sector management standards, encouraging people in public organizations to mobilize their idealism in order to bring profitable ventures into being that benefit social needs and can clearly target ecopreneurship (Isaak 2002a). Zero-sum fights for public-budget dollars often lead to proposals promising to reduce risks rather than proposals that foster risk-taking, creative solutions to public problems in a sustainable manner. For example, in 2000 I used the non-profit university sector to have students set up two profit-making eco-businesses which not only paid back their venture capital, but also contributed their profits to worthy environmental causes (Anderson 2000). Such pilot experiments transform normal passive learning into stakeholder motivations that get young and old to cooperate in helping to build sustainable local community initiatives. Local governments, for example, can sponsor competitions for the best green start-up business plan and provide seed-capital for the winning entry, contributing to 'green job creation'.

- *Use ecopreneurship as a strategy for boosting civic competency and social capital.* In a globalized era of increasing 'democratic deficits' (for example, more elite and fewer direct democratic controls), it is necessary to find simple, targeted means to bring people together for a common cause in a way that builds social capital (networks of collective learning and solidarity) and economic development while raising environmental consciousness. Ecopreneurship is such a strategy. Sustainability crosses party affiliations and is in the long-term interests of most constituencies. Non-governmental organizations can be called upon for support, ideas and the stimulation of networking for the sake of sustainability. To find new, green ways of doing things that a community needs to have done can attract positive media attention to local communities and be educational as well as financially rewarding. Research has demonstrated that, as agents of change, entrepreneurs are more likely to be able to 'fix' environmentalism within new businesses (Anderson 1998, p. 135).

- *Start a public campaign to delegitimize non-sustainable business results.* Corporate managers are moved by threats as well as positive incentives. The environmental damage done to the environment by corporate neglect or actions must be exposed and heavily fined. But, beyond this, social pressures must be increased. One novel example has been New York State Governor George Pataki's policy of exposing the linkages between abnormally high cancer rates and zip code areas in which corporate pollution has been particularly high. Public institutions must make it clear to collective perception that pollution will be exposed and punished while positive steps towards sustainability, such as ecopreneurship, will be praised and rewarded (Isaak 2002b).

Conclusion

Ecopreneurship is not just anybody's existentialism. Businesses that are not designed to be sustainable negatively affect our health, shorten our time on earth and destroy the heritage we leave for our children, no matter where we are located globally. On the other hand, green-green businesses are models that can help show the way to increase productivity while reducing resource use in a manner that is harmonious with human health and the sustainability of non-human species as well. Green start-ups make it easier to 'fix' environmental components and processes from the outset. Green subsidiaries of larger firms can foster innovation and bring back the heightened motivation of social solidarity to businesses where it has been all too easy to slip into cynicism in an era of global economic crises.

The choice is clear. The technology is there. Only the political will is lacking. Sustainability is the ultimate political commitment and epitomizes common sense from the perspective of corporate citizenship. Every time we invest we should think of our own personal values and use a 'blended value' approach combining social and environmental as well as financial objectives. Only in this way can 'serial ecopreneurship' thrive and be cultivated. The key is to bring 'green-green businesses' to a critical mass and thereby assure global sustainable development.

References

American Wind Energy Association (2002) *Global Wind Energy Market Report* (March), pp. 1–8.

Anderson, A.R. (1998) 'Cultivating the Garden of Eden: Environmental Entrepreneuring', *Journal of Organizational Change Management*, Vol. 11, No. 2, pp. 135–143.

Anderson, L. (2000) 'Learning to Give Something Back', *New York Times*, 10 September.

Emerson, J. (2000) 'The Nature of Returns: A Social Capital Markets Inquiry into Elements of Investment and the Blended Value Proposition', *Social Enterprise Series No. 17* (Working Paper), Boston, MA, Harvard Business School.

Fischer, K. and Schot, J. (eds) (1993) *Environmental Strategies for Industry*, Washington DC, Island Press.

Fowler, G. A. (2002) 'Green Sales Pitch isn't Moving Many Products', *Wall Street Journal*, 6 March, p. B1.

Gupta, A.K. (1997) 'The Honey Bee Network: Linking Knowledge-rich Grassroots Innovations', *Development*, Vol. 40, No. 4, pp. 36–40.

Isaak, R. (1998) *Green Logic: Ecopreneurship, Theory and Ethics*, Sheffield, Greenleaf Publishers.

Isaak, R. (2002a) 'Building Creativity and Entrepreneurship into Standards for Public Sector Management', in D. Bräunig and P. Eichhorn (eds) *Evaluation and Accounting Standards in Public Management*, Baden-Baden: Nomos Verlagsgellschaft, pp. 86–93.

Isaak, R. (2002b) 'Social Incentives for Corporate Sustainability: Beyond the Limits of Liberalism', paper presented at the 10th International Conference of the Greening of Industry Network: 'Corporate Social Responsibility – Governance for Sustainability, 23–26 June 2002 in Göteborg, Sweden. Available at: www.GIN2002.miljo.chalmers.se.

Kumlien, K. (2002) 'How the Milesnicks Found Markets: Fly-Fishing on a Cattle Ranch', PERC, June, at: www.perc.org.

Pastakia, A. (1998) 'Grassroots Ecopreneurs: Change Agents for a Sustainable Society', *Journal of Organizational Change Management*, Vol. 11, No. 2, pp. 157–170.

Roddick, A. (1999) *Body and Soul*, Crown, New York.

Schaper, M. (2002) 'The Challenge of Environmental Responsibility and Sustainable Development: Implications for SME and Entrepreneurship Academics' in U. Füglistaller, H.J. Pleitner et al. (eds) *Radical Changes in the World – Will SMEs Soar or Crash?*, Rencontres de St Gallen, St Gallen, pp. 541–553.

US Water News (2002) 'Salted Irrigation', PERC, June, at: www.perc.org.

von Wiezäcker, E., Lovins, A.B. and Lovins, H.L. (1997) *Factor Four: Doubling Wealth, Halving Resource Use*, Earthscan, London.

Whitford, D. (2002) 'Smith & Hawken Founder Paul Hawken Believes that Business is Destroying The World; Maybe that's Why the Author and Environmentalist Wants You to Turn Your Small Business Upside Down', *Fortune Small Business*, Vol. 12, Issue 4/5, pp. 40–47.

World Resources Institute (2002) 'Are Business and Industry Taking Sustainability Seriously?', 25 February, at: www.wri.org/trends/business. html, p. 1.

4

Beyond the Visionary Champion: Testing a Typology of Green Entrepreneurs

Liz Walley, David Taylor and Karen Greig

ABSTRACT

Amongst the wealth of research on entrepreneurship, there has, hitherto, been surprisingly little investigation until recently into the motives of and influences on green entrepreneurs (Schaper 2005). This is especially serious given the importance of green entrepreneurs in the transition of the United Kingdom towards a sustainable society. Assessing both the research on typologies of entrepreneurs generally and recent perspectives on green entrepreneurs in particular, we have argued (Taylor and Walley 2004) that green entrepreneurs are best characterized by a combination of internal motivations and external structural influences (Giddens 1984). We have previously presented a range of frameworks for understanding and investigating the provenance of green start-ups and have developed an exploratory typology of green entrepreneurs encompassing four 'ideal types': innovative opportunists, visionary champions, ethical mavericks and accidental 'enviropreneurs' (Taylor and Walley 2004).

This typology has been pilot-tested using semi-structured interviews with ten owner-managers of UK green businesses. The scope of this research is not restricted to businesses founded on the principle of sustainability, but encompasses all possible forms of green business. The analysis of the pilot case studies resulted in a roughly equal distribution between the four types in our typology. In other words, the results suggest that there are as many new green businesses set up with entirely economic motives as there are green start-ups established because of wider sustainability goals. Given that the most popular image of a green entrepreneur is probably the 'visionary champion' type – for example, Anita Roddick of The Body Shop fame – this preliminary research suggests there are in practice, as well as in theory, various

types of green entrepreneur 'beyond the visionary champion' category. The pilot
results also suggest there may be a link between the industry sector and the resulting
typology classification, relating to the external structural influences dimension. The
green entrepreneurs in certain sectors (for example, energy) were predominantly
influenced by hard structural factors, whereas in other sectors (for example, food
and farming) soft structural factors were apparently more influential.

Introduction

The last 20 years of the twentieth century saw the growth of substantial
research and academic literatures in the fields of both entrepreneurship and
the greening of business. Prior to this, surprisingly little had been written
about the provenance of green entrepreneurs (Hendrickson and Tuttle 1997;
Anderson 1998; Isaak 1998). Researchers are now increasingly recognizing that
green entrepreneurs are crucial change agents or champions in the movement
towards a more sustainable future through the creation of new green business
formations, or green start-ups (see, for example, the special edition of *Greener
Management International*, 2002, Issue 38; Taylor and Walley 2004; Schaper,
2005). Our contribution to this early work was to construct a matrix or
typology that represented the drivers, or inspirations, of green entrepreneurs.
The defining criteria for this conceptual typology were based on an analysis
of general entrepreneurship typologies (see, for example, Chell, Haworth and
Brearley 1991; Dana 1995; Thompson 1998), structuration theory applied to the
greening of business (Giddens 1984; Walley and Stubbs 2000) and different
conceptualizations of green businesses (Elkington 1999; Isaak 1998). Other
typologies of green entrepreneurs have been developed (Schaltegger 2005;
Linnanen 2005; de Bruin and Lewis 2005), but few researchers have so far
provided evidence beyond a limited number of case studies (Schaper 2005). By
contrast, recent research by Vega and Kidwell (2007) draws on an impressive
80 cases of new venture creators in the United States to test their typology, but
the scope is significantly different in that they focus on the similarities and
contrasts between business and social entrepreneurs, and the latter includes
not-for-profit enterprises.

What Constitutes a Green Entrepreneur?

The term 'entrepreneur' is used here as a kind of generic shorthand for any
individual who starts up, runs (and possibly, but not inevitably, grows) a new
business venture (Gartner and Shane 1995; Iversen, Jørgensen and Malchow-

Møller 2005). In academic literature, entrepreneurship is generally accepted as extending well beyond the small business owner-manager sector (Ricketts 2006; Swedburg 2000). Our use of the term avoids a narrow preoccupation with either growth-orientation or uniqueness of product or service, and, given that we are ultimately interested in the motivations of anyone inclined to start a green business, include both entrepreneurs and small business owner-managers, although we use the 'shorthand' of green entrepreneurs to include both.

It is apparent that our definition of green entrepreneurs – and therefore the scope of our typology and research – is wider than most other authors in this field (Schaper 2005). It is important therefore to explain that our scoping of green entrepreneurs relates to individuals who set up green businesses, so it is the definition of what constitutes a green business that is significant. In popular usage, the expression 'green' is used in both a relative and an absolute sense. So a green business could refer to a business that has been set up with the aim of contributing:

> to the move towards a sustainable society by adopting processes and producing products that do not impact on the environment, or one that has, over time, adapted its products and processes in order to lessen their impact on the environment and in so doing contributes to the move towards a sustainable society.

Greenness can also refer to either the product or the process, and it is this aspect that is important to the definitional differences. For example, we would argue that a solar energy business is a green business by nature of the product, no matter what the motives or circumstances of the founding individual might be. Our argument is that all types of green businesses contribute to the move towards a sustainable society and we are therefore interested in the motives and influences of all entrepreneurs who set up such businesses. Their motives may or may not include a green belief system, although this is one of the potential characteristics that our research aims to investigate. For the primary research, therefore, one of the challenges was to articulate a definition of what constitutes a green business.

Most other authors' conceptions of green entrepreneurs or ecopreneurs – these terms are sometimes used synonymously and sometimes differently – seem to require or include a green intentionality or belief system (Schaper 2005). For example, Isaak's ecopreneurs (1998) are individuals who set up businesses that are founded on the principle of sustainability. Schaltegger's (2005) ecopreneurs category includes only those committed to environmental progress and mass market growth. The definition which is perhaps closest to our own in its breadth of scope is Hendrickson's and Tuttle's (1997) definition of green entrepreneurs as entrepreneurial activity that benefits the environment.

Another sense in which our definition is broad is that we include in our scope those businesses which could be primarily identified as ethical/social businesses but clearly include some green credentials. In our experience, sustainability-related enterprises often have a mixture of green, ethical and social characteristics. Whilst green implies compliance with environmental legislation and continually striving to reduce the impact of products and processes on the natural environment, it is not easy or necessary – given the triple-bottom-line definition of sustainability (Elkington 1999) – to separate or prioritize them. Desjardins (2007) suggests that the three criteria for sustainability are economic, ecological and ethical factors. Given that Elkington calls the third bottom line 'social' and Desjardins calls it 'ethical', we do not distinguish between the terms but use the expression 'ethical/social' to describe this general area. Our interpretation of green businesses also assumes a profit orientation and therefore excludes charitable, voluntary and public-sector organizations. To summarize, our working definition of what constitutes a green entrepreneur is an individual founder of a new, for-profit, significantly green business. 'Significantly green' is taken to mean green either by virtue of the nature of the product (for example, renewable energy), or substantially green policies and practices within the business (for example, The Body Shop).

The Typology

It can be argued that the most relevant explanatory variables for characterizing different types of green entrepreneurs are the external context (structural influences) and the entrepreneur's personal orientation or motivation (see Figure 4.1 opposite). This is based on our review of general entrepreneurship typologies and green entrepreneurship literature (Taylor and Walley 2004). This approach is underpinned by Giddens's (1984) ideas of structure and action, in the sense that green entrepreneurs' activities emerge from the mutually producing relationship between action and organization (social structure). Structure shapes the action of the green entrepreneur, and ecopreneurial action in turn shapes structure. In other words, green entrepreneurs do not operate in isolation, but will be influenced by the evolving economic and social structures around them and, in turn, are influencing those structures. This theme – of the interplay between individual motivations and the broader economic/ social context – is also found elsewhere in the ecopreneur literature (Schick, Marxen and Freimann 2002; Beveridge and Guy 2005). The structure axis in our typology ranges from hard structural influences at one end (for example, regulation and economic incentives) through to soft structural influences at the other (for example, past experiences, family and friends). These are illustrated in Figures 4.1 and 4.2.

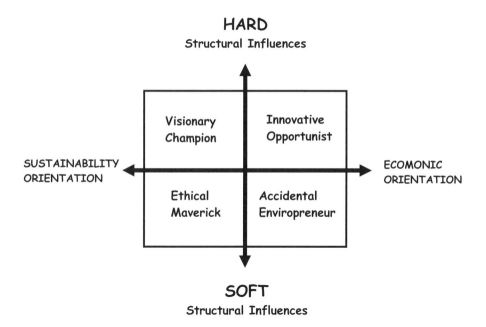

Figure 4.1   Green entrepreneur typology

In Figure 4.1 the 'orientation' axis, as described in Taylor and Walley (2004), arises from the exploration of what constitutes a green business, and is influenced by Thompson's (1998) paradigm perspective. The economic-orientation end of the axis represents the type of founder who set up the business with only profit motives (but who 'qualifies' as falling within the scope of the study because the business has already been classified as a green business, probably because of the nature of the product). The alternative set of orientations identified in the typology is one that combines economic, green and social/ethical motives, represented in the typology as a sustainability orientation. The matrix formed by these two axes – motivation and influences – thus produces four 'ideal types' of green entrepreneurs.

The 'visionary champion' type embraces a transformative, sustainability orientation. This champion of sustainability sets out to change the world, operates at the leading edge and has a vision of a sustainable future that envisages hard structural change.

The 'innovative opportunist' type is a financially-oriented entrepreneur who spots a green niche or opportunity and has been mainly influenced by hard structural drivers, such as regulation.

The 'ethical maverick' type is influenced predominantly by friends, networks and past experience rather than visions of changing the world. With their values-driven motivation comes a tendency to set up alternative-style businesses on the fringes of society rather than mainstream operations.

The motivation of the 'accidental enviropreneur' is largely financial rather than values-driven, and personal networks, family and friends influence them most.

The structural influences axis of the typology warrants further explanation, and this is presented visually in Figure 4.2. Interactions between personality and such factors as past experience, existing competence and the immediate context have proven decisive to the understanding of entrepreneurship (Blundell and Smith 2001). This integrated social–psychological approach to entrepreneurial behaviour (Chell, Haworth and Brearley 1991) focuses, amongst other things, on the way people respond to experience and crucial dimensions of the business context. Figure 4.2 conveys the range of potential influences in the external environment of the nascent green entrepreneur.

In Figure 4.2 the black inner circle illustrates the view, as reflected in the entrepreneurship literature, that the influence of the external environment is mediated by the individual characteristics of the entrepreneur – such as personality and competence. The circular arrows indicate the mutually producing relationship (Giddens 1984) between and within levels of structure and the entrepreneur. All these factors will impact on the nature of the green business that emerges. The 'question marks' remind us that we do not know what all the influences might be.

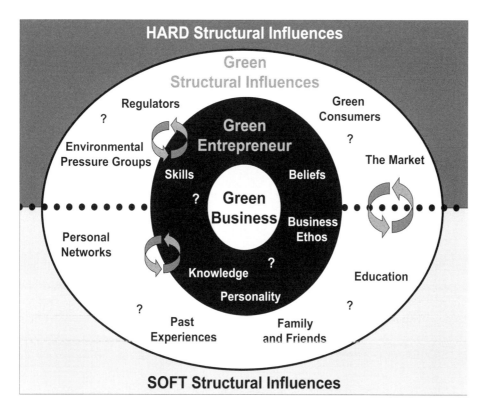

Figure 4.2   Influences on the green entrepreneur

The typology is intended to provide a useful framework for further research into the influences on, and motivations of, green entrepreneurs. For example, what are the significant external influences that impact on potential green entrepreneurs? To what extent do new green entrepreneurs fit the theoretical types proposed in the model and (if they do) what is the relative proportion of champions, opportunists, mavericks and accidentals? This research is intended to provide insights for policy-makers and educators into ways of fostering green entrepreneurship. For example, are green businesses more likely to be established by entrepreneurial types who are educated or trained to identify green opportunities, or by green enthusiasts who are encouraged or trained to become entrepreneurs?

Testing the Typology

One could critique the research so far on green entrepreneurs as being mainly conceptual and speculative without much supporting empirical evidence. Our own typology (Taylor and Walley 2004) was illustrated with examples taken from secondary published data, not primary research. With an appropriately-sized dataset one can begin to assess how relevant and useful the typology might be. Hence we embarked on primary research – in the form of interviews with green entrepreneurs – in January 2007, in order to test the appropriateness of the typology presented.

The first challenge was to identify a population of green businesses in the United Kingdom. A number of alternative sources were considered, but we chose *The Green Guide Directory* (www.greenguide.co.uk) as a starting point. This is a British online directory of approximately 12,400 nationwide eco-friendly goods and service providers.

For the pilot interviews we chose the three largest industrial sectors: energy, recycling and pollution; food and farming; and toiletries, cosmetics, clothing and fashion. With the exception of farming businesses, we also set aside companies that were established over 25 years ago, because we needed to talk to the founders of the businesses about their motives and circumstances at the time they set up the business, and, pragmatically, with an older company the founder was less likely to still be around. Having identified the founder of qualifying green businesses, we asked for telephone or face-to-face interviews.

The interview process, whilst very wide-ranging, was designed to obtain sufficient information about the founder so that their position on the typology could be determined. For example, there were questions relating to hard and soft structural influences, and we asked respondents to also rank themselves on the economic–sustainability continuum scale.

The data from the interviews was analysed using an agreed analytical process which included, *inter alia*: classifying influences cited as either soft structure or hard and assessing which was the dominant set; noting any 'new' structural influences (to add to the set identified in Figure 4.2); and plotting the orientation score on the continuum. This 'mapping' exercise resulted in a position or classification within the typology as illustrated in Figure 4.3. A second approach to classification – operating as a kind of check on the analytical process – was to check the descriptions associated with each typology type and see which matched the overall picture gained from the 'story' the respondent told.

All research methodologies are to some extent a compromise between what to include and what not to include, and are in that sense limited. The approach taken will inevitably exclude some of the possible routes that could have been followed. It is clear, for example, that our methodology so far does not include any other perspectives than that of the entrepreneur themselves (and our interpretation of that perspective). There have been no interviews with support organizations nor consideration of the role of support mechanisms, other than as perceived by the respondents in the context of significant influences. The focus at this stage is on the influences/motivations as perceived by the individual entrepreneur *at the time the business was conceived*, not, for example, on what happened next (Beveridge and Guy 2005). It therefore excludes, for now, the (potentially influential) role of their team, interpersonal relations and partnerships with external bodies. It does not address such research themes as network-building, trust and communication, other than as perceived by the individual respondents. Similarly, the research does not consider different socioeconomic contexts other than as influences perceived by the respondents themselves.

The aspects of the methodology being reported on here are based on testing an interpretation of structuration theory, or society–individual dualism. Some of the semi-structured questions were a directed testing of the typology, and this approach is not likely to give rise to grounded theory-type insights. In this sense, the data cannot readily be used to construct superior analytical tools to this typology-driven approach. All of these limitations suggest areas for further complementary research, in due course.

Results

Following the analysis of the ten sets of data from these pilot interviews (see Tables 4.1, 4.2 and 4.3), the typology classification results were as follows: two visionary champions, two innovative opportunists, three ethical mavericks and three accidental enviropreneurs.

In Figure 4.3, E1–E4 are the energy-sector cases, F1–F3 are food/farming entrepreneurs and T1–T3 are in the toiletries sector (see also Tables 4.1–4.3). The position of the case within each box is random – in other words, there has been no attempt at this stage to finely grade each case *within* the respective type box.

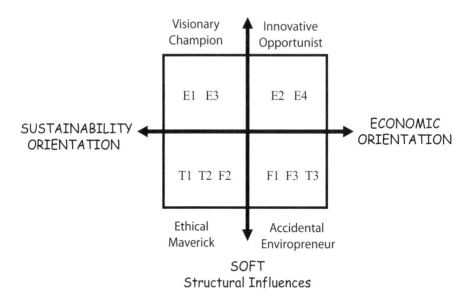

Figure 4.3   Classification of pilot case studies

Table 4.1   Energy-sector case studies

Energy-sector Case Studies	Case E1 Renewable Energy Supply and Consultancy	Case E2 Planning and Consultancy	Case E3 Solar Water Heating	Case E4 Scientific Laboratory
Company profile	Suppliers, distributors and project coordinators for solar PV and wind turbine systems. Established in 2002. Two employees.	Planning and environmental consultancy provider within an architect, surveyor and planner partnership. Established 2001. Three employees (50 within the partnership).	Installs affordable solar water heating systems in the UK and exports kits worldwide. Established 1998. 16 employees.	Environmental analysis laboratory specializing in accredited services for the environmental sector. Established 1990. Approx. 200 employees.
Green credentials	All products supplied are renewable energy products.	Services provided focus mainly on gaining planning permission for renewable energy projects.	100% solar water heating systems.	80–90% of business is environment related – e.g. monitoring and analysis of landfill.

Table 4.1   *Concluded*

Energy-sector Case Studies	Case E1 Renewable Energy Supply and Consultancy	Case E2 Planning and Consultancy	Case E3 Solar Water Heating	Case E4 Scientific Laboratory
Main influences at start-up	• Opportunity – didn't see anyone else doing this in the UK • Belief that renewables will go mainstream • Job/lifestyle change.	• Opportunity – renewals consultancy was a growing part of the market • Responding to client enquiries • Previous job and education.	• Offered the UK technology licence. • Previous employment • Winner of DTI Smart award – seed core funding	• Saw the idea operating successfully in another country • One founder was unemployed • Forthcoming EU/UK environmental legislation.
Orientation	Between 'light' and 'deep' green; motivation both economic and environmental.	Business established for commercial/profit reasons.	Deep green; very sustainability– oriented.	Motives totally economic.

Table 4.2   **Food- and farming-sector case studies**

Food/ Farming-sector Case Studies	Case F1 Health Food Retailer	Case F2 Organic Arable Farm	Case F3 Trout Farm
Company profile	Retailer of health-food supplements. Physical and online shop. Business bought as a going concern in 1988. Business founded in 1973. Employs 25 part-time staff.	Sells firewood logs and hay produced on the farm. Business taken over by current farmer (grandson of founder) in late 1980s. Business founded in 1915. Employs one part-time staff.	Trout farm founded in 1981 by current owner-manager. Business organic since 1991. Employs nine people. Trout supplied nationwide to retailers, box schemes, mail order and caterers. Also supplies organic salmon. Also sports fishing, tackle shop and fishing lessons.
Green credentials	50% of product line from green sources. Recognized as green by council due to level of recycling.	The farm was the first to go organic on the Wirral (1984). Currently considering a return to organic vegetable production. No chemical or artificial fertilizer on land since 1984.	Trout are grown to Soil Association standard. Operates an environmental action and animal welfare plan. Core market (95%) in 25-mile radius (reducing carbon footprint). From 1981 to 1990 almost completely self-sustaining. All equipment made from locally produced wood.

Table 4.2   *Concluded*

Food/ Farming-sector Case Studies	Case F1 Health Food Retailer	Case F2 Organic Arable Farm	Case F3 Trout Farm
Main influences at start-up	• Wife's medical condition • Desire for independence • Location of business.	• Father did not believe in chemical farming • Visit to Pimhill (organic estate of 1300 acres) in late 1970s • Member of CND and Green Party.	• Desire for control • Smallholding in South America • On Management and Trustee Board of Soil Association.
Orientation	Profit first.	Welfare of cattle (before farm went arable); premium value of organic produce.	Profit; lifestyle; sustainable through economic necessity.

Table 4.3   Toiletries-sector case studies

Toiletries-sector Case Studies	Case T1 Fair-Trade Gifts Retailer	Case T2 Manufacturer and Retailer of Natural Skincare Products	Case T3 Essential Oils Online Retailer
Company profile	Retailer of fair-trade products. Physical and online shops. The business was established in the late 1980s by the current owner with the aim of improving the livelihoods of disadvantaged people through fair and ethical trade with craft producers in developing countries. Employs 70 staff.	Natural skincare manufacturer and retailer established in the 1970s by the current owner. Employs around 30 staff. Supplies products to retailers and direct to online customers.	A mail-order/online supplier of essential oils established by the current owner-manager in 1993 and employs two people, including the owner-manager.
Green credentials	Proactively promotes fair and ethical trade and environmental protection. Over 50 % of craft producer partners are members of International Federation of Fair Trade (IFAT).	The company is a member of Groundwork which has audited its waste management process.	Both product and process are green. Packaging used is minimal and recyclable.
Main influences at start-up	• Experiences while travelling abroad • Previous employment.	• Family encouragement • An interest in 'alternative' skincare products.	• Previous employment in family company. • Own research into essential oils.

Our open-ended questions to the green entrepreneurs relating to potential 'influences' elicited some more factors which might be added to Figure 4.2 in due course if they occur regularly in the bigger sample. For example, in the hard structure category, respondents quoted influences relating to the (then) current business environment and the ecological environment. On the soft structure side, the data suggests that we will be able to be more specific about which particular types of 'past experiences' are quoted most often. For example, employment history was often talked about and employment insecurity (in various forms). Similarly, we hope to be able to make generalizations about the most influential networks – for example, nuances associated with family and friends. We could then potentially conduct follow-up interviews with members of each entrepreneur's networks (Taylor and Pandza 2003).

Based on this analysis of our initial pilot interviews of green entrepreneurs, we have a complete mix of 'types' – that is, at least two each in all four segments of the typology, namely visionary champions, innovative opportunists, ethical mavericks and accidental enviropreneurs. Since the data does not result in any 'empty boxes' in the typology, this gives some positive endorsement of the explanatory variables used. Given this balance, the results also suggest that there are as many new green businesses set up with entirely economic motives as there are green start-ups established because of wider sustainability goals. In the interviews, our respondents clearly identified – either explicitly or implicitly – their underlying motivation on the economic-sustainability orientation axis. We found it more difficult to place them on the hard–soft structural influences axis. Most of our respondents quoted both hard and soft structural influences as being significant in their decision to start the business. We sometimes therefore had to make a judgement based on both the overall balance of factors – to determine whether we placed them on the hard or soft end of the 'influences' axis – and on which 'type' description seemed to best fit the individual. For example, two of the renewable energy entrepreneurs appeared to have finely balanced combinations of both hard and soft structural influences, but it was their 'vision' of the future scope/scale of the business that placed them in the 'visionary champion' rather than 'ethical maverick' category.

It is interesting that, in this small pilot sample, there appears to be a link between the industry sector and the resulting typology classification. Two out of three of the toiletries-sector interviews resulted in ethical maverick classifications and, similarly, two out of three of the food/farming cases were accidental enviropreneurs. All the food/farming and toiletries cases appear in the bottom half of the matrix in Figure 4.3 – that is, the area of predominantly soft structural influences. The renewable-energy-sector entrepreneurs were either innovative opportunists or visionary champions – in other words, all appearing in the top half of the matrix where hard structure is most influential. With the benefit of hindsight, it is clear that certain contexts are more likely to result in stronger 'soft structure' influences: for example, in the farming sector, individuals invariably inherit the business, generation-to-generation, and so, perhaps almost by definition, will be (or appear to be) more influenced by soft structure factors such as family, personal networks and experiences. Similarly, businesses in certain sectors – for example, renewable energy – perhaps have more innate potential to grow and bring about a transformative 'sea change' than businesses in, say, the agricultural sector.

Conclusion

Our primary research results so far have highlighted some limitations and some positive attributes of both the methodological approach and the typology framework. For example, we have had to exclude from our sample large, evolving businesses – such as large engineering firms which have significant environmental or renewable energy divisions – because of the difficulty of identifying the point at which the business may have become significantly green and the existence of an identifiable 'entrepreneur/intrapreneur' within the business. Surprisingly, it has sometimes seemed like the two underlying parameters in our typology 'overlap' in the interpretation. For example, what about a farmer who does not want to kill his or her cows? Is this a motivation or the result of an influence? We believe that this is how structuration theory – the interplay between structure and action – manifests itself in practice.

Whilst acknowledging these issues and limitations, they do not appear to undermine the research approach being taken. The sample source, selection procedure, research questions and analytical approach are producing results which are illuminating the typology and giving us inspirational insights into the genesis of new green businesses. The results suggest that green entrepreneurial behaviour is not limited to 'visionary champion' types and that there are interesting stories and insights beyond the visionary champion. Having modified the research approach in light of experiences from this pilot study, we plan to continue this primary research with green entrepreneurs in a wider range of industrial sectors and geographical areas to the point when the volume of results supports firmer generalizations to be made about the influences and motivations of green entrepreneurs in the UK.

References

Anderson, A.R. (1998) 'Cultivating the Garden of Eden: Environmental Entrepreneuring', *Journal of Organizational Change Management*, Vol. 11, No. 2, pp. 135–144.

Beveridge, R. and Guy, S. (2005) 'The Rise of the Eco-preneur and the Messy World of Environmental Innovation', *Local Environment*, Vol. 10, No. 6, pp. 665–676.

Blundel, R. and Smith, D. (2001) 'Business Networks: SME's and Inter-firm Collaboration', *Report to the Small Business Service*, Research Report RR003/01.

Chell, E., Haworth, J. and Brearley, S. (1991) *The Entrepreneurial Personality*, Routledge, London.

Dana, L-P. (1995) 'Entrepreneurship in a Remote Sub-Arctic Community', *Entrepreneurship Theory and Practice*, Vol. 20, No. 1, pp. 57–72.

de Bruin, A. and Lewis, K. (2005) 'Green Entrepreneurship in New Zealand: A Micro-Enterprise Focus' in M. Schaper (ed.), *Making Ecopreneurs: Developing Sustainable Entrepreneurship*, Ashgate, Aldershot, pp. 61–71.

Desjardins, J.R. (2007) *Business Ethic, and the Environment: Imagining a Sustainable Future*, Prentice Hall/Pearson Education, Upper Saddle River, NJ.

Elkington, J. (1999) *Cannibals with Forks: The Triple Bottom Line of 21st Century Business*, Capstone, Oxford.

Gartner, W.B. and Shane, S.A. (1995) 'Measuring Entrepreneurship over Time', *Journal of Business Venturing*, Vol. 10, pp. 283–301.

Giddens, A. (1984) *The Constitution of Society: Outline of the Theory of Structuration*, Polity Press, Cambridge.

The Green Guide Directory (2006) at: www.greenguide.co.uk (accessed August 2006).

Hendrickson, L.U. and Tuttle, D. (1997) 'Dynamic Management of the Environmental Enterprise: A Qualitative Analysis', *Journal of Organizational Change Management*, Vol. 10, No. 4, pp. 363–382.

Isaak, R. (1998) *Green Logic: Ecopreneurship, Theory and Ethics*, Greenleaf, Sheffield.

Iversen, J., Jørgensen, R. and Malchow-Møller, N. (2005) 'Defining and Measuring Entrepreneurship', DP 2005-17, Centre for Economic and Business Research, at: http://www.cebr.dk/Publications%20submenu/Discussion%20Papers/2005/DP%202005-17.aspx (accessed 15 January 2008).

Linnanen, L. (2005) 'An Insider's Experiences with Environmental Entrepreneurship', in M. Schaper (ed.) *Making Ecopreneurs: Developing Sustainable Entrepreneurship*, Ashgate, Aldershot, pp. 72–85.

Ricketts, M. (2006) 'Theories of Entrepreneurship: Historical Development and Critical Assessment' in M. Casson, B. Yeung, A. Basu and N. Wadeson, (eds) *The Oxford Handbook of Entrepreneurship*, Oxford University Press, Oxford, pp. 33–58.

Schaltegger, S. (2005) 'A Framework and Typology of Ecopreneurship: Leading Bioneers and Environmental Managers to Ecopreneurship' in M. Schaper (ed.) *Making Ecopreneurs: Developing Sustainable Entrepreneurship*, Ashgate, Aldershot, pp. 43–60.

Schaper, M. (ed.), (2005) *Making Ecopreneurs: Developing Sustainable Entrepreneurship*, Ashgate, Aldershot.

Schick, H., Marxen, S. and Freimann, J. (2002) 'Sustainability Issues for Start-Up Entrepreneurs', *Greener Management International*, Vol, 38, pp. 59–70.

Swedburg R. (ed.) (2000) *Entrepreneurship: The Social Science View*, Oxford University Press, Oxford.

Taylor, D.W. and Pandza, K. (2003) 'Network Capability: The Competitive Advantage of Small Firms' in O. Jones and F. Tilley (eds) *Competitive Advantage in SMEs: Organising for Innovation and Entrepreneurship*, John Wiley and Sons, Chichester, pp. 156–173.

Taylor, D.W. and Walley, E.E. (2004) 'The Green Entrepreneur: Opportunist, Maverick or Visionary?', *International Journal of Entrepreneurship and Small Business*, Vol. 1, Nos 1/2, pp. 56–69.

Thompson, J.L. (1998) 'Will the Real Entrepreneur Please Stand Up!', Professorial Inaugural Lecture, October 1998, University of Huddersfield.

Vega, G. and Kidwell, R.E. (2007) 'Toward a Typology of New Venture Creators: Similarities and Contrasts between Business and Social Entrepreneurs', *New England Journal of Entrepreneurship*, Vol. 10, Issue 2, pp. 15–28.

Walley, E.E. (2000) 'Environmental Politicking: Skill Strategies for Environmental Champions', *Proceedings of the Business Strategy and the Environment Conference*, University of Leeds, pp. 412–419.

Walley, L. and Stubbs, M. (2000) 'Termites and Champions: Case Comparisons by Metaphor', *Greener Management International*, Issue 29 (Spring), pp. 41–54.

5

A Framework and Typology of Ecopreneurship: Leading Bioneers and Environmental Managers to Ecopreneurship

Stefan Schaltegger[1]

ABSTRACT

This chapter proposes a framework to position ecopreneurship in relation to other forms of environmental management. The framework can also be easily adapted to corporate sustainability. The framework provides a reference for managers for introducing ecopreneurship. Five basic positions are distinguished according to the degree of environmental orientation of a company's core business and market impact: environmental administrators, environmental managers, alternative activists, bioneers and ecopreneurs.

The chapter suggests an approach to the qualitative operationalization of ecopreneurship and sustainable entrepreneurship and how to assess the position of a company in a classification matrix. The degree of environmental or sustainable orientation in the company is assessed on the basis of environmental goals and policies, the ecological profile of the range of products and services, the organization of environmental management in the company, and the communication of environmental issues. The other examined dimension of ecopreneurship, the market impact of the company, is measured on the basis of market share, sales growth and reactions of competitors.

1   I would like to thank the EU, the Ministry of Science and Culture of Lower Saxony and the German Federal Ministry for Science and Education for funding of the basic research behind this chapter. I am furthermore grateful to Holger Petersen for his impressive contribution to a German report on the concept of ecopreneurship. Many thanks also to the students of the CSM sustainable entrepreneurship seminar for their company analyses.

The approach was then applied to seven company case studies. The case studies showed that the basic concept of ecopreneurship is applicable. The company representatives evaluated the approach as helpful in clarifying their position in ecopreneurial terms. The main benefit of the approach is that it provides a framework for self-assessment and indications for improvement.

Introduction

Innovations can radically alter the economy and society. Cars, computers and the Internet have changed the world more fundamentally than most political programmes. Being innovative means providing organizational and technical improvements which can be sold successfully in the marketplace. Creating innovations requires firms to overcome thresholds.

In a market system, sustainable development requires sustainable innovations and entrepreneurs who can achieve environmental goals with superior innovations that are successful in the marketplace. Market innovations driving sustainable development do not occur by accident, but have to be created by leaders who put them into the core of their business activities. Actors and companies making environmental progress to their core business can be called *ecopreneurs*. They generate new products, services, techniques and organizational modes which substantially reduce environmental impacts and increase the quality of life.

Joseph Schumpeter (1934) referred to such entrepreneurial activities as creative destruction. Ecopreneurs destroy existing conventional production methods, products, market structures and consumption patterns, and replace them with superior environmental products and services. They create the market dynamics of environmental progress.

This chapter attempts to provide a typology of ecopreneurship and to distinguish it from other forms of corporate environmental activities. This is summarized with a positioning matrix of ecopreneurship which allows management to assess its state of environmental and economic activities in relation to others. The next section defines the term 'ecopreneurship' and its derivation from entrepreneurship. The section after this discusses the elements of the positioning matrix of ecopreneurship and a first approach to assessing ecopreneurship. This approach is distinguished from eco-ratings and environmental assessments. The final section presents examples of companies and their management that have made a self-assessment of their ecopreneurial position. The company examples represent a sample of organizations which were regarded as potential ecopreneurial companies and invited by the RIO management forum, a Swiss-based non-governmental organization promoting eco-efficiency and environmental management in industry, to present their activities. The case studies illustrate the conceptual approach and demonstrate its usefulness as a self-assessment tool for company leaders.

What is Ecopreneurship?

THE FOUNDATION NOTION OF ENTREPRENEURSHIP

Economics and management theory neglected the phenomenon of entrepreneurship for a long time, as did the environmental management literature. However, for the last couple of years, more and more authors have started to deal with entrepreneurship following the work of Schumpeter (1934) and Kirzner (1973).

The word 'entrepreneur' derives from French and can be taken to mean 'taking the initiative to bridge'. Entrepreneurs are the catalysts who bring together money, people, ideas and resources. Whereas all entrepreneurs deal with bridging activities between suppliers and customers to create and change markets, ecopreneurs differ from conventional entrepreneurs in that they also build bridges between environmental progress and market success. Entrepreneurship can describe various phenomena (Lambing and Kuehl 1997):

- Many authors concentrate on the process of a start-up company (Bennett 1991; Boons and Roome 2005; Ripsas 1997). In this view entrepreneurs are actors opening a new company, and entrepreneurship is the process of creating and establishing a new company.

- Another aspect of entrepreneurship is that of striving for growth (Kyrö 2001; Timmons 1986; Wuestenhagen 2003). Entrepeneurs are viewed as actors enlarging companies and expanding businesses.

- Entrepeneurship has also been interpreted as a social movement or another kind of environmental grassroots movement (Bennett 1991; Bright, Fry and Cooperrider 2006; Pastakia 1998). In this perspective entrepreneurs are actors changing existing consumption and production patterns on basis of individual initiatives.

- Entrepreneurs are sometimes distinguished from traditional companies by their capability to innovate and create competitive advantage (Desa and Kotha 2006; Gruber and Henkel 2006; Risker 1998; Schaltegger and Wagner 2007; Schumpeter 1934; Staber 1997; Wiklund 1999; Wuestenhagen et al. 2008). Entrepreneurship links inventions with market success.

- Finally, entrepreneurship is characterized by the personal characteristics of a leader, such as ambition, leadership, team–building capability, personal involvement and commitment (Keogh and Polonsky 1998; Stevenson and Gumpert 1998).

The term 'ecopreneurship' is a combination of two words, 'ecological' ('eco') and 'entrepreneurship'. Ecopreneurship can thus be roughly defined as 'entrepreneurship through environmental lenses'. It is characterized by some fundamental aspects of entrepreneurial activities that are less oriented towards management systems or technical procedures and focus more on the personal initiative and skills of the entrepreneurial individual or team to realize market success with environmental innovations. After a first wave of literature beginning in the 1990s, only recently have some authors started to deal with environmentally-oriented entrepreneurship in more detail (cf. Anderson and Leal 1997; Bennett 1991; Berle 1991; Blue 1990; Isaak 1999; Keogh and Polonsky 1998; Kyrö 2001; Larson 2000; Lober 1998; Pastakia 1998; Schaltegger and Petersen 2001; Staber 1997; Wiklund 1999).

NARROW AND WIDE DEFINITIONS OF ECOPRENEURSHIP

Entrepreneurial thinking first starts with individuals, since environmental preferences are personal concerns. This is why ecopreneurs like Claus Hipp (founder of the Hipp company, one of Europe's largest producers of baby food), Gottlieb Duttweiler (founder of Migros, the largest food supplier in Switzerland), Ernst Pfenninger (founder of Trisa, a leading European producer of brushes and brooms) and Peter Kowalsky (owner of Bionade, the third largest soft-drinks company in Germany) embody the combination of strong environmental and social values with an energetic entrepreneurial attitude. Ecopreneurs show personal mastery (see Senge 1996) and consider their professional life as a creative act. Differences between personal goals and the perceived reality are considered as a challenge and not as a problem (Senge 1996, p. 175). Ecopreneurs influence their company substantially with their personal goals and preferences in such a way that these are reflected in the company's goals. This is more often and to a larger extent the case with start-up companies and small companies than with larger enterprises. Whereas environmental managers can leave a company without the firm losing substantial character, ecopreneurs constitute and shape the 'face' of their company. Because of the strong influence of the company leader's (or leaders') personality on company goals, ecopreneurship and the status of an ecopreneur can also be important to the whole company. As a consequence, ecopreneurship – narrowly defined – deals with a start-up of a very innovative company supplying environmental products and services (for a similar definition of entrepreneurship, see Ripsas 1997).

However, ecopreneurs can also be seen in established firms, since the process of creating substantial market success with environmental products and services also exists in established companies (for example, in the process of building up profit centres, spin-offs and so on). Defined more widely, ecopreneurship can thus be described as an innovative, market-oriented and personality-driven form of value creation by environmental innovations and products exceeding the start-up phase of a company. This wide definition of ecopreneurship takes *intrapreneurs* (Pinchot 1988) as an important subgroup of ecopreneurs into account, since intrapreneurs represent actors inside an organization who substantially change and shape the environmental and business growth development of an existing company. Similarly, *interpreneurs* (Fichter 2005), as actors starting networks and undertaking entrepreneurial activities with their network, are covered by the concept and term of ecopreneurship. Furthermore, ecopreneurs can act in the roles of intrapreneurs, founders and interpreneurs in parallel or over time.

Ecopreneurship (and sustainable entrepreneurship as the complementary theme on sustainable development) must be distinguished from *social entrepreneurship* (see, for example, Schwab Foundation 2006) which covers the societal activities of non-profit organizations with the means of entrepreneurship but without market-related economic goals.

In the following section, ecopreneurship is distinguished from other forms of corporate environmental development by the company's vivid commitment to environmental progress and its strong desire for business growth.

Where do Ecopreneurs Position their Companies?

This section shows in more detail what can be understood by ecopreneurship and how it is distinguished from other kinds of environmental activities undertaken by companies. Following an introduction to the positioning matrix of ecopreneurship, the two main dimensions of a model (priority of environmental goals and market effect) are discussed in more detail.

THE POSITIONING MATRIX OF ECOPRENEURSHIP

Companies contribute most to the overall environmental progress of an economy and society if their core business deals with environmental solutions and environmentally superior products, and if their innovations substantially influence the mass market. This is the main thesis for the empirical investigation detailed later and the basis for the definition of what we call ecopreneurship.

A positive environmental influence by companies calls for a real and substantial contribution to environmental improvement. A real improvement can only be created if the production processes, products and services are environmentally superior. To make a substantial contribution the company needs to exert a significant influence on the market by having a large market share or by influencing competitors and other market actors (such as suppliers) to adopt superior environmental solutions. Ecopreneurs run companies which fulfil both requirements (see Figure 5.1). Ideally, ecopreneurship pulls the whole market towards further environmental progress. Ecopreneurs strive for business success through environmental solutions for the mass market.

To measure how well a company has done, both dimensions of ecopreneurship can be further subdivided. The priority of environmental goals (the vertical axis in Figure 5.1) can range from low priority (environmental protection as a trustee duty) to medium priority (environmental issues as a supplement to conventional business issues) and high priority (environmental issues as an integral part of core business activities). The market effect of the company and its businesses (the horizontal axis) can be small in the alternative scene, medium with the successful occupation of an eco-niche and large through a strong influence on the mass market.

The combination of these dimensions provides the positions in Figure 5.1 and allows us to distinguish ecopreneurship from other forms of corporate environmental activities.

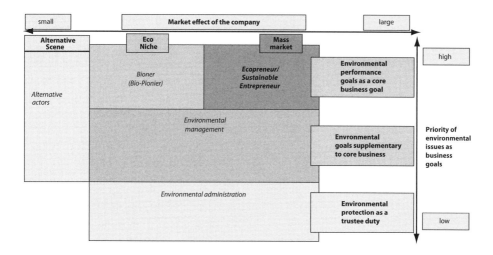

Figure 5.1   Positioning matrix and typology of ecopreneurship
Source: Schaltegger and Petersen (2001, p. 10).

Organizations in which environmental issues are of low priority consider these as a trustee duty and concentrate on the implementation of given environmental regulations and standards. Environmental issues are left to the legal department and to bureaucrats who administer the issues according to formally defined rules and regulations.

Company leaders who consider environmental issues as a supplementary aspect of business establish environmental management systems and departments which attempt to pilot and control environmental impacts in the most efficient manner. Cost reduction, the improvement of competitiveness and eco-efficiency, image campaigns and the differentiation of products and services are major goals of environmental management.

Companies in the upper level of Figure 5.1 treat environmental issues as central to their core business because their economic success is strongly linked to their environmental performance.

On the horizontal level of Figure 5.1 the market effect is distinguished between alternative scenes, eco-niches and mass markets. Suppliers characterized by alternative economic modes (for example, non-monetary swapping) act in an alternative scene or eco-scene amongst themselves. Turnover is supposed to secure personal living style. Market goals are non-existent.

Eco-niches mirror medium-sized market segments and are occupied by *bioneers*. The expression 'bioneer' is a combination of 'bio' and 'pioneer' and attempts to express not only the central role of research and development, but also the attempt to find customers with high preferences for their inventions and innovations. Bioneers focus on attractive market niches with their customer-focused eco-products.

In comparison, ecopreneurs and their companies aim for a large and growing market share, and for a high or increasing turnover in mass markets.

THE IMPORTANCE OF ENVIRONMENTAL ISSUES FOR THE CORE BUSINESS

Having discussed the typology and defined the dimensions of ecopreneurship, we can proceed to an initial qualitative approach to measuring ecopreneurship.

The strong environmental focus of the core business is the first major dimension of ecopreneurship. Three stages or positions are distinguished: administration, management and entrepreneurship.

Stage 1: Environmental administration   The administrative approach is of a stabilizing character and can be interpreted in line with the aim to preserve the capital of nature. Environmental administration stresses the conservation aspect of environmental issues and nature. It reminds management of its duty to act as a trustee of nature.

However, in the corporate context, administration is focused on the correct implementation of guidelines and instructions. This often accompanies bureaucratic structures and procedures. Environmental administration reflects a defensive approach. Its aim is to achieve minimal change in market conditions and to safeguard the status quo. Environmental protection is then seen as a duty which has to be dealt with because of external (legal, market or social) pressure. New social or legal requirements and technical inventions are seen as menacing developments questioning what has been achieved.

In concrete terms, this usually means the appointment of an environmental officer to supervise emission standards, regulations and formal company internal procedure protocols. Documentation is a core activity of environmental administration, and it is an integral part of the standards for environmental management systems such as ISO 14001 and EMAS. One of the main advantages of environmental administration is the safeguarding of legal compliance. The main disadvantage is the lack of focus on environmental performance and the creation of paperwork and environmental manuals which can destroy the motivation to undertake substantial environmental improvements.

Although environmental administration can be useful for securing legal compliance, it stands in opposition to the innovation necessary for substantial environmental progress. To improve eco-efficiency and eco-efficacy requires financial investments and commitment.

Stage 2: Environmental management   In comparison with environmental administration, environmental management is defined as more actively tackling problems. To 'manage' can be translated as taking something in one's hands and gaining control over it. The intention is to shape the company and its products and services, and to take advantage of technical and social opportunities. This requires the optimally efficient allocation of scarce resources like time, money, energy and environmental resources. Efficiency gains, not conservation, are the focus of environmental management. A major goal of corporate environmental management is to increase eco-efficiency as the relation between value added and environmental impacts added (Schaltegger and Sturm 1990). To achieve this, management approaches and tools, such as life-cycle assessment, environmental accounting and eco-control (Schaltegger and Burritt 2000), a sustainability balanced scorecard (Figge et al. 2002; Schaltegger and Dyllick 2002) and environmental management systems (Tibor and Feldman 1996), have been developed to control material and energy flows in the most systematic way. In contrast to standards such as ISO 14001, these tools focus on the improvement of environmental performance rather than on the correct functioning of a management system.

To improve the environmental quality in a market system a substantial increase of eco-efficiency is necessary. However, this will not be sufficient as long as relative improvements are overcompensated by larger amounts of sold and consumed products that do not contribute to environmental progress themselves. This leads to the entrepreneurial challenge of substantially contributing to higher environmental quality with eco-effective products and services.

Stage 3: Environmental quality as an entrepreneurial challenge   To make sure that eco-efficiency gains are not overcompensated by higher production, ecopreneurs must also focus on eco-efficacy. Eco-efficacy describes how well the reduction of environmental impacts is achieved in absolute terms (BMU, Econsense and CSM 2007; Schaltegger and Burritt 2000). Are the environmental impacts caused by a product throughout the whole market reduced effectively? This goal is not equal to the supply of environmental technologies, as the suboptimal effect of end-of-pipe technologies illustrates.

The entrepreneurial challenge is thus to be economically successful with the supply of products and services which change – on a purely voluntary basis – consumption patterns and market structures, leading to an absolute reduction of environmental impacts. Unlike bioneers, ecopreneurs are generally not inventors. Instead of spending time in laboratories, ecopreneurs search for inventions which they can shape and place on markets to create turnover (Murphy 2000) and influence market structures and even regional development (Boons and Roome 2005; Staber 1997). Only in exceptional cases are successful inventors simultaneously ecopreneurs. However, ecopreneurs often work with bioneers to convert inventions into market successes. The core activity of ecopreneurs is thus to search for business ideas created by environmental problems and solutions, to identify the market potential of inventions, and to realize market success with them.

In the extreme, ecopreneurship can thus be defined similarly to Timmons's concept:

> ... as a human act that builds something of value from practically nothing. It is the pursuit of opportunity regardless of the resources, or lack of resources, at hand. It requires a vision and a passion and commitment to lead others in the pursuit of that vision. It also requires a willingness to take calculated risks. (Timmons 1994, p. 48)

THE MARKET EFFECT OF ENVIRONMENTALLY-ORIENTED COMPANIES

The second dimension of ecopreneurship in the positioning matrix is the market effect. Corporate solutions to environmental problems have little effect if they remain in market niches or if the market introduction fails (Villiger, Wuestenhagen and Meyer 2000). Many company examples which are discussed as leading cases have had little meaningful market impact. Figure 5.2 shows three positions of market influence that reflect environmentally-oriented companies in practice.

1. Production in the alternative scene   Autonomy in management without bosses, the renunciation of hierarchies, craftsmanship instead of industrial production, and the integration of leisure time and work characterize the goals of the alternative scene, which attempts to create a counter-culture to the conventional economy (see Conti 1984). The attraction of the alternative scene is to break out of normality and obligations of any kind, and to create a small world of self-assuring structures and procedures (see Schulze 1996, p. 747). However, the total environmental effect is not of interest, as any large-scale imitation would contradict the intentions and motivations of the actors creating the alternative scene. Nevertheless, the environmental movement of the 1970s and 1980s has created alternative structures which, in some cases, have survived for three decades and have provided the background for many entrepreneurs and bioneers who have entered market niches in the last couple of years.

2. Focusing on eco-niches   Niche-market suppliers are companies which specialize in specific customer preferences (Kotler 1998; Porter 1999). The competition strategy is to focus on one precisely defined area of the market which is big enough to be economically successful and small enough to be neglected by the mass market suppliers. The suppliers serve exclusive target groups with a consequent differentiation strategy. This requires innovation of not only the products and services supplied, but also production technologies and organizational concepts. Large competitors neglect these niches because they do not recognize them, do not consider them to be attractive enough, or are unable to fulfil the specific customer preferences well enough.

Since the 1980s many autonomous producers and green activists left the alternative scene and started to enter commercial market niches (Horx 1985). Some suppliers (for instance, some organic wine producers) have similar characteristics to those in the alternative scene. However property rights are clearly more defined amongst eco-niche suppliers. A leader, who makes the investment, takes the decisions and wants to earn money characterizes the company. The customers show a strong interest and are willing to pay premium prices for the products.

Suppliers driven by environmental invention can be called bioneers – they play the role of a pioneer by opening new paths of environmental development in markets. This is why they never consider the usual mass-market marketing and communication approaches. Apart from having higher incomes and environmental preferences, the customers usually need substantial market and product knowledge and more time to find the products they are looking for.

Many examples of bioneers can be found in the environmental high-tech sector (solar and wind energy), energy contracting and the textile industry. Another group of bioneers are traditional SMEs which develop their products and services according to environmental criteria. They are often led and strongly shaped by a company owner or family authority striving for harmony between environmental, social and financial goals.

Although bioneers serve an important function in the environmental development of products, their direct impact remains small. The majority of customers and the main flow of materials and energy in the mass markets are not affected by the activities of bioneers. However, with their innovations, bioneers can influence competition in the mass market. Whereas in the past many environmentalists have subscribed to the view that 'small is beautiful', the environmental management literature has recently started to step out of niche-market terms and to 'think big' in order to gain a substantial environmental impact in mass markets (Schaltegger and Petersen 2001; Villiger, Wuestenhagen and Meyer 2000).

The Measurement Approach and Case Studies

Given the general description and distinction of ecopreneurship, the question arises: how can ecopreneurship be measured in practice?

This question is distinctly different from the usual environmental rating or environmental assessment approaches, as the attempt is not primarily to measure a specific status of corporate environmental impact or to check the existence of environmental management systems. Instead, it is to investigate how well the process of ecopreneurship is realized.

TOWARDS A MEASUREMENT APPROACH

To measure ecopreneurship and to test the positioning matrix we operationalized the two dimensions (environmental priorities and market effect) in the following way (Schaltegger and Petersen 2001, p. 26ff).

Programmes of activities Business policies, environmental statements, corporate strategy papers and activity programmes reflect the strategy and the importance given to environmental issues in the core business. They provide the objectives for operative management. Concrete assessment questions to measure this aspect of ecopreneurship are:

- Are environmental principles part of the business policy?

- Are these principles reflected in the strategy papers?

- Have quantitative goals and timetables been defined on the basis of these principles and strategies?

Range of products and services   The range of products reflects how well the company has been able to convert its policies into concrete market actions. The main question to check this requirement of ecopreneurship is: how environmentally-oriented are the company's products and services compared to those of its competitors? A problem with this issue is that it is generally not feasible to reliably measure the environmental impacts of a product using life-cycle assessment. The following indicators can be used to approximate this aspect:

- An easy measure is the number of explicitly labelled environmentally-oriented products compared to the total range of products of the company.

- Another proxy is to measure how well the goals defined by the company have been achieved. This indicator requires that the goals have been defined precisely enough to be measured and that they are made public.

The product range and production processes can be compared with the main competitors. Environmental benchmarking fails in most cases because of a lack of data. However, the question of whether there is a substantial difference for the majority of production processes and products can often be answered more easily.

One proxy is to check the opinion expressed by environmental experts, assessment companies and media. This includes whether environmental criteria of external assessment organizations have been met and whether eco-labels and awards have been received.

In addition, a comparison over time is necessary to get a picture of whether ecopreneurial progress exists.

Organization and communication processes   Ecopreneurship is only possible if environmental issues are dealt with at a top management level and integrated into all business activities. Possible assessment questions are:

- Are environmental issues an integrated part of every management level and business unit in the company or are environmental matters delegated to an environmental, legal or PR department with a bureaucratic organization structure?

- Is the company involved in scientific environmental research and development projects and do these projects address core business activities?

- Are environmental issues and the relation to economic performance addressed in the company's core communication activities (financial report, advertisements and so on)? In many cases, ecopreneurs tend to give oral communication by the company leader a high priority.

Market effect   One main market effect is directly measurable as market share or sales of the company. Indirect market effects occur when environmental innovations are copied by competitors or when an environmental product feature becomes a standard in the market. Ecopreneurial companies have a large market share and/ or a strong influence on product standards and company behaviour. One main requirement for achieving this is to reduce the price of the environmental products to the existing market level. Sometimes companies can also extend or develop a market by influencing change in legal and political conditions, as has happened in the market for wind energy in northern Europe. Among the main questions leading the assessment of the market effect as part of ecopreneurship are:

- Does the company have a substantial market share? Is the growth of market share and sales larger than the average market growth?

- Have the company's innovations been copied by competitors?

- Do the prices of the company's products fall in the medium range of the market or do they reflect a niche strategy focusing on an exclusive group of customers?

- Has the company been able to extend the market for environmental products? This is achieved in some cases by political means (Kotler 1986).

These ways of qualitatively measuring ecopreneurship have been tested on case studies, which are described below.

CASE STUDIES ON THE ASSESSMENT OF ECOPRENEURSHIP

The following cases are of companies which were selected as being leading companies in terms of environmental and economic performance by students of the Centre for Sustainability Management at the Leuphana University of Lueneburg (see Brix, Bromma and Jaenisch 2006). The students' empirical investigation was based on a questionnaire developed earlier with this concept of ecopreneurship (Schaltegger and Petersen 2001). The questionnaire was answered by company representatives and supplemented by informational material, such as company policy data, environmental statements and reports, advertisement and communication materials, which we asked for in a preparation phase. Table 5.1 provides an overview of the 11 case studies, which are mainly European companies. Some of them are internationally-oriented

Table 5.1   Companies involved in the case studies on measuring ecopreneurship

Name of Company	Industry/ Market	Market Position/Size/ Sales	Employees approx. (2005–06)	Geographic Focus
Auro	Colours	Leader in organic colours, €8 million	55	Mainly Germany
Ben & Jerry`s	Ice cream	Leader in super-premium ice cream, €250 million	n.a.	World
Demeter	Organic food organization	The world's largest supplier organization of organic food	3,500 farms	Europe
Lichtblick	Electric power retailer	Largest 'green' power supplier in Europe – 190,000 households	220	Germany
Toyota	Automobiles	The world's largest producer, €110,000 million	> 400,0000	World
The Body Shop	Furniture textiles	Cosmetics, €1,300 million	15,000	World
SCA	Paper	Largest paper producer of Europe, € 9,500 million	51,000	World
Otto	Retail	The world's largest mail-order retailer, €1,000 million	53,000	World
Hipp	Baby food	Europe's market leader, 6,000 farms	1,000	Europe

and others are more focused on their national market. For most companies the entrepreneurial leader is well known to the public. All companies have environmental or sustainability reports and these are often presented in the media. Each of them is either included in the portfolio of sustainability funds or of sustainability venture funds.

In addition to the questionnaire and the examination of further company publications and documents, the students were asked to position the companies in the ecopreneurship positioning matrix. To do so, the students established contact with company representatives. In a next step the students were challenged in a workshop by the author and other students. In some cases, the position was changed in mutual agreement after a discussion of all considered documents and arguments.

The results of the case studies are shown in Figure 5.3. The stars show the current position.

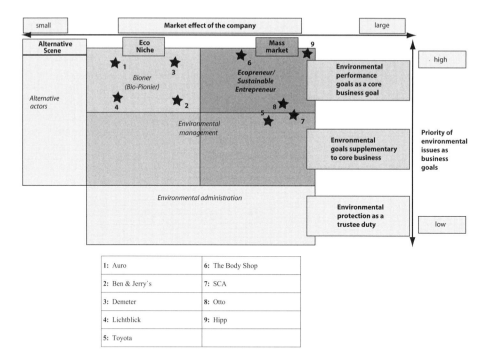

1: Auro	6: The Body Shop
2: Ben & Jerry's	7: SCA
3: Demeter	8: Otto
4: Lichtblick	9: Hipp
5: Toyota	

Figure 5.3   Ecopreneurial positions

Source: Brix, Bromma and Jaenisch (2006).

The results show very different positions in the matrix of ecopreneurship for the companies identified as environmental and economic leaders by students. In many cases, the role of intrapreneurs was seen as being as important as the role of the company leader in driving the process of ecopreneurship. The assessment helped identify possible steps to improve the ecopreneurial position. In some cases, company internal measures are necessary to further develop the position. In other cases, further technological and external political developments can create the desired market breakthrough.

Conclusions

The proposed classification can be used for both external assessment and self-assessment to support bioneers and environmental managers in their attempts to realize ecopreneurship in practice. Furthermore, the approach provides not only a framework for classification and terminology, but also a first step towards the measurement of ecopreneurship. The case studies showed that the basic concept of ecopreneurship and the approach of (self-) assessment is indeed applicable.

The aim of the assessment approach is not to judge and distinguish 'good' from 'bad' companies. The main benefit of assessing the ecopreneurial position is to provide a framework for (self-) assessment and indications for improvement.

References

Anderson, T. and Leal, D. (1997) *Enviro-Capitalism: Doing Good While Doing Well*, Littlefield Publishers Inc., Lanham, MD.

Bennett, S.J. (1991) *Ecopreneuring: The Complete Guide to Small Business Opportunities from the Environmental Revolution*, Wiley, New York.

Berle, G. (1991) T*he Green Entrepreneur: Business Opportunities that Can Save the Earth and Make You Money*, Liberty Hall Press, Blue Ridge Summit, PA.

Blue, J. (1990) *Ecopreneuring: Managing for Results*, Scott Foresman, London.

BMU, Econsense and CSM (eds) *Sustainability Management of Corporations*, BMU, Econsense and CSM, Berlin/Lueneburg.

Boons, F. and Roome, N. (2005) 'Sustainable Enterprise in Clusters of Innovation – New Directions in Corporate Sustainability Research and Practice' in S. Sharma and J.A. Aragón-Correa (eds) *Environmental Strategy and Competitive Advantage*, Edward Elgar Academic Publishing, Northhampton, MA, Chapter 12.

Bright, D.S., Fry, R. and Cooperrider, D.L. (2006) 'Transformative Innovations for Mutual Benefit in Business, Society and Environment', paper presented at the Academy of Management Meeting, Atlanta, 11–16 August.

Brix, K., Bromma, M. and Jaenisch, J. (2006) *Sustainable Entrepreneurship*, Fallstudien und empirische Überprüfung, CSM, Lueneburg.

Conti, C. (1984) *Abschied vom Bürgertum: Alternative Bewegungen in Deutschland von 1890 bis heute*, Rowohlt, Reinbeck.

Desa, G. and Kotha, S. (2006) 'Technology Social Ventures and Innovation: Understanding the Innovation Process at Benetech', paper presented at the Academy of Management Meeting, Atlanta, 11–16 August.

Fichter, K. (2005) *Interpreneurship. Nachhaltigkeitsinnovationen in interaktiven Perspektiven eines vernetzten Unternehmertums*, Metropolis, Marburg.

Figge, F., Hahn, T., Schaltegger, S. and Wagner, M. (2002) 'The Sustainability Balanced Scorecard', *Business Strategy and the Environment*, Vol. 11, No. 5, pp. 269–284.

Gruber, M. and Henkel, J. (2006) 'New Ventures Based on Open Innovation: An Empirical Analysis of Start-up Firms in Embedded Linux', *International Journal of Technology Management*, Vol. 33, No.4, pp. 256–372.

Horx, M. (1985) *Das Ende der Alternativen*, Hanser, Munich.

Isaak, R. (1999) *Green Logic: Ecopreneurship, Theory and Ethics*, Kumarian, West Hartford, CT.

Keogh, P.D. and Polonsky, M.J (1998) 'Environmental Commitment: A Basis for Environmental Entrepreneurship?', *Journal of Organizational Change Management*, Vol. 11, No. 1, pp. 38–49.

Kirzner, I. (1973) *Competition and Entrepreneurship*, University of Chicago Press, Chicago.

Kotler, P. (1986) 'Megamarketing', *Harvard Business Review* (Autumn), pp. 117–124.

Kotler, P. (1998) *Marketing Management: Analysis, Planning, Implementation and Control*, Prentice Hall, Englewood Cliffs, NJ.

Kyrö, P. (2001) 'To Grow or not to Grow? Entrepreneurship and Sustainable Development', *International Journal of Sustainable Development and World Ecology*, Vol. 8, No. 1, pp. 15–28.

Lambing, P. and Kuehl, C. (1997) *Entrepreneurship*, Prentice Hall, Upper Saddle River, NJ.

Larson, A.L. (2000) 'Sustainable Innovation through an Entrepreneurship Lens', *Business Strategy and the Environment*, Vol. 9, pp. 304–317.

Lober, D.J. (1998) 'Pollution Prevention and Corporate Entrepreneurship', *Journal of Organizational Change Management*, Vol. 11, No. 1, pp. 26–37.

Pastakia, A. (1998) 'Grassroots Ecopreneurs: Change Agents for a Sustainable Society', *Journal of Organizational Change Management*, Vol. 11, No. 2, pp. 157–173.

Pinchot, G. (1988) *Intrapreneuring*, Wiesbaden, Gabler.

Porter, M. (1999) *Competitive Advantage*, Campus, Frankfurt.

Ripsas, S. (1997) *Entrepreneurship als ökonomischer Prozess*, Gabler, Wiesbaden.

Risker, D.C. (1998) 'Toward an Innovation Typology of Entrepreneurship', *Journal of Small Business and Entrepreneurship*, Vol. 15, No. 2, pp. 27–42.

Schaltegger, S. and Burritt, R. (2000) *Contemporary Environmental Accounting*, Greenleaf, Sheffield.

Schaltegger, S. and Dyllick, T. (2002) *Nachhaltig managen mit der Balanced Scorecard*, Gabler, Wiesbaden.

Schaltegger, S. and Petersen, H. (2001) *Ecopreneurship. Konzept und Typologie*, CSM/Rio Management Forum, Lueneburg/Lucerne.

Schaltegger, S. and Sturm, A. (1990) 'Ökologische Rationalität', *Die Unternehmung*, Vol. 4, No. 90, pp. 273–290.

Schaltegger, S. and Wagner, M. (2008) 'Types of Sustainable Entrepreneurship and Conditions for Sustainability Innovation' in: R. Wuestenhagen, J. Hamschmidt, S. Sharma. and M. Starik (eds) *Sustainable Innovation and Entrepreneurship*, Edward Elgar Publishing, Cheltenham.

Schulze, G. (1996) *Die Erlebnisgesellschaft*, Campus, Frankfurt am Main.

Schumpeter, J. (1934) *Theorie der wirtschaftlichen Entwicklung*, New Pring, Berlin.

Schwab Foundation for Social Entrepreneurship (2006) *Outstanding Social Entrepreneurs*, Schwab Foundation, Colgny.

Senge, P. (1996) *Die Fünfte Disziplin: Kunst und Praxisder lernenden Organisation*, Klett-Cotta, Stuttgart.

Staber, U. (1997) 'An Ecological Perspective on Entrepreneurship in Industrial Districts', *Entrepreneurship and Regional Development*, Vol. 24 No. 1, pp. 37–48.

Stevenson, H. and Gumpert, D. (1998) 'Der Kern unternehmerischen Handelns' in G. Faltin et al. (eds) *Entrepreneurship. Wie aus Ideen Unternehmen werden*, C.H. Beck Verlag, Munich, pp. 93–112.

Tibor, T. and Feldman, I. (1996) *ISO 14000: A Guide to the New Environmental Management Standards*, Irwin Professional Publishers, Chicago.

Timmons, J. (1986) 'Growing Up Big' in D. Sexton and R. Smilor (eds) *The Art and Science of Entrepreneurship*, Ballinger, Cambridge, MA.

Timmons, J. (1994) *New Venture Creation: Entrepreneurship for the 21st Century*, Irwin, Boston, MA.

Villiger, A., Wuestenhagen, R. and Meyer, A. (2000) *Jenseits der Öko-Nische*, Birk-
    häuser, Basel.

Wiklund, J. (1999) 'The Sustainability of the Entrepreneurial Orientation
    Performance Relationship', *Entrepreneurship, Theory and Practice*, Vol. 24,
    No. 1, pp. 37– 48.

Wuestenhagen, R. (2003) 'Sustainability and Competitiveness in the Renewable
    Energy Sector: The Case of Vestas Wind Systems', *Greener Management
    International*, Vol. 44, pp. 105–115.

Wuestenhagen, R., Hamschmidt, J., Sharma, S. and Starik, M. (eds) (2008)
    Sustainable Innovation and Entrepreneurship, Edward Elgar Publishing,
    Cheltenham, UK, and Lyme, US.

6

Little Acorns in Action: Green Entrepreneurship and New Zealand Micro-Enterprises

Anne de Bruin and Kate Lewis

ABSTRACT

This chapter examines green entrepreneurship in New Zealand, with a special focus on small and micro-sized firms.* It uses one particular industry – the waste recycling and minimization sector – to illustrate some of the factors which work to promote and hinder green entrepreneurship within the country. It then presents a conceptual framework for identifying and classifying ecopreneurial firms, which seeks to capture the multiplicity of responses and orientations that make up the green actions of entrepreneurs in New Zealand. A selection of short cases on micro-enterprises is used to illustrate different dimensions of the framework. Three firms – the WasteWise Trust, Waste Not Consulting and Brookby Herbs – are profiled.

---

*   The definition of SMEs varies across countries and within countries. New Zealand government agencies such as the Ministry of Economic Development define 'small' firms as those with 19 or fewer FTEs. Micro-enterprises are those with less than six employees.

Introduction

'Clean and green' is a catch-cry that increasingly resonates around the world. It reflects in a concise fashion the complex nature of the global drive for sustainable development. This push for sustainability has also resulted in the creation of a whole new entrepreneurship paradigm relating to how to do business in an environmentally responsible fashion (Schaper 2002). The focus on understanding best business practice, in terms of environmentalism and sustainability, has revealed that such a 'green' orientation can be rewarding in terms of the business bottom line as well as conservation of the world's resources (Dixon and Clifford 2007; Menguc and Ozanne 2005).

In New Zealand 'clean and green' is more familiar as a description of what the country has to offer (such as its agricultural products and its tourism industry), rather than as a term applied to the practices of its businesses. However, increased global consciousness in terms of sustainable business practice has also begun to have an effect on the country's businesses and markets. It is to be expected, therefore, that increasing numbers of New Zealand businesses would endeavour to act more responsibly in terms of the environment and more responsively to the needs of environmentally-oriented consumers. There is, however, no firm evidence to back up this expectation, and a green business image could well be more rhetoric than reality. However, as one of the only pieces of empirical evidence on New Zealand firms and their environmental practices shows, many firms in the country still have a long way to go (Knuckey and Johnston et al. 2002). For example, an assessment of measures taken to reduce the environmental impact of business activities over a three-year period indicated that only 47 per cent of surveyed firms had implemented measures to reduce environmental impacts. 'Leading' firms (those in the top quintile, based on overall scores for business practice and outcomes) performed better at 71 per cent, whilst only 21 per cent of 'laggers' (the bottom quintile) had put in place environmental measures. Furthermore, a low 9 per cent have, or plan to gain, environmental certification.

Defining Green Entrepreneurship

Green entrepreneurship may be viewed as synonymous with 'environmental entrepreneurship' which, following Hendrickson and Tuttle (1997, p. 363), is defined simply as 'entrepreneurial activity that benefits the environment'. Yet this perspective is not particularly useful as it can encompass practices that are environmentally friendly but form part of the ordinary, or necessary, operation of a business (for example, complying with government or industry regulations such as those required under the Kyoto Protocol). More useful, however, is Hendrickson's and Tuttle's (1997) elaboration on environmental businesses, which distinguishes three distinct types:

1.   those that are environmental due to the inputs and resources used in their products and services (for example, use alternative energy sources, or recycled products or make an everyday product in an environmentally friendly way);

2.   those that are environmental due to their impact through products or services on the 'transformation process' (for example, they help other companies to reduce waste in manufacturing processes, or help identify toxic waste problems, or design waste reducing products); and

3.   those that are environmental because of the goods or services they produce (for example, they assist with waste clean-up or deal with waste in an environmentally friendly manner).

Complementing the Hendrickson and Tuttle categorization is that of Linnanen (2002). His eco-business classification (2002, pp. 72–73) may also be used as a convenient means of grouping green businesses into four segments: nature-oriented businesses; producers of environmental technology; providers of environmental management services; and producers of environmentally friendly products. Green entrepreneurship can be further refined according to shades of green or strength of commitment to environmental goals and strategies. According to Walley and Taylor (2002, p. 31) 'in popular usage the expression "green" is used in both a relative and absolute sense'. So the label of 'green business' can refer to one that has been set up on a green basis or one that has become relatively green, and greenness can also refer to either the product or the process. Work by Isaak (2002) has also contributed to the development of a differentiation between so-called 'green' and 'green-green' businesses. 'Green businesses' did not start out that way: instead, owners or managers became aware of the cost, innovation and marketing advantages and so implemented the changes necessary to become 'green'. In contrast, 'green-green businesses' are those that were designed to be green in terms of both processes and products from the outset, and are also 'intended to transform socially the industrial sector in which it is located towards a model of sustainable development' (Isaak 2002, p. 82). Isaak (1998) therefore defines ecopreneurs as being those individuals who found or set up green-green businesses, and Schaltegger (2002) suggests that ecopreneurs differ from conventional entrepreneurs only in that they also build bridges between environmental progress and market success.

The New Zealand Context

New Zealand is an island nation comparable in size to the United Kingdom, but with a population of only approximately 4 million people. In 2007, 89 per cent of the country's 463,380 enterprises were micro in size. The Kyoto Protocol was ratified by New Zealand in 2002, and it binds the country to reduce greenhouse gas (GHG) emissions to 1990 levels between 2008 and 2012. The government introduced a GHG emissions trading scheme as part of the 2007 Climate Change Act to address this obligation.[1]

The case of the waste recycling and minimization sector is used in the next section to emphasize that in order to better understand green entrepreneurship (specifically in the context of micro-enterprises), it is necessary to grasp the range of contexts in which this entrepreneurial activity can potentially occur. More specifically, however, this section is used to demonstrate that the use of any categorizations of green micro-entrepreneurship is critically dependent on an understanding of its contextual underpinnings, be that at a global, national or local scale. Market orientation and entrepreneurial actions are a result of the manner in which green entrepreneurs interpret and react to intrinsic or personal environmental concerns and passions, and to the external forces that constantly shape and reshape these responses. Thus '… commitment to environmental concerns can be considered both a process and a resultant' (Keogh and Polonsky 1998, p. 41).

As Thornton aptly puts it, entrepreneurship occurs 'as a context-dependent, social and economic process' (1991, p. 20). At a core level, therefore, both green entrepreneurship and its purer cousin, entrepreneurship, can be conceived as parts of the wider social milieu. The de Bruin and Dupuis (2003) approach to entrepreneurship emphasizes entrepreneurship as an activity 'embedded' (Granovetter 1985) in ongoing social relations. In relation to the green theme, Anderson (1998, p. 139) goes so far as to suggest that the very 'notion of embeddedness is why entrepreneurship is most likely to sustain environmentalism than any other form of imposed change'. Thus the popularity of the green movement embodies shifts reflecting individual intentions of citizens and the collective intentions of societies to focus more on preserving, rather than consuming, their environs. This global trend augurs well for the overall success of green entrepreneurship and provides increasing business opportunities (see, for example, Hawken, Lovins and Lovins 1999). Nevertheless, more specific contextual factors at the local, national and global levels can both help and hinder entrepreneurial endeavours. In order to illustrate this, the rest of this section comprises an examination of a particular green sector in New Zealand – the recycling industry.

---

1   See www.stats.govt.nz for more information on New Zealand.

Advocacy of the so-called 3Rs (reduce, reuse, recycle) has rapidly grown in prominence in the developed world. During the early years of the recycling movement (the late 1960s and early 1970s) resource recycling was fostered as a change-seeking movement on the basis of non-profit, volunteer organized practices, and in terms of a community-building model. However, as recycling came to be institutionally supported, particularly through state and regulatory actions, the industry evolved into its contemporary status as major for-profit industry in the United States and elsewhere. It is now a core activity of numerous multinational corporations operating in the international arena (Lounsbury, Ventresca and Hirsch 2003; Weinberg, Pellow and Schnaiberg 2000). Murray explains the transformation of the recycling industry, and the implication of this for small business, vividly:

> The world of municipal collection, small firm disposal and the rag-and-bone man suddenly came into contact with a wider economy. ... Multinationals are taking an increasing interest in waste. Privatization has opened up new markets in collection. The new standards of treatment and the industrialization of waste management require resources beyond the means of small and medium-sized firms. (Murray 1999, p. 20)

In New Zealand the general climate is now conducive to recycling. Many recycling initiatives are at the local grassroots level and are often the result of community partnerships and also part of the wider national effort to create jobs for those who are disadvantaged in the labour market..[2] Local government bodies are also increasingly committed to the philosophy of maximizing recycling and waste minimization, with well over 50 per cent of local governments adopting 'zero waste' targets. As the zero-waste philosophy rapidly gains worldwide acceptance, in New Zealand there is momentum for the movement. The Zero Waste New Zealand Trust (www.zerowaste.co.nz) was established in 1997 to support a growing network of groups working on waste minimization initiatives and to help develop innovative strategies to deal with New Zealand's growing waste problem. The role of supportive networks such as Zero Waste networks (see also www.grrn.org) in maintaining both business viability and the drive for environmental goals should not be underestimated.

Despite the governmental commitment to supporting small businesses and regional development, New Zealand remains subject to global market forces and also to several multilateral environmental agreements. Micro-enterprises can be

---

2   For more detail and examples of community job creation partnerships in the recycling industry, see de Bruin and Power (1999).

particularly constrained by these overarching considerations. Within the recycling industry, this issue was poignantly brought home by the fate of the Christchurch-based battery recycling operations of the Dominion Trading Company in 2003. When Exide Batteries (a multinational with a US parent) cut its prices, the financial viability of these activities was threatened, even though Dominion had collected most of New Zealand's used lead acid batteries, such as car batteries, over the past 40 years (Collins 2003). This also meant that any micro-business operators that collected these batteries were also affected. Differing environmental standards and regulations within countries and international codes of practice are also an inherent part of business operation in a global age. Hence export or import of hazardous wastes such as used batteries must comply with international agreements such as the Basel Convention, OECD Decision and Waigani Convention relating to the transboundary movement of these wastes. The Ministry of Economic Development therefore rejected a 2003 application to export used batteries to Australia, as they could be recycled domestically. Exide thus retained its position as the monopoly buyer. Ironically, in the previous two years small shipments of used batteries to a Philippines recycling plant were allowed, even though environmental regulatory compliance standards there are lower than in New Zealand. Currently, however, Dominion Trading has permits to export used lead acid batteries to the Philippines (expiring July 2010) and the Republic of Korea (expiring January 2010), while Exide Technologies currently holds a permit to import these batteries to Australia. This illustrates that environmental regulations conditions are subject to frequent change and creates a great deal of uncertainty for eco-enterprises.

A Framework for Examining Green Entrepreneurship

The green entrepreneurship framework put forward in this chapter not only allows matching of enterprises to different existing typologies, but also allows for the many enterprises that might not readily slot into a specific category. In addition, it accommodates both individual (for example, entrepreneurs and/or ecopreneurs) and collective enterprise (for example, firms, trusts, cooperatives and so on). The framework portrayed in Figure 6.1 is also designed to address issues that we feel have been given inadequate consideration in the literature to date. Common to the green entrepreneurship typologies in the green literature is their typically one-dimensional nature and their focus on delineating one dominant aspect, behaviour or single characteristic; they use the firm (rather than the individual) as the unit of analysis of description; and create discrete categories into which a green entrepreneur is expected to fit (in other words, they facilitate no overlap or progression between categories over time).

To redress these issues a multidimensional framework that can be used to 'classify' green entrepreneurship is described. The framework also has the potential to be used to capture the evolution of firms in terms of both environmental responses and chronological development. The value of this SME-specific framework, if only as a starting point, is great, particularly given that small and micro-firms represent 96.4 per cent of all New Zealand businesses (Ministry of Economic Development 2007) and that their collective environmental impacts are therefore of significance. Also, while many green entrepreneurship responses start out at a micro-level (in terms of the number of people involved) they can quickly evolve to represent an impact that is disproportionate to the size of the SME or initiative.

As Figure 6.1 shows, the vertical axis (labelled the 'green micro-entrepreneurship response') indicates that green entrepreneurship may be: a) a response to personal environmental concerns; b) a business opportunity orientation linked to environmental benefit; or c) a collective or group eco-response, often resulting in a community enterprise. Thus, green entrepreneurship endeavours can have sole or multiple drivers. The horizontal axis of the figure (labelled 'market orientation') categorizes market orientation and reveals that green enterprises may: a) not be market-oriented (for example, a not-for-profit initiative); b) be on the market fringes (for example, what has in other typologies – for example Schaltegger (2002) – been classed as an alternative enterprise); c) be tailored to a niche market (for example, oriented to

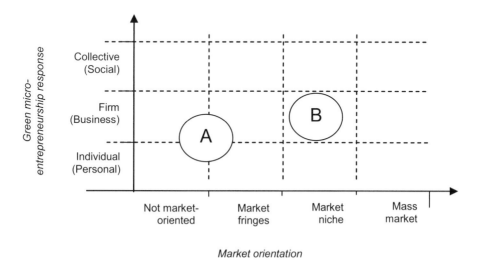

Figure 6.1   The green entrepreneurship framework

the organics niche of the market); or d) be developed with the mass market in mind (that is, not targeted specifically at the green segment of the market).

This framework has been developed on the basis that most green entrepreneurship in New Zealand begins on a micro-scale (that is, it manifests in firms that employ fewer than six FTEs), but acknowledges that, in some instances, it evolves into another form (that is, potentially something larger, if not always in terms of business size). Consideration has also been given to the fact that micro-entrepreneurs in New Zealand rarely fit into a single discrete category either in terms of market or entrepreneurship orientation. The examples A and B on the framework in Figure 6.1 reflect this. Example A is a non-market oriented/sometime market fringe green micro-entrepreneurship response that springs from an individual green micro-entrepreneur who has founded a part-time business. In contrast, B is a profit-driven business that is oriented to a specific niche of the market (that is, not socially- or purely environmentally-oriented). As the circle representing example B shows, it fits 'within' the boundaries of two categories, whilst the circle representing example A illustrates how the framework can capture the fact that some examples span boundaries of categories.

Operationalizing the Framework

The following three short New Zealand cases are included as examples of some of the multiple dimensions of the framework depicted in Figure 6.1. They are positioned according to the framework and depicted in Figure 6.2.

LINDA LEE AND THE WASTEWISE TRUST

Linda Lee, a solo mother, runs workshops and demonstrations on how to create, design and develop worm farms and grow organic food. Her belief that money (or a lack of it) is not an obstacle to participating in environmentally responsible behaviour is the basis for her opinion that everyone can convert his or her waste into a resource at no cost. Linda has been involved in organics for almost two decades, and began thinking about developing a vermiculture education, research and development centre after attending a workshop on resource recovery in 1998. That year she launched a business that was to be a learning experience that cost her financially and jolted her confidence. However, an opportunity arose when, through a chance meeting, she was offered two large tunnel houses and a garage. In 1999 the WasteWise Trust was established

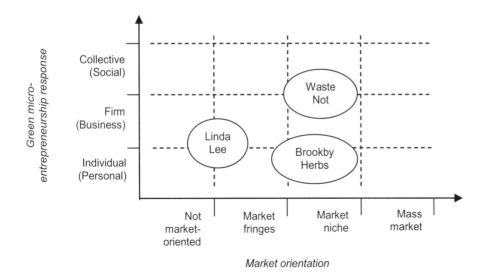

Figure 6.2   Empirical facets of the framework

as the education arm of the farm, and the worm farm itself has developed into a working model of vermiculture. Free to visit, the Pukaki Worm Farm attracts visitors from both New Zealand and overseas (case adapted from CEG 2001).

In terms of the framework, the position of Linda's enterprise is depicted in Figure 6.2. As the diagram shows, Linda's response can be classed as a personal response to environmental concerns, but also as a response that has evolved into a business opportunity (hence the circle overlaps two categories on the vertical axis). Linda's market orientation also spans two categories: non-market-oriented and on the fringes on the market. As Linda's enterprise evolves, or expands, it is likely that her 'position' on the framework may also shift – illustrating the advantage of the flexibility of the descriptive framework that has been devised.

WASTE NOT CONSULTING

Based in Auckland, Waste Not Consulting (www.wastenot.co.nz) is a for-profit company that is focused on waste and resource efficiency. Previously operated by the Waste Not Auckland Trust, the consultancy is now employee-owned. It specializes in consulting relating to solid waste and provides the following services: waste audits; policy and strategy development; design and implementation of recovery systems; integrated waste management plans; environmental management systems; cleaner production programmes;

environmental education and waste service analysis for local government and territorial authorities.

As Figure 6.2 shows, Waste Not Consulting can be described as a firm (business) in terms of its entrepreneurial response (on the vertical axis) and targeting a market niche in terms of its market orientation (on the horizontal axis). Readers will note that the edge of the circle representing Waste Not Consulting also encroaches into the space representing a social or collective entrepreneurship response; this is to account for the fact that the company is affiliated with a socially-oriented charitable trust.

JACKIE RIVE AND BROOKBY HERBS

In Clevedon (in the southern area of Greater Auckland) Jackie Rive, with her husband Wayne, runs her business, Brookby Herbs (www.brookbyherbs.co.nz), from the family home. In 1992 in response to a perceived niche and the desire to be self-employed, Jackie starting growing the herb echinacea for the human health market. At the time, the business thrived on the strong demand for the product, and Jackie and Wayne successfully grew up to three acres at a time for the domestic and export markets (Meade 2003). However, as more growers entered the market Jackie realized that, without diversification, her business was going to fold.

Spurred by this prospect and the impending birth of her second child, Jackie arrived at a new business concept – herbs for animals – and so in 1999 Brookby Herbs was born. The firm specializes in the production and distribution of organic (BioGro certified) herbal remedies to improve equine and canine health. Its products are 100 per cent natural and contain no artificial fillers or additives. Brookby Herbs is a family micro-business that blends the ethical values of its owners with an ecopreneurial approach to both a product and doing business. As Figure 6.2 shows, Brookby Herbs can be 'classified' as spanning a number of quadrants within the framework due to both the intentions and values of the owners and the origins of the business itself. In terms of market orientation the firm is predominantly market niche, but it also has characteristics of the market fringe category. In terms of a green micro-entrepreneurship response Brookby Herbs is depicted as being mostly in the category of individual (personal) response, as the business operations are so congruent with the values and practices of its owners.

Concluding Comments

In this chapter a novel schema that can be used to study green micro-enterprises has been suggested. However, while this schema is inherently conceptual, the stories of New Zealand green entrepreneurs presented here demonstrate that this framework need not be purely theoretical; it can also reflect the actual endeavours of small (micro-) business owners and the dynamic evolution of their businesses. The framework is a valuable contribution to the debate on green entrepreneurship, since earlier examples of typologies in the literature have predominantly focused on larger organizations. It is hoped that this new framework will go some way towards helping incorporate the perspectives of the micro- and smaller business into the theoretical discourse of green entrepreneurship. It is at least a starting point for diverging from the path of thought that immediately places micro-enterprises in the same frames of reference as larger firms.

For the green entrepreneurs described in the chapter, their passion for the 'green cause' means that their willingness to serve social goals in some instances might even exceed their desire to reap a profit, or is at the very least an integral part of their business practice. It is therefore often difficult to objectively assess the success of green enterprises and entrepreneurs, since the performance of such firms must be measured by multidimensional success criteria, including non-financial outcomes. Devising appropriate performance indicators and a matrix for measuring their 'success' is an area of research that demands attention in the future.

References

Anderson, A. (1998) 'Cultivating the Garden of Eden: Environmental Entrepreneuring', *Journal of Organizational Change Management*, Vol. 11, No. 2, pp. 135–144.

Coase, R. (1988) 'The Nature of the Firm: Influence', *Journal of Law, Economics and Organizations*, Vol. 4, pp. 33–47.

Collins, S. (2003) 'Battery Collectors Call it Quits as Prices Drop" *New Zealand Herald*, 7 July, p. A4.

Community Employment Group (CEG) (2001) 'Living The Dream', *Employment Matters*, Vol. 12, No. 6 (June), p. 1 and 3.

de Bruin, A. and Dupuis, A. (eds) (2003) 'Introduction: Concepts and Themes' in A. de Bruin and A. Dupuis, *Entrepreneurship: New Perspectives in a Global Age*, Ashgate, Aldershot, pp. 1–24.

de Bruin, A. and Power, G. (1999) 'The Partnership Approach to Local Employment Generation' in P.S. Morrison (ed.) *Labour Employment and Work in New Zealand: Proceedings of the Eighth Conference*, Victoria University of Wellington, New Zealand, pp. 239–245.

Dixon, S.E.A. and Clifford, A. (2007) 'Ecopreneurship – A New Approach to Managing the Triple Bottom Line', *Journal of Organizational Change Management*, Vol. 20, No. 3, pp. 326–345.

Granovetter, M. (1985) 'Economic Action and Social Structure: The Problem of Embeddedness', *American Journal of Sociology*, Vol. 91, No. 3, pp. 481–510.

Hawken, P., Lovins, A. and Lovins, L.H. (1999) *Natural Capitalism – Creating the Next Industrial Revolution*, Little, Brown & Company, Boston, MA.

Hendrickson, L.U. and Tuttle, D.B. (1997) 'Dynamic Management of the Environmental Enterprise: A Qualitative Analysis', *Journal of Organizational Change Management*, Vol. 10, No. 4, pp. 363–382.

Isaak, R. (1998) *Green Logic: Ecopreneurship, Theory and Ethics*, Greenleaf Publishing, Sheffield.

Isaak, R. (2002) 'The Making of the Ecopreneur', *Greener Management International*, Vol. 38, pp. 81–91.

Keogh, P.D. and Polonsky, M.J (1998) 'Environmental Commitment: A Basis for Environmental Entrepreneurship?', *Journal of Organizational Change Management*, Vol. 11, No. 1, pp. 38–49.

Knuckey, S. and Johnston, H. (eds) with Campbell-Hunt, C., Carlaw, K., Corbett, L. and Massey, C. (2002) *Firm Foundations: A Study Of Business Practices and Performance in New Zealand*, Ministry of Economic Development, Wellington, NZ.

Linnanen, L. (2002) 'An Insider's Experiences with Environmental Entrepreneurship', *Greener Management International*, Vol. 38, pp. 71–80.

Lounsbury, M., Ventresca, M. and Hirsch, P.M. (2003) 'Social Movements, Field Frames and Industry Emergence: A Cultural–Political Perspective on US Recycling', *Socio-Economic Review*, Vol. 1, No. 1, pp. 71–104.

Meade, B. (2003) 'Hooked On Herbs', *Next* (July), pp. 144–149.

Menguc, B., and Ozanne, L.K. (2005) 'Challenges of the "Green Imperative": A Natural Resource-based Approach to the Environmental Orientation–Business Performance Relationship', *Journal of Business Research*, Vol. 58, pp. 430–438.

Ministry of Economic Development (2007) *SMEs in New Zealand: Structure and Dynamics*, Ministry of Economic Development, Wellington, NZ.

Murray, R. (1999) *Creating Wealth from Waste*, Demos, London.

Schaltegger, S. (2002) 'A Framework for Ecopreneurship: Leading Bioneers and Environmental Managers to Ecopreneurship', *Greener Management International*, Vol. 38, pp. 45–58.

Schaper, M. (2002) 'The Essence of Ecopreneurship', *Greener Management International*, Vol. 38, pp. 26–30.

Thornton, P. (1999) 'The Sociology of Entrepreneurship', *Annual Review of Sociology*, Vol. 25, pp. 19–46.

Walley, E.E. and Taylor, D.W. (2002) 'Opportunists, Champions, Mavericks? A Typology of Green Entrepreneurs', *Greener Management International*, Vol. 38, pp. 31–43.

Weinberg, A.S., Pellow, D.N. and Schnaiberg, A. (2000) *Urban Recycling and the Search for Sustainable Community Development*, Princeton University Press, Princeton, NJ.

7

An Insider's Experiences with Environmental Entrepreneurship

Lassi Linnanen

ABSTRACT

This chapter argues that most of the normal entrepreneurial laws are valid also in environmental ventures. However, the value-based leadership often rightly associated with environmental entrepreneurs gives a special flavour to these businesses. Including hands-on practical experience and insightful theoretical orientation, the chapter analyses typical environmental business features and its main segments, and presents a typology of ecopreneurs.

Introduction

Is environmental entrepreneurship something different from ordinary entrepreneurship? The right answer might be both 'no' and 'yes'. Most of the normal entrepreneurial laws, such as the correlation between risk and profit, right timing of market entry, and the need for adequate financial and human capital, are valid also in environmental ventures. To be successful, environmental entrepreneurs should move fast, motivate others and take risks, as well as anticipate and supply what large numbers of people want. However, the value-based leadership often rightly associated with environmental entrepreneurs gives a special flavour to these businesses.

In this chapter, the phenomenon of ecopreneurship is examined from two different sides. The practical side is that I have over ten years' personal experience in the creation and management of environmentally-oriented business ventures in Finland. This experience is drawn upon to provide many of the hands-on observations cited in the chapter. The second side is academic:

I also hold a professorship in environmental economics and management at Lappeenranta University of Technology,[1] and continue to support and advise young academic entrepreneurs. All of the recent start-ups with which I have been involved also have something in common: a quest for more sustainable products and services.

Due to the sensitiveness and confidentiality of the information behind the real-life examples, most of the companies and individuals referred in this chapter remain anonymous.

Ecobusiness Classification

Environmental businesses can be classified into four different segments. Each has a distinctive character, and their emergence has been influenced by a different combination of drivers. Three main drivers for environmental business and technology can be identified as follows:

- *The geographical area of influence*, ranging from local to regional to global. The balance has shifted from local point-source pollution, such as wastewater treatment, to global and more complex issues such as climate change.

- *Reason for market emergence*, either by regulation or by voluntary decisions of market actors. Besides the traditional command-and-control approach, market-based instruments and voluntary actions have become increasingly important.

- *Degree of enforcement*, varying from high to low. The degree of enforcement differs from country to country and from one law to another.

Based on the premises of these drivers, I am inclined to propose that at least the following segments can be identified among environmental businesses:

- *wildlife habitat preservation*, eco-tourism and other close-to-nature concepts that utilize economic and human resources to improve the state of environment.

---

1   See Linnanen (1998) for research background.

- *environmental technology*, which is driven by the legislative pressure towards communities or industrial enterprises to reduce their environmental load to water, air and soil;

- *environmental management services*, which aim to advise corporations on utilizing environmental excellence as a source of competitive edge.

- *environmentally friendly products*, which are differentiated from other existing products by better environmental performance over the product life cycle.

The purest segment of environmental entrepreneurs might be those trying to make their living through sustainable natural resource use. These businesses are often run by individuals with alternative lifestyles, or by individuals otherwise dedicated to serving good causes. They offer voluntary and local means to practise environmental resource management.

The public perception of environmental business is often limited to environmental technology, an industry segment that is usually compliance-driven. Tightening national legislation levels are the most important drivers of these firms. However, the importance of market-based growth drivers is becoming increasingly evident in environmental technology businesses. Tightening international regulations may result in less binding agreements than nationally enforced laws, but they force global businesses to react more quickly and voluntarily.

A typical ecobusiness environmental technology scenario is to overestimate the legislation push and underestimate the need for market pull, as the following case illustrates.

In the mid-1990s a start-up company planned to enter the waste rubber tyre market. At that time, a car-tyre recycling scheme had been established in Finland by legislative measures. The company quite rightly assumed that there would be a significant and cheap flow of material resulting from approximately 3 million waste tyres a year. It prepared a production and investment plan for rubber sheets based on their patented technology and expected price of the raw material. However, they failed to recognize the fact that the remanufactured products, like all other products, do not automatically have commercial value. There needs to be a market for them. After a more careful market study it was revealed that the intended production capacity was approximately a hundred times higher than the existing

> market demand. Even with a 100 per cent annual growth rate it would have taken almost ten years before the plant could be run at full capacity. The investment would clearly have been a failure, and the investment plan was cancelled.

Environmental management services achieve their goals by taking into account environmental protection criteria in all the company's planning, implementation and control activities, aiming at decreasing the environmental load and achieving long-term corporate objectives. This segment includes, but is not limited to, environmental management system consulting, environmental accounting and communication, legal services and life-cycle assessments. More recently, environmental management has expanded to cover the triple bottom-line approach.

Environmentally friendly products have markets as their driver. The demand for these products is derived from consumers' increasing environmental awareness. These consumers comprise 10–20 per cent of all consumers in Western societies and are willing to pay the environmental premium in the purchasing price (Peattie 1993). In addition to environmental criteria, this differentiation can be achieved by social criteria, like fair-trade products.

Table 7.1 summarizes the drivers of these four environmental business segments.

Table 7.1   Drivers of ecobusiness segments

	Geographical Influence	Reason for Market Emergence	Degree of Enforcement
Nature-oriented enterprises	Local	Market	Low
Environmental technology	Local to regional	Regulation	High
Environmental management services	Global	Regulation and market	Low
Environmental products	Global	Market	Low

Barriers to Ecopreneurship

It appears that there are a few critical issues that successful ecopreneurs must address and which conventional entrepreneurs do not. These can be classified into three broad categories:

1.   the challenge of market creation;

2.   the finance barrier; and

3.   the ethical justification for existence.

THE CHALLENGE OF MARKET CREATION

The diffusion of environmental awareness is an important factor in supporting market creation for environmental technology, products and services. The diffusion of environmental awareness and, to an even greater extent, the change in consumer behaviour have proved slow (Meffert and Kirchgeorg 1993). One potential explanation for this slowness lies in the complicated nature of the sustainability challenge. Environmental management and sustainable development are still fairly discredited concepts in public discourse, and it is therefore a natural inclination to require greater proof of a new or more provocative idea than the one already believed to be true (Sutton and Staw 1995).

One problem in communicating environmental problems is the difficulty in providing clear cause-and-effect relations. Consider the following imaginary example with regard to carbon dioxide emissions:

> *When you drive a car to a local hypermarket you will add to global carbon dioxide emissions, which contribute to global warming, which in turn might lead to food scarcity as the conditions in many productive agricultural areas will decline and, therefore, your food price rises in the long term. And, of course, you should calculate the fuel cost, which has a direct impact on the price of your food.*

When you hear the argumentation above for the first time, would you buy the idea and reduce your driving in order to keep your food prices down? Considering the plausibility of the causal relations, probably not. Luhmann (1986) argues that it is impossible for a society to respond to even grave environmental problems until they become public by means of the social communication system. Environmental threats become social threats through communication. This socialization of threats is also a prerequisite for their elimination.

A newly established company always faces a major challenge: the good business idea should be realized in practice. Market creation requires strong belief in the entrepreneur's own vision and capabilities. The need to create a new market for new products often proves difficult, as the following case demonstrates.

> A profound example of the challenges of timing one's market entry can be drawn from the fresh-water trade. By logical deduction, this seems to be one of the huge markets of the future. All the predictions argue that water availability is the world's most pressing resource issue, as fresh water is growing scarce amidst competing human needs (see, for example, Doering et al. 2002). The demand is expected to rise, making margins higher and, at a certain threshold level, making bulk fresh-water shipments profitable on a global scale. However, it is next to impossible to predict when this threshold level is achieved.

When the market creation challenge is combined with high-level capital investments to enable industrial-scale production, small companies often end up facing substantial financial barriers to launch and growth.

> Nanotechnology is argued to be one of the future markets that will support sustainable development. A technology centre staff developed a number of nanotechnology innovations related to surface treatment of materials (atomic layer epitaxy). The method provides a significant eco-efficiency potential in several application areas – for example, through product life extension. The business potential was recognized, resulting in a spin-off company from an existing corporation. However, this company experienced hard times during its first years of existence. The capital investments required were high, and there was as yet no existing market. Finally, a couple of industrial companies that could potentially use this new surface technology in their products decided to acquire minority stakes in the company. This simultaneously gave the company a more solid financial ground and created a market channel.

THE FINANCE BARRIER

Environmental entrepreneurs with drive and ideas often find it difficult to find investors who share their objectives and ideals. On the other hand, people interested in directly investing in environmental businesses encounter difficulties in finding enterprises which they can believe in and support. Many environmental companies seem to know little about the investment community, and many investors believe that ecopreneurs lack knowledge about the realities of financial markets and fail to grasp the investor's interests. And whether these prejudices are justified or not, they create an obstacle to placing and obtaining capital (IISD 2002).

Many ecopreneurs express the need for a longer period of product development to reach a market breakthrough than typical venture capitalists, who may seek to exit their investment after two to three years. This may be not enough for eco-innovations to become commercially viable. As a result, environmental venture capital is marginal. Randjelovic, O'Rourke and Orsato (2002) have estimated the amount of green venture capital to be around 0.1 per cent of the mainstream. One venture capital executive put it quite bluntly in a discussion: 'The environment may be a successful screening criterion to find possible growth companies, but after that it does not influence [investment] decision making. The problems and solutions are found from three areas: management, management, and management.' However, the recent rise of energy and climate technologies as a viable option for venture capital investments significantly changes the overall picture.

In my experience, it is difficult to sell investors a novel business concept containing positive environmental arguments. Persistence is needed to beat the resistance to change.

A start-up company aimed to replace the distribution chain of the high-school textbook market by reusing books. The business is especially interesting because of its high margins and its effectiveness in reaching the customer with an accurate provision of books. The company's core success factor is an information system which is designed to gather data as to where, when, what and how many books can be acquired and are needed in the following school terms. According to this information, the correct items are taken to schools and regional bookstores. The benefit to the customer is significantly lower prices, combined with a better service. However, raising finance for the company proved to be a difficult task, since there was no prior example of this earning logic. This raised doubts among venture capitalists. After several unsuccessful approaches, a group of private investors were able to provide the needed €0.5 million for the company to roll out the business to cover Finland.

The case cited here indicates an important trend. An emergent channel for ecopreneurs to raise venture capital is the stock of high-net-worth investors ('business angels') who seek sustainability-related investment because of their environmental and social beliefs and their understanding of the potential double dividends (Randjelovic, O'Rourke and Orsato 2002).

THE ETHICAL RAISON D'ÊTRE

Financial and market considerations are essential to all entrepreneurs. Therefore, maybe the most distinctive feature of many ecobusinesses is their explicitly expressed ethical reasoning. This has both positive and negative effects on business and corporate governance. The ethical dimension is a major issue to take into account when mainstreaming environmental businesses and innovations.

On the positive side, most of the ecopreneurs I have personally met are highly committed to their business. Their reason for running an enterprise is not solely money-making, but also a willingness to make the world a better place to live in. Personal commitment also increases marketing credibility and trustworthiness as a business partner.

Another issue is that sometimes this willingness to serve good purposes even exceeds the desire to make money. Ecobusinesses are indeed measured by multidimensional success criteria, many of them non-financial. The combination of fact-based and value-based issues linked with various impact levels – from an individual level up to a global level – leaves room for a broad diversity of performance indicators and makes it difficult to define success. Integrating the financial and ecological perspectives has proved to be difficult, if not impossible. The current lack of clarity of sustainability criteria leads to 'good business' being continuously open to multiple interpretations.

It is also possible to identify negative issues related to the ethical *raison d'être*. First, a quest for ethical issues complicates management. For example, recruitment and outplacement decisions are never easy, but they might be even more difficult in value-led enterprises. People coming in should naturally be talented and productive, but also show an ability to commit themselves to the world-improving value base. Then, if the company faces a need to reduce its workforce, it is difficult to fire people on the grounds of rational reasoning alone.

Second, many of those companies with a high ethical profile seem to resemble non-profit associations more than business organizations in terms of their governance and decision-making. A somewhat surprising link can be found between established family enterprises and environmental enterprises. Mustakallio (2002) identifies family business characteristics as having: 1) a low mobility of shares and controlling ownership; and 2) an emotional dimension with mixed self-interests and altruistic behaviours. Many of the ecopreneurs share these two characteristics.

The link between financial sector values and ecopreneurial values deserves a special mention. It is sometimes unclear whether the entry of venture capitalists into ecobusinesses is solely a positive phenomenon. Too often, blind money-making intentions overrule the ethical orientation that is one of the positive features of many ecopreneurs.

An environmental management software application provider offered holistic solutions to its customers' environmental management challenges by using web-based technology, automating environmental management basic routines such as data collection. The business concept of this company was a lucrative mix of environmental management and information technology, and the company's initial start-up finance was easily raised. Unfortunately, it soon transpired that the investor selected was only interested in the human capital of the young entrepreneurs, not so much in developing the company itself. Soon after the start-up stage, the investor announced a plan to employ these entrepreneurs directly. The company proved to be a market and financial success, but this happened at a high ethical price. In this case, forcing the young enterprise and its founders to abandon their original vision and values by strict contractual policy and by overuse of negotiating power was an unwanted side-effect imported from the financial community.

Developing a Typology of Environmental Entrepreneurs

Several definitions of ecopreneurship can be found in the literature. Some of them have a rather limited scope. For example, Anderson and Leal (1997, p. 3) define ecopreneurship as 'entrepreneurs using business tools to preserve open space, develop wildlife habitat, save endangered species, and generally improve environmental quality'. Schuyler (1998) provides a more generic definition by stating that 'the term ecopreneurs has been coined for entrepreneurs whose business efforts are not only driven by profit, but also by a concern for the environment'.

Taking into account the considerations in the above discussion, ecopreneurs can be classified according to two criteria: first, their desire to change the world and improve the quality of environment and life; and, second, their desire to make money and grow as a business venture. These two dimensions seem to be independent. The first dimension of pursuing the good life, like sustainability, is an acceptable goal as such, but it is primarily an inefficient business concept. It is often argued in management practice that the more focused the business idea, the better it is in terms of commercial success. The second dimension emerges from a reasonable assumption that economic success factors are no different in ecobusinesses than in any other business. Successful ecopreneurs are expected to move fast, take risks with prospective gains, motivate others, and anticipate and supply what large numbers of people want.

The typology of environmental entrepreneurs is shown in Figure 7.1, and analysed below.

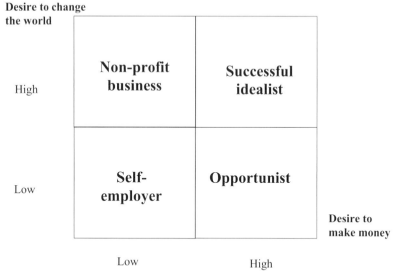

Figure 7.1   Typology of environmental entrepreneurs

SELF-EMPLOYER

An important characteristic shared by ecopreneurs who do not financially prosper is an unwillingness to grow. Many of these ecopreneurs have founded companies as an alternative to the dream of continuous growth, which is usually found in 'normal' business enterprises. Among this type of ecopreneur there is often a low desire to proceed along the same pattern and 'to repeat the same mistakes the capitalist system always does when assuming an infinite and ever-growing system'. Without entrepreneurial drive it is self-evident that substantial growth will not take place. It should also be borne in mind that the majority of small-scale entrepreneurs are self-employers. They are satisfied with a cash-flow level sufficient to guarantee a reasonable living standard. Out of the ecobusiness segments presented earlier, ecopreneurs who advocate nature-oriented business ideas are most likely to belong to this category.

NON-PROFIT BUSINESS

Among this type of ecopreneur, the distinction between business and non-profit organizational roles is often unclear. They usually have a strong commitment to changing existing business and consumer behaviour. However, good citizenship often overtakes the quest for high-performance financial results. In other words, these people often have a high willingness to influence society but a low willingness to grow as a venture. A typical example of such an enterprise is a sustainability think-tank that usually remains as a fairly small expert organization but has an influence much bigger than its size might suggest.

OPPORTUNIST

Opportunists are rather recent entrants among ecopreneurs. They typically have a professional background in traditional industries or they are 'ordinary' entrepreneurs expanding into ecobusiness in order to increase their profits. Driven by pure economic considerations, their business ideas are not linked to changes in the entrepreneur's value base. Opportunists are most likely to be involved in environmental technology, which provides the most direct promise for economies of scale.

SUCCESSFUL IDEALIST

Taking the growth leap needs an internal ambition, and sometimes ecopreneurs succeed. The successful ecopreneur builds a dynamic balance between two virtues: making money and making the world a better place. These ecopreneurs could be labelled as successful idealists. Their desire to improve the world leads to a motivation to create markets. The cycle is reinforced by positive feedback from the customers and other stakeholders, providing additional momentum for positive business results and further strengthening the entrepreneurial motivation. This virtuous cycle is illustrated in Figure 7.2.

Figure 7.2   The virtuous cycle of ecopreneurship

Conclusions and Discussion

Environmental entrepreneurs share many features of ordinary entrepreneurs. Similar to mainstream businesses, the ecopreneurial success cycle is quite unstable and can easily shift to becoming vicious. The less successful cycle does not emerge or collapse as a result of good intentions but because of failure in the market test. Consequently, this decreases motivation, paralyses further competence development and impairs the ability to serve markets. However, a few differences can be shown between ecopreneurs and ordinary entrepreneurs. Market creation is even more difficult than with non-environmental business ideas, since the financial community may not yet be mature enough to finance environmental innovations, and the role of ethical reasoning leaves room for confusion among the mainstream business community.

Maybe the most distinctive feature of many ecobusinesses is their explicitly expressed ethical reasoning. Being highly ethical brings certain difficulties in today's business culture which is dominated by a mistaken assumption that most decisions are value-free. Luckily, these attitudes are gradually softening as socially responsible investing and other value-driven commercial successes demonstrate the win–win option. Hall describes a responsible entrepreneur:

> The popular thinking was that to succeed, one must be tough, selfish, and ready to whatever it takes to beat the other side … to the contrary, many entrepreneurs who are nice, decent people build better relationships and, in turn, accomplish great things for that very reason. (Hall 2001, p. 19)

There is also one other factor that helps partially explain why the creation of environmentally-driven markets is difficult. The barrier arises from the inherently different logic between academia and the business community. Companies and their managers often expect some kind of prescriptive recommendations drawn from the research. Entrepreneurs tend to look for specific examples of successful management, an inventory of success stories as well as suitable tools needed when aspiring for success. In contrast, academic researchers and policy-makers are more interested in consistent and systematic data on environmental performance and in the drivers of change. What appears as an interesting success story of environmental management for a businessperson might just 'add yet another case study to the literature' in the eyes of an academic. Such an imbalance of expectations does not make the complex issue any easier, and it needs to be addressed.

References

Anderson, T.L. and Leal, D.R. (1997) *Enviro-Capitalists: Doing Good While Doing Well*, Rowman & Littlefield Publishers, Inc., Lanham, MD.

Doering, D.S., Cassara, A., Layke, C., Ranganathan, J., Revenga, C., Tunstall, D. and Vanasselt, W. (2002) *Tomorrow's Markets: Global Trends and their Implications for Business*, World Resources Institute, Washington, DC.

Hall, G. (2001) *The Responsible Entrepreneur*, Career Press, Franklin Lakes, NJ.

IISD International Institute for Sustainable Development (2002) 'Perception Barriers', at: http://www.bsdglobal.com/markets/rm_barriers.asp (accessed 31 August, 2002).

Linnanen, L. (1998) 'Essays on Environmental Value Chain Management : The Challenge of Sustainable Development', *Studies in Computer Science, Economics and Statistics*, Vol. 46, *University of Jyväskylä. Jyväskylä*, Finland.

Luhmann, N. (1986) *Ecological Communication*, Polity Press, Cambridge.

Meffert H. and Kirchgeorg, M. (1993) *Marktorientiertes Umweltmanagement. Grundlagen und Fallstudien*, Schaeffer-Poeshel, Stuttgart.

Mustakallio, M.A. (2002) 'Contractual and Relational Governance in Family Firms: Effects on Strategic Decision-making Quality and Firm Performance', PhD dissertation, Helsinki University of Technology, Institute of Strategy and International Business, Espoo, Finland.

Peattie, K. (1993) *Green Marketing*, Pitman Publishing, London.

Randjelovic, J., O'Rourke, A.R. and Orsato, R. (2002) 'The Emergence of Green Venture Capital', paper presented at the Greening of Industry Network Conference, Göteborg, 23–26 June.

Schuyler, G. (1998) 'Merging Economic and Environmental Concerns through Ecopreneurship', ED434220 No. 98-8, at: http://www.celcee.edu/products/digest/Dig98-8.html (accessed 31 August 2002).

Sutton, R. and Staw, B. (1995) 'What Theory is Not', *Administrative Science Quarterly* (September), pp. 371–384.

PART TWO

Contexts and Conditions

8

Ecopreneurship in India: A Review of Key Drivers and Policy Environment

Astad Pastakia[1]

ABSTRACT

Market systems have adversely affected the environment by: a) failing to deal with negative environmental externalities and b) undervaluing natural resources, leading to their overexploitation and depletion. Governments have sought to deal with the problem through a mix of command-and-control and market-based instruments, with limited success. One of the most potent alternatives for dealing with such market failures is ecopreneurship, which refers to a process by which entrepreneurs introduce eco-friendly (or relatively more eco-friendly) products and process into the marketplace. In this chapter a theoretical framework to assess the emergence of ecopreneurship in a given society or industry is presented. The framework identifies both internal forces (sustainability values, competitive advantage of eco-friendly products/processes) and external forces (powers of the discerning consumer, the discerning investor, enabling policies, regulatory agencies and civil society). A discussion of the Indian case serves to demonstrate the utility of such a framework. The study shows how revitalization of strong cultural values for nature, coupled with a proactive judiciary and incentives under international protocols such as carbon trading, are all converging to facilitate the emergence of ecopreneurship in the country.

Introduction

With growing awareness about the causes of environmental externalities, business corporations are placed in the unenviable position of having to face pressures

---

1   The author is grateful to Tapan Patel, Centre for Integrated Development, Ahmedabad for assistance in reviewing the literature.

from both below (local communities, consumers, shareholders, employees) as well as from above (international protocols, bans on hazardous products and services, stricter governmental regulations against polluting processes and products). The responses to these mounting pressures have been varied.

While some have relied on good public relations and lobbying techniques, which can grant them a new lease of life to carry on business as usual, a small minority have chosen to innovate in order to internalize their environmental externalities. Through their pioneering efforts, the latter group of firms has shown that the problem of environmental externalities is not totally insurmountable. Apart from the ongoing enterprises that attempted to reorient themselves, there were also new entrants that sought to popularize or scale-up eco-friendly ideas, innovations, products and processes. In an earlier study of grassroots entrepreneurs in the Indian context, I referred to the latter as ecological entrepreneurs or ecopreneurs for short (Pastakia 1998). In this chapter, the definition of ecopreneurs has been broadened to include both types of enterprise.

India is among the few Asian countries that have registered impressive economic growth in recent times. Its growth rate of around 9 per cent has been fuelled largely by dramatic growth in its information communication technology as well as economic reforms that started around the early 1990s resulting in the growing competitiveness of Indian companies. If the Indian economy (as, indeed, other growing economies like China, Brazil and so on) is to grow in an environmentally sustainable manner, then perhaps the only way to achieve it is to create strong incentives for ecopreneurship leading to rapid transformation in the very manner in which business is conducted. However, given the present policy environment and levels of participation of citizens in environmental protection, what are the chances of ecopreneurship emerging as a major force to bring about such a transformation? What is the level of preparedness of government, civil society and other major stakeholders in witnessing such a green revolution? These are precisely the questions this chapter seeks to answer.

The study has two main objectives:

1.   To assess the existing policy environment in India with respect to ecoprensurship and to bring out the extent to which existing policies are conducive for its growth.

2.   To assess the key drivers for ecopreneurship in a developing country like India.

Framework for Assessing Key Drivers of Ecopreneurship

The theoretical framework adopted for the study visualizes ecopreneurship emerging from the net effect of both internal and external forces on a given business organization (see Figure 8.1). While *internal forces* deal mainly with ideological and strategic concerns of the ecopreneur and his/her organization, the *external forces* can be traced to the socioeconomic–legal environment in which the business is embedded. The latter may include pull factors (powers of the discerning investor and consumer, power of enabling policies) or push factors (power or regulatory agencies, power of judicial activism and civil society) that bring pressure to bear on the organization.

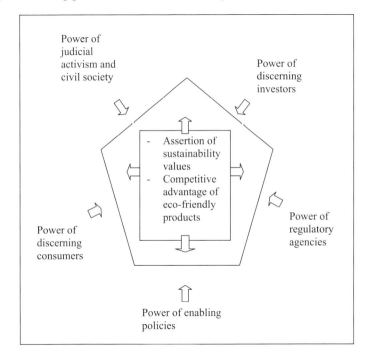

Figure 8.1   Framework for assessing key drivers of ecopreneurship

Note: Drivers within the pentagon are internal forces, while drivers outside the pentagon are external forces.

The former can be viewed as change coming from within, guided by the vision of the organization's leadership for a business that contributes to the sustainable development of society. A potential ecopreneur is one who harbours sustainability values,[2] but finds a dissonance between the espoused

2   For a more detailed discussion on sustainability values, see Norgaard (1984) and Pastakia (1996).

and practised values. Needless to say, if the dissonance is high it is likely to lead to introspection and a search for alternative modes of conduct. However, this internal urge to assert sustainability values can remain suppressed for a long time if the industrial environment does not offer the scope to derive a competitive advantage out of alternative products and processes. Ecopreneurs have been found to use a number of heuristics in identifying green business opportunities. Some of these include developing alternative (non-polluting or pollution-minimizing) goods and services, developing alternative sources of energy, waste utilization and waste minimization.[3]

While both internal and external forces can lead to change, the internal forces may be considered superior and more likely to lead to ecopreneurship of the highest order. External forces may also bring about change in the vision of the leadership over time and therefore be translated into an internal force.

The framework can be applied at various levels, ranging from entire economies to specific industries. In the case of specific industries, there may be a few industry-specific characteristics that affect the behaviour of various stakeholders differently. For instance, industries that have been declared as most polluting would be under a stricter regulatory regime, and such industrialists may feel more vulnerable in the face of growing public awareness and criticism about social and environmental costs that are being externalized by the industry. However, this in itself may not be a sufficient condition for innovating and coming up with more socially acceptable ways of conducting business. Other forces may play an equally important role. In as much as the social fabric and legal infrastructure of a given country remains the same, the framework has greater potential for bringing out inter-country, rather than intracountry, differences.

The Case of India

EXTERNAL FORCES

Power of regulatory agencies   India's active involvement in the United Nations Conference on the Human Environment, held at Stockholm in 1972, marked the beginning of serious governmental efforts aimed at environmental protection. India is among the few countries in the world to have provided

---

3   The list of heuristics shown here is only illustrative. A more rigorous study of the subject would help make explicit the entire range of heuristics currently in use or with potential for future.

constitutional safeguards for protection of the environment. Since the passing of the Constitution (42nd amendment) Act in 1976 by the federal parliament, it became an obligatory duty of the state and every citizen to protect and improve the environment. Three constitutional provisions bear directly on environmental matters:

> *'The State shall endeavour to protect and improve the environment and to safeguard the forests and wildlife of the country.' (Article 48 A)*

> *'... it shall be the duty of every citizen of India to protect and improve the natural environment including forests, lakes, rivers and wildlife and to have compassion for living creatures.' (Article 51 A)*

> *'No person shall be deprived of his life or personal liberty except according to procedure established by law.' (Article 21) (quoted from Rosencranz and Rustomjee 1996, p. 75)*[4]

To ensure that these constitutional rights do not remain mere aspirations, the central (national) and state governments have enacted a large number of laws and regulations governing the environment. Over 200 statutes having a bearing on environmental protection have come into existence during the past two decades (National Productivity Council n.d.).

The Ministry of Environment and Forests, created in 1985, oversees the integration of environmental dimensions into planning and development, and administers different laws related to the environment. Among the important legislation overseen by the MoEF is the Water Act[5] which provides for the establishment of the Central Pollution Control Board and State Pollution Control Boards (SPCBs) in the respective states. The SPCBs are given wide-ranging powers to regulate the environmental impact of industry. Some of these include the power to issue directions for closure, prohibition or regulation of any industry, operation or process, or the stoppage or regulation of supply of electricity, water or any other service to industry in the prescribed manner.

---

4   The provisions of the 42nd constitutional amendment remained largely untapped until the early 1990s. Citizens' rights to a healthful environment were first explicitly recognized by the Indian Supreme Court in the 1991 case of *Subhash Kumar* v. *State of Bihar*. The Court declared that the right to life guaranteed by Article 21 includes the right to enjoy pollution-free water and air. This paved the way for making Public Interest Litigation (PIL) for violation of fundamental rights the most preferred instrument for judicial activism (Rosencranz and Rustomjee 1996).

5   The Water (Prevention and Control of Pollution) Act, 1974 (as amended in 1978 and 1988).

SPCBs also have the right to refuse or withdraw consent for discharge of effluents.

Despite these elaborate arrangements, the regulatory mechanism has by and large proven ineffective in curbing industrial pollution, which has increased by leaps and bounds. Some of the major constraints faced by enforcement agencies are inadequate staffing, lack of technical knowledge, resistance to change within industry and lack of financial resources (National Productivity Council n.d.). Rent-seeking behaviour among officers of the SPCBs is also considered as one of the limitations of these agencies. For instance, the Supreme Court censured the Uttar Pradesh Pollution Control Board for using wrong standards in measuring pollution levels in the Ganges river. In the case of the West Bengal Pollution Control Board, the court ordered a vigilance inquiry, and the officials found guilty were suspended by the state government (Mehta 1996).

The Government of India has reiterated its commitment to waste minimization and control of hazardous wastes, both nationally and internationally. The Basel Convention on the Control of Transboundary Movements of Hazardous Wastes and their Disposal was signed by India in 1990. As per the convention, and a recent Supreme Court order which covers countries that have not ratified the same, imports of hazardous wastes are banned except for the purpose of reuse as raw material.

Stringent and effective implementation of environmental laws provides the necessary pressure for entrepreneurs to internalize their externalities. Clearly, this is not the case in India, which has some of the best laws in place but a poor to moderate track record of implementation.

Power of judicial activism and civil society   The ineffective regulatory system of the 1980s had resulted in large-scale and blatant violations of the pollution prevention regulations (Mehta 1996). The worst offenders were the 3 million small-scale industry (SSI) units (National Productivity Council n.d.), which were accustomed to a variety of concessions from the government. In the mid-1980s and 1990s a spate of public-interest petitions, spearheaded by eminent environmentalist and advocate M.C. Mehta,[6] succeeded in changing this scenario. Examples include the protection of the Taj Mahal and 225 historical monuments from pollution caused by the Mathura refinery and other

6   M.C. Mehta, a recipient of the prestigious Goldman Environment Prize for 1996, is a Delhi-based public-interest lawyer who has successfully fought and won over 40 landmark cases in the Supreme Court since 1984.

industries, the relocation of 600 tanneries from the congested city of Kolkatta to a leather complex outside, strictures against 50,000 industrial units and over 250 townships that were discharging untreated sewage and/or effluents into the Ganges river (M.C. Mehta Environment Foundation 2008).

In the case of SSIs, the courts ruled that such industrialists could not absolve themselves from their responsibility towards society and the natural environment merely on the grounds that it was not economically feasible for them to do so (see, for instance, Kirpal and Gokahle1995). The courts directed all SSI units located in clusters to set up common effluent treatment plants (CETPs), while passing strictures on the erring regulatory authorities. The judgments brought about a significant change among small-scale entrepreneurs. Several of the industrial estates in Gujarat, for instance, established CETPs in the wake of the Kirpal–Gokahle judgment. In 1996 the Supreme Court ordered the closure of 1,300 major polluting and hazardous industries from Delhi and the relocation of about 90,000 units to neighbouring states (M.C. Mehta Environment Foundation 2008).

In 1992 the Supreme Court delivered another landmark judgment that changed the face of vehicular pollution in Delhi and other major cities. Orders for providing lead-free petrol and then use of compressed natural gas (CNG) and other types of fuel in vehicles were passed and carried out. From April 1995 all new cars have been fitted with catalytic converters. Outlets have been set up to provide CNG as clean fuel and Euro 2 norms have been adopted. In the process, Delhi became the first city in the world to have its complete public transport system running on CNG.

The power of public pressure created by civil society organizations and individuals can be gauged by the fact that, in the last few decades, major toxic products have been phased out of the market not through conventional command-and-control mechanisms or economic instruments, but because the public has become informed about the environmental damage being caused by these products. The banning of dicholorodiphenyltrichloroethane (DDT) and certain carcinogenic dye intermediates, the push for chlorine-free bleaching in the paper industry, among other initiatives,. have all happened as a result of public pressure. In fact, it was this realization that prompted the Delhi-based Centre for Science and Environment (CSE) to launch its Green Rating Project (see 'The Power of Discerning Investor' below) which uses the 'reputational incentive' by publicly disclosing ratings on environmental performance.

An active civil society operating in the world's largest democracy continues to put pressure on both the regulating agencies and the legislature. For instance in 1997 an NGO, Srishti, succeeded in influencing the policy for biomedical wastes. It began to work with manufacturers on developing appropriate technologies and products for a small 30-bed hospital in Delhi, which was used as a model. It was effective in demonstrating the potential market size for products in environmental management like microwave machinery, waste shredders, coloured non-PVC bags, bins, needle-cutters and workers' safety gear. In 1998 the national Law for Bio-medical Rules was passed by parliament, making it mandatory for all institutional healthcare providers to segregate their waste in specified categories, disinfect and transform hazardous products and arrange for their safe disposal (Sawhney 2004).

So far, there is no specific legislation pertaining to the management of e-waste.[7] According to one estimate, India produces around 1.5 million tones of e-waste annually (IRG Systems 2006). People discard their computers every three years and refrigerators every five to seven years. The Electronics Industry Association has predicted that e-waste will increase by 11 times by 2012 (IRG Systems 2006). Unorganized recycling and backyard scrap trading form close to 100 per cent of total e-waste processing. Apart from plastics, the waste that is recycled includes many metals such as nickel, silver, copper, gold and platinum. Although the sector creates substantial value by collecting and repairing disused equipment, some recovery processes employed are extremely dangerous for the workers and the environment (Bibhu Ranjan Mishra 2006).

It is in such areas where legislation falls short that civil society steps in, creating awareness and compelling industrial organizations to commit themselves to an extended liability. In September 2006 the IT Products and Services Division of Wipro Infotech, one of India's largest computer manufacturing companies, was compelled to introduce an e-waste disposal service when Greenpeace challenged its e-waste policy. The company identified and set up 15 locations across the country where its executives collect the e-waste from its customers and safely dispatch it to certified agencies such as Trishiraya Recycling and Ash Recyclers for recycling and disposal. Formal e-waste recyclers are in a nascent stage. Bangalore-based E-Parisara, said to be India's first scientific e-waste recycling unit, was founded by P. Parthasarthy. With an investment of about US$ 0.2 million (PTI, 2005), it has won the Frost

---

7   Refers to waste generated by discarded electronic goods such as computers, refrigerators, TV
     sets etc.

and Sullivan Excellence Award for the Best Entrepreneurial Company of the year 2009 in the Waste Management Services Vertical (see company website).

Judicial activism in India has played a crucial role in raising awareness about the costs of environmental pollution. It has also brought pressure on both the polluters and the regulatory agencies. In a few cases, civil society organizations have gone beyond lobbying by demonstrating new models and ways of dealing with environmental issues.

Power of enabling policies   However, in the long run, end-of pipe solutions are not very economical for entrepreneurs because they involve additional recurring costs that eat into profitability. This has forced many an entrepreneur to examine their waste stream and search for alternative solutions to reduce, minimize, recover, recycle or convert wastes into useful byproducts. The impetus for this kind of change has also come, to some extent, from international donor agencies, which are making funds available to less industrialized countries for minimizing wastes and shifting towards cleaner technology.

In the early 1990s, UNIDO/UNEP selected the National Productivity Council of India as the location for the National Cleaner Production Centre (NCPC). The NCPC was established to:

- demonstrate-cleaner production concepts in Indian industries, particularly small-scale industries;

- conduct demonstration projects;

- conduct training programmes/workshops;

- disseminate information on cleaner production; and

- make policy-level interventions (NCPC 2007).

NPC also launched its Waste Minimization Circle programme among small-scale industries with considerable success. This has prompted many state governments to follow suit by establishing state-level Cleaner Production Centers (SCPCs). SCPCs have initiated capacity-building activities for environmental auditing and related topics.

India has become a signatory to several international protocols and conventions. The impact of some of these has been quite significant, as demonstrated by the cases of the Montreal and Koyoto Protocols. The provisions of the Montreal Protocol became effective in India from 1992. In 1993 an Ozone Cell was established within the Ministry of Environment and Forests (MoEF) largely to facilitate the proper utilization of bilateral funds to modernize old plants that generated ozone-depleting gases (ODS) through the adoption of new technology that was free of such emissions. The use of ODS is to be phased out by the year 2010, as per the schedule of the Protocol. The government adopted fiscal measures, such as exemption from customs and excise duty on goods required for ODS phase-out and on new investments in non-ODS technology. The Reserve Bank of India issued guidelines to financial institutions not to finance new projects with ODS technology, and the licensing system was adjusted to regulate the expansion of ODS technology. By 2001 investments in 39 projects had helped to phase out 1,877.3 ODP MT. Additional investments of US$ 11.1 million during the following year were planned in order to phase out an additional 1,635 ODP MT (MoEF Annual Report 2001–02). Significantly, India hosted the 18th Meeting of Parties of the Montreal Protocol in 2006 (MoEF 2007).

More recently, the implementation of the Kyoto Protocol has emerged as a huge business opportunity for ecopreneurs in developing countries like India. Under the pact, developed countries agreed that, if their industries could not reduce carbon emissions in their own countries, they will pay others like India (a signatory to the Protocol) to do it for them and help them meet their promised reduction quotas in the interest of worldwide reduction of greenhouse gases. The Clean Development Mechanism (CDM) programme permits companies from the industrialized world to offset their carbon emissions by investing in clean-energy projects elsewhere. The UN Framework Convention on Climate Change (UNFCCC) registers projects allowing a company in a developing country to offer CERs[8] produced by its project to a prospective buyer. In 2006 CERs worth an estimated US$ 30 billion were traded, three times more than those traded in the previous year (World Bank 2007). China dominated the market with a 61 per cent share of volumes transacted, while India stood a distant second at 12 per cent. During 2007 India registered 282 CDM projects – the largest number for any country. However, in terms of market share, China continues to dominate (Vaish 2007).

---

8   The currency for this trade is called Carbon Emission Reduction (CER). One unit of CER is
     equivalent to one tonne of carbon dioxide emission and its price ranges from about US$ 11.5
     for early-stage projects to US$ 24.0 for issued units.

Both public and private companies are taking advantage of the opportunity created by carbon trading. Gujarat Fluorochemicals Ltd has made about US$ 166.75 million by selling over 9 million CERs. It has set up a system to decompose HFC23, a potent greenhouse gas. The GMR Group uses bagasse and biomass to power its sugar project instead of depending on the national grid or fossil fuel. It earned US$ 0.75 million from the sale of CERs in 2006. The Delhi Metro Rail Corporation uses regenerative braking. Capitalizing on the modal shift from roads to rail, it expects to generate US$ 18.5 million from the sale of CERs. Indian Railways expects to earn 1.1 million CERS from using lightweight coaches, solar lighting at crossings and bio-diesel. The benefits of carbon trading could go beyond reducing CO_2 emissions. For instance, it could help reduce poverty in rural India through reforestation. In 2004 Powerguda, a village in Andhra Pradesh, sold CERs worth US$ 645 to the World Bank – a first for an Indian village – by extracting biodiesel from Pongamia trees (Vaish 2007).

Another source of change that is beginning to make an impact is ISO certification for Environmental Management Systems (ISO 14001). Studies show that the number of ISO 14001 certified companies grew from about 275 in 2000 (Peglan 2007) to 2,016 in 2006 (ISO 2006). It is mostly the large export-oriented companies that recognize the need to comply with international standards of environmental safety and quality in order to compete in the international market, which have opted for certification. The examples provided below suggest that ISO certification also leads to a variety of innovations, leading to substantial savings and gains for the company.

- Arvind Mills Pvt Ltd, a leading player in the global denim market, was among the first textile companies in the country to obtain ISO 14001 for its denim plant at Ahmedabad. The establishment of an Environment Management System (EMS) led to the creation of a corporate culture in which innovative approaches to the problems of waste management and resource conservation were encouraged. This in turn led to several innovations particularly in the field of solid waste reduction, which was brought down from 6 per cent (of annual production) in June 1998 to about 2.5 per cent in December 1999. One of the steps taken was to develop a vendor who could recover most of the waste yarn. The total savings through various incremental innovations were worth US$ 0.15 million, whereas the total investment cost of establishing the EMS was less than US$ 0.87 million (Israni 2000).

- Around the same time Kirloskar Oil Engines Ltd (KOEL), the famous Pune-based manufacturer of diesel and gas engines, decided to go green. It established an EMS at a total cost of 4 million rupees. As a result of the innovations that took place, KOEL has become a zero discharge company. Its Pune plant, which manufactures diesel engines in the 20–270 h.p. range, is an ISO 14001 certified unit. In 2000 the annual savings resulting from this investment were worth about US$ 0.325 million (*Economic Times* 2000).

In recent years, a number of enabling policies and programmes have given an impetus to ecopreneurship and better environmental management. In particular, the CDM under the Koyoto Protocol has created opportunities which both public- and private-sector entrepreneurs have been quick to take advantage of.

THE POWER OF THE DISCERNING CONSUMER

Environmentalists often hope that the discerning consumer will compel producers to produce eco-friendly products and use cleaner processes. In order to make this a reality, a significant number of consumers should be willing to exert a choice in favour of such products.

The Forrester Survey, on US technology consumers with a sample size of 5,000 adults, identified three distinct segments of consumers. The first, consisting of the 'bright greens' who are concerned about the environment and are willing to pay more for eco-friendly products, represent 12 per cent of the population. The second group, accounting for 41 per cent of the population, consists of people who have concerns about environmental issues, but do not strongly agree that they would pay more for eco-friendly products. The remaining 47 per cent 'do not (yet) share the greens' concerns about the environment or global warming' (Mines 2007).

Similar data for the Indian consumer is not readily available. However, according to a global food packaging survey conducted by The Nielsen Company,[9] despite a growth in eco-friendly living, a shop's environmental friendliness is the last consideration for Indian consumers (21 per cent) in

---

9   Conducted in mid-2007, the study surveyed 26,486 Internet users in 47 markets from Europe, Asia Pacific, the Americas and the Middle East, on the factors that influenced their choice of grocery store.

determining where to spend money, while value for money (65 per cent) ranks as the number one influencer of store choice (Anon, 2008).

Previous research with ecopreneurs in India (Pastakia 1998) has revealed that there is an initial resistance to green products and services when these appear in the marketplace. The extent of resistance depends on the nature of product/service, as shown in Table 8.1.

Table 8.1   Resistance to green products

Green Offerings	Consumer Resistance	Criteria for Preference
Substitute product	Low	Economic>Normative
Products/services that require change in system	Medium	Economic = Normative
Products/services that imply change in lifestyle	High	Economic<Normative

Source: Pastakia (1998).

The least resistance is offered to substitute products where the dominant criteria for selection are economic rather than normative. A farmer switching from a chemical pesticide to a herbal pesticide would not be overconcerned about normative issues as long as the herbal pesticide offers a better prospect for preserving his or her crops. The degree of resistance rises when the consumer is expected to change not just a product, but the entire system associated with the product (for example, getting rid of the entire wiring system to put in place a new eco-friendly domestic energy and heating system). The highest level of resistance is faced when products and services imply a change in lifestyle. At this level the consumer would respond to normative appeals more than economic ones.

In an article focusing on consumer behaviour in India, Dasgupta (2007) concluded that it would take time for the Indian consumer to evolve into a green consumer. The three critical factors on which this transition would hinge are convenience, cost and concern for the environment. Companies are stated to be drawing up innovative marketing and awareness strategies around these major influences:

- *Convenience*. Being easy to spot, simple to use, and available at the right place at the right time go a long way in gaining consumer acceptance of a product. This is especially true for organic foods, energy-saving lightbulbs and other such products. Godrej Agrovet, a company that runs eight retail outlets under the Nature's Basket brand stocks a wide range of organic and health products. Sales have been growing by 15–20 per cent annually. Among other things, its success is attributed to convenience, which draws in the customer and builds loyalty. (Dasgupta 2007).

- *Cost*. Cost is still an overriding concern of the Indian consumer. Philips India had to bring down the cost of CFLs by seven times before the Indian consumer accepted these. The product line is now growing at a healthy 25 per cent per annum. A strategy used by architects of green buildings is to look at life-cycle costs rather than price value. According to Karan Grover,[10] an architect and promoter of green buildings, in India the incremental cost of green buildings is paid back in three to five years due to the savings in energy and water. This is apart from the other benefits of improved health, comfort of occupants and environmental protection. In 2007 buildings rated as green by Leadership in Energy and Development (LEED) had grown from occupying a meagre 20,000 sq. ft to 1.6 million sq. ft, according to data from the India Green Building Council (IGBC) (Dasgupta 2007).

- *Concern for the environment*. Considerable investment in educating the Indian consumer about the ecological impacts of products and processes will be called for before he/she can start making choices in favour of green products and processes. Organizations such as the CSE, Delhi, Centre for Environmental Education, Ahmedabad, Sristi, and many others are doing this in their own way. The CSE's exposé of pesticide contaminants in leading Indian soft drink brands in 2003 helped educate a large number of consumers while making the companies more responsible. Ecopreneurs, too, can play an important role by educating the consumer and joining hands with such social entrepreneurs.

This is in line with the current thinking in the corporate world, which is now seriously eying the huge untapped market potential at the 'bottom of the pyramid'. The change in thinking is inspired by management guru C.K. Praladh,

---

10 Hyderabad's CII-Sohrabji Business Center designed by Grover, is rated as one of the world's greenest buildings on the LEED (Leadership in energy and development) scale.

who stresses the importance of continuous innovation to achieve quantum jumps in the 'performance–price' ratio for the customer, while ensuring that the technologies used are sustainable (Prahalad 2006).

The Indian consumer is yet to evolve into a green consumer. Until this happens, most green products will have to occupy niche markets. In the Indian context, the green consumer is unwilling to compromise on price and convenience. In addition, ecopreneurs must invest in educating the consumers. This makes it all the more difficult to market a green product in India. While it is easier to tap into the niche markets comprising mostly of the educated and affluent class, the real challenge lies in reaching to the masses of poor and middle-class consumers.

Power of the discerning investor   There is a growing trend, at least in the more industrialized countries towards voluntary disclosure through corporate environmental reporting. Through these reports corporations strive to communicate qualities such as environmental leadership, credibility and greater responsiveness to a variety of stakeholders, especially investors.

In India, the practice of corporate environmental disclosure is yet to be adopted in a big way. According to Shainesh (2007) less than 40 per cent of websites of the top 500 businesses in India have a web page on environmental performance. However, an interesting system of voluntary disclosure for the purpose of green rating was initiated on an experimental basis by the Centre for Science and Environment (CSE), New Delhi, in 1996, with support from MoEF and UNDP (CSE 1999). The first report of its kind was done for the Indian paper and pulp industry. Subsequently, similar exercises were carried out for the automobile, the chlor-alkali and the cement industries (CSE 2007). The goal of the green rating project (GRP) is to improve industry's environmental performance. It benchmarks a company's environmental performance on the basis of theoretical best practice. Then, at the end of each rating process, it lays down clear guidelines for the industry to improve its performance. According to the CSE, the recommendations resulting from the first green rating project helped in upgrading the environment. Many paper and pulp companies started buying wood from farmed forestries rather than from natural forests. Water consumption per tonne of paper produced declined and certification under ISO 14000 increased significantly.

The centre uses what it calls the 'reputational incentive' to induce voluntary disclosure. It also employs a 'default option' under which those companies that do not automatically come forward are rated as the worst. Such ratings are expected to influence the investment decisions of perceptive shareholders and financial institutions, as well as influencing the company's corporate image. According to Jewell (2007), who reviewed corporate environmental performance in India, the GRP method is extremely time-intensive and relies on a network of volunteers for data collection. The weights given to impact indicators vary across sectors, and each company is qualitatively evaluated against global and local standards. In his view, the method is impractical for investors who want to rapidly and quantitatively compare companies' environmental performance and disclosure across sectors. However, as an alternative, companies can opt for the Global Reporting Initiative (GRI), a UNEP partner, where such comparison becomes possible due to the quantitative and standardized indicators adopted. Currently only 13 out of the 2,600 sustainability reports listed with GRI are from Indian companies. The GRI framework, however, can become a starting point for creating an industrial environmental performance ratings system (Jewell 2007).

In another instance, CRISIL, a leading rating agency in India, helped select firms for ABN AMRO's Sustainable Development Mutual Fund, India's only sustainability-related mutual fund (Jewell 2007). Such voluntary disclosures and rating schemes are likely to exert a certain measure of pressure on companies to improve their environmental performance in future. At present, environmental performance does not seem to be an important criterion for the average individual investor. Perhaps the only investors who factor in environmental performance in investment decisions are the financial institutions. However, efforts made by institutions like the CSE have gone a long way towards creating awareness among the investors.

Despite some interesting initiatives on green rating and corporate environmental reporting, the typical Indian investor seldom bases her/his decision on the environmental performance of a company. The lack of a reliable system that generates comparative data is a major stumbling block. Under the circumstances, the impetus for ecopreneurship is unlikely to emerge from the side of the investors.

INTERNAL FORCES

Value dissonance and assertion of sustainability values   My earlier work at the grassroots level (Pastakia 1998) showed that ecopreneurship is alive and well, especially at the micro-level. Six cases of innovative farmers and other change agents who struggled against all odds to scale up and diffuse eco-friendly pest management innovations among the farming communities of the states of Gujarat and Maharashtra in western India were documented. Many of the innovators rejected chemical farming on the grounds that this went against traditional systems and beliefs, in which humankind was expected to live in harmony with nature. In fact Haribhai, one of the innovators from the Junagadh district of Gujarat, claimed that he refused to allow other farmers to draw water from his well if it was for the purpose of spraying toxic chemical pesticides.

Indian culture (drawing values from the dominant Hindu world-view, as well as from other faiths such as Buddhism and Jainism) has, over the ages, demonstrated a strong concern for the conservation of natural resources and their use (Banwari 1992). In their bid to steer Indian society once again towards sustainable pathways, these grassroots agents of change seek to relocate lost values and restore faith in traditional world-views. This augers well for the country as a whole, for sustainable development can only be achieved on the bedrock of such values.

However, it is also a fact of life that little industrial production is in the hands of people such as Haribhai. While large-scale export-oriented units are affected by pressures to conform to international norms for environmental performance and safety, small- and medium-scale operators tend to take environment and society for granted. When faced with a conflict between traditional and modern values and ways of working, Indian industrialists tend to resort to coping mechanisms such as 'compartmentalization of work-space and family-space' (Singer 1972). The industrialists most affected by this value dissonance are those who are most likely to respond when eco-friendly manufacturing alternatives are proposed. However, this is subject to the alternatives being economically as feasible and attractive as the current operations.

The traditional Indian world-view promotes eco-friendly values which, however, are being eroded by modern values of consumerism and short-term gains. Revitalizing these traditional values may be the key to creating a new generation of ecopreneurs, green consumers and green investors.

Competitive advantage of green products   Ecopreneurs have the knack of identifying green business opportunities and converting them into viable enterprises. They use a wide range of heuristics in identifying business opportunities. A few examples are provided below.

- *Developing alternative (pollution reducing/ non-polluting) products and services*. The development of Reva, a zero-emission car by the

Bangalore- based Maini group, is a case in point. This battery-operated vehicle was launched in late 2000 in Bangalore City (Anon 2000). Currently, the company has a manufacturing capacity of 6,000 cars per annum. Plans are underway to double this capacity. The company is in the process of setting up the world's largest electric car manufacturing plant with an annual capacity of 30,000 units. Production is expected to begin in the first quarter of 2010–11 (Aurora, 13 August 2009). General Motors (GM) has joined hands with the Maini Group to manufacture electric vehicles for the Indian market. By making India a global hub for affordable environmentally friendly vehicles, GM also hopes to emerge as a major manufacturer of electric vehicles (Anon, 24 September 2009).

Inspired by Reva's success, Electrotherm India Ltd established Indus Elec-trans, a division to manufacture EVs. Now, Indus has commenced the manufacture of electric two-wheelers, YO bikes, at Kutch in Gujarat. Other types of EVs are on the anvil (Indus Elec-Trans 2007). More recently, leading automobile manufacturer Tata Motors disclosed plans to put a fleet of clean and new technology vehicles on the road. It has drawn up an eight-year timeframe to deliver the standard Indica, its successful trucks and buses and other vehicles in their green avatars. Some of these would run on blended fuels, some on hydrogen-based hybrid engines and yet others on four different fuels at the same time (Seth 2007)

- *Alternative energy*. Tlusi Tanti, an ecopreneur from Gujarat established SUZLON Energy, the fourth largest wind turbine maker in the world. In the late 1990s, Tanti bought two wind turbine generators to meet the energy needs of his textile company. Impressed by their performance and looking to the potential growth of this alternative energy source, in 2001 Tanti sold off his textile manufacturing firm and entered the field of wind turbine generators. Within six years, Tanti found his way into *Time* magazine's list of global environmental champions (*Times of India* 2007).

The biodiesel industry is poised to make important contributions to meet India's energy needs by supplying clean, eco-friendly fuel using *Jatropha curcas* and other non-edible oilseeds as feedstock. Recognizing the global need for biodiesel to combat depleting fossil fuel reserves and escalating pollution, a private firm, Naturol Bioenergy Ltd, was incorporated in the state of Andhra Pradesh in October 2007, to set up an integrated oleochemical complex at the port town of Kakinada. This is India's first biodiesel plant. Its entire annual production of 30 million gallons is tied up for exports to customers in the United States and Europe (Surendra 2007). This venture has opened up scope for the large-scale use of many non-edible oils in India, such as *neem, karanj* and *jatropha.* As part of its backward integration strategy, Naturol has formed a subsidiary, Naturol Biosciences Ltd, to focus on research into improved strains of energy crops sourced locally. It has started entering into Memoranda of Understanding (MOUs) to buy back Jatropha seeds from farmers in Andhra Pradesh; these MOUs cover up to 0.3 million ha of plantations (Naturol Bioenergy Limited 2007). The Indian Bio-fuel Policy, long in the making, was finally announced on 23 December 2009. The policy in its present form appears to be merely aspirational as it lacks definite targets and financial commitments (Lele n.d.). The National Mission on Biodiesel that envisaged committing 4 million ha of land to biodiesel crops such as Jatropha and sweet sorghum has been left mid-way due to apprehension about large-scale acquisitions of land by big energy majors (Dey and Jaiswal 2008).

- *Waste minimization.* An organization that actively seeks to create green opportunities through creative design is Core Emballage, based in Ahmedabad. Core has revolutionized the packaging industry in India by offering customers a total packaging solution. Its design studio is constantly creating new solutions for improved packaging strength with minimal wastage of material (Handa p.c.).

- *Waste to wealth.* In 2002 a personal finance news magazine, *Intelligent Investor,* carried a cover story on six enterpreneurs who have made small fortunes from waste (Karunakaran 2002). Some of these are more conventional and could be termed green by default. For instance, Gupta Enterprises of Chennai achieves a turnover of US$11.0 million by converting human hair into wigs and toupees. The company has bagged export awards for the past 14 years. A less conventional waste to wealth enterprise is that of Jitendra Pareek whose Eco-Vision Industries uses 26 tonnes of fly ash[11] a day to manufacture bricks and blocks. Over 70 million tonnes of fly ash is generated annually from over 80 thermal power stations in India. The National Thermal Power Corporation supplies free fly ash to entrepreneurs and the State Government of Orissa has even banned the use of topsoil for brick manufacturing within a 70 km radius of thermal power stations. Consequently, over 50 fly-ash brick-manufacturing units have been founded in the state. The success of most such ecopreneurs is dependent either on a niche market or on governmental support of the type indicated above.

- *Environmental performance support services.* Providing services to improve environmental performance is a field with tremendous potential. Pune-based Thermax India Ltd is a global solution provider in energy and environment engineering, which has been helping customers improve their processes, conserve energy, increase their competitiveness and adhere to environmental norms for over three decades. With a turnover of US$ 800 million, Thermax offers products and services in heating, cooling, waste heat recovery, captive power, water treatment and recycling, waste management and performance chemicals to clients in over 75 countries (Thermax India 2010).

The comparative advantage of green products/services is the greatest in sectors where conventional goods and products are unable to meet the global and national environmental standards and statutory requirements. In addition, green products become competitive if they can also compete on conventional criteria like price, performance, convenience and so on. At present, most green products are restricted to niche markets, but, with the rapidly changing economic and legal environment in the country, this could change in the short to medium term.

Conclusion

Theoretically, the existence of any one or more of the forces described in this chapter can trigger change and promote ecopreneurship. However, whether such change can be sustained over longer periods of time will depend on the support gained from other forces. In the case of India we find three external

---

11 A residue created from the combustion of coal.

forces strong enough to bring about change: the power of judicial activism; the power of enabling policies; and, to a lesser extent, the power of regulatory agencies. Internal forces are also favourable in as much as basic religious and cultural values militate against the abuse of nature, leading to high levels of dissonance. However, at present the competitive and economic advantages of going green are not very strong. This may change in the near future, once the introduction of incentives under the Koyoto and Montreal Protocols have begun to make a definite impact. Measures such as CDM and carbon trading have elicited the active participation of industry across the board and are likely to go a long way towards the greening of industry.

At the grassroots level, where economic stakes are not very high, expression of values in favour of the ecology seem to be less inhibited – a situation which also applies to the upper end of industry, where large industrial houses and multinationals have to meet international standards to remain competitive. For the bulk of India's small and medium-sized firms, however, it is business as usual.

The Indian government is making substantial efforts to strengthen external forces, especially with respect to establishing national standards for the quality of environment and the implementation of these regulations. It is also taking some proactive measures through the state-level Cleaner Production Centres and tapping into international bilateral funding to support the phasing out of products and processes that are known to contribute to global warming and ozone depletion.

Much needs to be done to strengthen the consumer movement in India. Ultimately, it is the education of producers, consumers and regulators that will pave the way for a major transformation of industry. This is as much a responsibility of entrepreneurs and civil society as it is of the government. In the Indian context, creating a concern for the environment is often not sufficient for success as an ecopreneur. Innovation at all levels of the value chain in order to make the price–performance ratio attractive to large number of customers at the bottom of the pyramid appears to be the key to success. Convenience is another factor to lure the customer and build loyalty.

The framework for analysis presented here has been illustrated with the case of a developing country, but could be applied to other economies as well. Such an analytical framework can help in identifying the areas in which policy-makers must focus their efforts if they are to strengthen the various drivers of change.

References

Anon (2000) 'Reva-lution! Reva Electric Car', *Autocar India* (May) pp. 49–53.

Anon (2008) 'How Green is Our Consumer?', news section of the Nielson Company website, 13 February, at: http://in.nielsen.com/site/NielsenIndia-News-PressReleases-14August2007.shtml (accessed 3 March 2010).

Anon (2009) 'GM Ties up with Reva for Electric Car Production', 24 September, at: http://www.domain-b.com/companies/companies_g/General_Motors/20090924_gm_ties_up.html (accessed 3 March 2010).

Aurora Nihit (2009) 'Reva Car: World's Largest Car Manufacturing Plant in India', 13 August, at: http://www.autoblogs.in/2009/08/reva-cars-worlds-largest-car-plant.html (accessed 3 March 2010).

Bangalore Medical Trust v. Mudappa and Others, AIR 1991, SC 1902.

Banwari (1992), *Panchwati: Indian Approach to Environment*, Shri Vinayaka Publications, New Delhi.

Bibhu Ranjan Mishra (2006) 'India: A Dumping Ground for E-waste', 15 August, at: http://www.rediff.com/money/2006/aug/15ewaste.htm (accessed 3 March 2010).

Center for Science and Environment (1999) 'The Green Rating Project', *Down to Earth* (31 July), pp. 20–32.

Center for Science and Environment (2007) 'GRP Not a Theoretical Exercise: Impact of Green Rating Project', at: http://www.cseindia.org (accessed 20 October 2008).

Dasgupta, Arundhati (2007) 'Pushing Green', *Business India*, at: http://www.businessworld.in/content/view/2124/2191 (accessed 30 October 2008).

Dey, Sushmi and Jayaswal, Rajeev (2008) 'Biodiesel Mission Set to Pull Down Shutters', 4 August, at: http://economictimes.indiatimes.com/News/News_By_Industry/Energy/Oil__Gas/Biodiesel_mission_set_to_pull_down_shutters/articleshow/3322496.cms (accessed 3 March 2010).

Economic Times (2000) 'Kirloskar Oil Engines Go Green, Save Rs 1 crore', 17 February.

Gonsalves, Joseph (2007) 'An Assessment of the Biofuels Industry in India' for UN Conference on Trade and Development, Geneva, 17 February, at: http://www.unctad.org/en/docs/ditcted200066_en.pdf.

Green Rating Project (2007) Center for Science and Environment, at: http://www.cseindia.org (accessed 30 October 2008).

Handa, Sunil, CEO, Core Emballage, personal communication.

Indus Elec-trans, (2007) Company Profile, at: http://yobykes.in/electrotherm.aspx?pg=cinf&sb=et (accessed 3 March 2010).

IRG Systems, South Asia, Survey (2006) at: www.rediff.com/money/2006/aug/15ewaste.htm.

ISO (2006), ISO Survey at: http://www.iso.org/iso/survey2006.pdf (accessed February 2010).

Israni, Haresh (2000) Personal communication with Head of Denim Operations, Arvind International Division of Arvind Mills Ltd.

Jewell, John Paul (2007) 'Corporate Environmental Performance in India', Center for Developmental Finance, Institute for Financial Management and Research, at: http://ifrm.ac.in/cdf/CDF_CEP_Sept07.pdf (accessed 22 October 2008).

Karunakaran Naren (2002) 'How to Create Wealth from Waste', *Outlook Money*, 31 March, at: http://money.outlookindia.com/printarticle.aspx?87461 (accessed 3 March 2010).

Kirpal, B.N. and Gokhale, H.L. (1995) 'Pravinbhai J. Patel vs. State of Gujarat', Special Civil Application No. 770 of 1995 *Gujarat Law Reporter*, Vol. XXXVI, No. 2, pp. 1210–1257.

Lele, Satish (n.d.) 'Biodiesel in India', at: http://www.svlele.com/biodiesel_in_india.htm (accessed 3 March 2010).

M.C. Mehta Environment Foundation (2008) 'Landmark Cases', at: http://www.mcmef.org/landmark_cases.html (accessed 3 March 2010).

Mehta, M.C. (1996) 'Judicial Activism: Unexpected Saviour', *The Annual Hindu Survey of the Environment*, p. 207.[12]

Mines, Christopher (2007) 'In Search of Green Technology Consumers: Why Tech Marketers Should Target this Emerging Segment', *Forrester Survey*, 30 November, at: http://www.forrester.com/rb/Research/in_search_of_green_technology_consumers/q/id/43729/t/2 (accessed 3 March 2010).

Ministry of Environment and Forest, Ozone Cell, (2007) 'India Success Story – 2007', at: http://www.ozonecell.com (accessed 25 October 2008).

National Cleaner Production Center (2007) at: http://www.npcindia.org/NationalCleaner.aspx (accessed 3 March 2010).

National Productivity Council (n.d.) *Training Package for WMC Facilitators*, National Productivity Council, New Delhi, p. 2.

Naturol Bioenergy Limited (2007) at: http://www.naturol-bio.com (accessed 3 March 2010).

Norgaard, Richard B. (1984) 'Coevolutionary Development Potential', *Land Economics*, Vol. 60, No. 2, (May), pp. 160–173.

Pastakia, A.R. (1996) 'Grassroots Innovations for Sustainable Development: The Case of Agricultural Pest Management', unpublished dissertation, Indian Institute of Management, Ahmedabad.

12 This is the annual news magazine of the newspaper *The Hindu* published out of Chennai in South India.

Pastakia A.R. (1998) 'Grassroots Ecopreneurs: Change Agents for a Sustainable Society', *Journal of Organizational Change Management*, Vol. 11, No. 2 (May), pp. 157–173.

Peglan, Reinhard,(2007) Federal Environmental Agency, Berlin, at: http://www.riet.org/research (accessed 22 October 2008).

Prahalad, C.K. (2006) *The Fortune at the Bottom of the Pyramid*, Dorling Kindersley (India) Pvt Ltd, New Delhi, publishing as Pearson Power (Indian edition).

PTI (2005) 'An Eco-friendly Unit to Handle E-waste in IT Hub', 10 April, at: http://news.indiainfo.com/2005/04/10/1004e-waste.html.

Rosencranz, Armin and Rustomjee, Shiraz (1996) 'Citizens' Right to a Healthful Environment under the Constitution of India', *National Law School Journal*, Vol. 8, pp. 75–85.

Sawhney, Aparna (2004) *The New Face of Environmental Management in India*, Ashgate Studies in Environmental and Natural Resource Economics, Ashgate, Aldershot.

Seth, Nitin (2007) 'Tata Readies Plan for Green Car', Times Business, *Times of India*, 26 November.

Shainesh G. (2007) 'Environment Friendly Tag is Not Yet a Selling Point in India', at: http://www.economictimes.indiatimes.com, (accessed 7 October).

Singer, Milton B. (1972) *When a Great Tradition Modernizes: An Anthropological Approach to Indian Civilization*, Praeger, New York.

Surendra, T. (2007) 'Naturol Bioenergy to Start India's First Bio-diesel Plant', Times Business, *Times of India* at: http://www.riet.org/research/iso – com.htm (accessed 12 October 2008).

Thermax India (2007) Company website, at: http://www.thermaxindia.com/About-Us.aspx (accessed 3 March 2010).

Times of India (2007) 'Two Indians Make it to Time's Global Champions List – Rajkot's Tanti among Heroes of Environment', 23 October.

Vashi, Nandani (2007) 'The Greener Side of Carbon', *India Today*, 19 November.

World Bank (2007) *The State and Trends of the Carbon Market*, World Bank Institute and International Emissions Trading Association, Washington, DC.

9

Sustainability in the Start-up Process[1]

Jürgen Freimann, Sandra Marxen and Hildegard Schick

ABSTRACT

The concept of entrepreneurship covers many types of organizational and individual activities, but takes its most obvious form in the decision by an entrepreneur to start a new business. In recent years, researchers from different perspectives have focused more attention on the entrepreneurial activity involved in starting one's own business. Sociologists, psychologists and economists have all tried to give answers to questions such as 'What conditions support business start-ups?', 'Why do individuals decide to become entrepreneurs?' and 'What impacts do start-ups have on the economy?'. Environmental business management research has not yet concentrated on start-ups, although this early stage of a business enterprise's life might be a sensible starting point for environmental management.

This chapter is a report of an empirical study into start-up processes, designed to discover whether there are opportunities for implementing more sustainable business practices from the very beginning of new business ventures. Start-up entrepreneurs, as well as start-up business advisers, were interviewed in order to identify points where environmental management could be incorporated into the start-up process. In the group of entrepreneurs interviewed, both conventional and ecologically-oriented entrepreneurs were represented. The different orientations made it possible to compare their respective approaches to the adoption of more sustainable business practices.

---

[1] The chapter reports on the current results of a research project carried out on behalf of the German Ministry of Education and Research. The project is named 'start-up-to-sustain' and aimed to discover possibilities and develop measures for green start-ups and the greening of common start-ups. For further details (mostly in German) see http://www.ibwl.uni-kassel. de/fnu/start-up-to-sustain/index.htm.

It was found that starting a new business venture is a very complex process. Start-up entrepreneurs have to comply with a variety of external demands. Business advisers and banks, as well as market conditions, often interfere with the pursuit of ecological business practices. Information on how to start an ecologically-oriented business venture is notably not provided by institutions that support start-ups. The comparison of ecologically-oriented start-ups with conventional start-ups showed that the most crucial factor for environmental considerations in the start-up process is the entrepreneur him- or herself.

Turning the Focus to Start-ups

Various levels of ecological awareness and activity can be seen in corporate practice. Most companies still practise a more or less defensive strategy. They comply with legal obligations and try not to attract special attention from local residents, environmental activists or the general public (Belz and Strannegård 1997). On the other hand, there are a few eco-pioneers whose environmental performance is much better than that of the average company.[2] They save energy and resources and, as a consequence, substantial costs. Furthermore, these entrepreneurs look for opportunities in their respective markets to develop goods and services for environmentally aware customers. They are on their way to sustainability.[3] However, although most of them are also successful in economic terms, other companies do not necessarily follow their example. The green enterprise is still an exotic enterprise.

Since 1995–96 a new wave of the greening-of-industry process has occurred in Europe and the industrialized world. For example, standardized environmental management systems (EMS), mainly of the EMAS- or the ISO 14001-type, have been developed and implemented within more than 40,000 companies worldwide.[4]

However, the positive environmental effects of EMSs are rather small (see, for example, Dyllick and Hamschmidt 2000; Morrow and Rondinelli 2002). The normal state of organizational practice does not match the state of the

---

2   Other authors call them green-green businesses, ecopreneurs or enviro-capitalists. See Anderson and Leal (1997) and Isaak (1999).

3   If we allude to sustainability rather than to ecology, we recognize that this term – although it has its origin in ecology – includes the balance between ecological, social and economic aspects. Since ecological aspects are the very basis of sustainability and, in addition, most of our interviewees in the companies did not understand the term 'sustainability', we looked for ecological awareness as the most important step on the way to a sustainable economy.

4   For exact current figures see http://www.ecology.or.jp/isoworld/english/analy14k.htm.

art in organizational theory, either. EMSs are expert-based systems, in which corporate environmental care is dictated in a top-down way. It is rare to find substantial changes in corporate culture arising from the adoption of EMSs. In practice, the implementation of more sustainable business measures into an already existing organizational culture is often an arduous and lengthy process. It results in conventional additional environmental conservation measures that do not reach beyond daily operating procedures (Freimann and Schwedes 2000; Freimann and Walther 2002).

Promoting sustainability in start-up businesses seems to be a more promising approach, for a number of reasons. New businesses have yet to develop an organizational culture. As examples of green-green businesses founded with the clear objective of profitability through serving ecological and social aims show, there are opportunities for developing sustainable corporate cultures from the very beginning of a new venture. According to this argument, it should be easier to 'infect' founders of new businesses with the idea of sustainability than to rebuild established corporate cultures of existing companies.

Thus, the focus should not only be on the few ecopreneurs who convert their ideas of sustainable enterprises from the very first moment they think about building up their own businesses. It should also be on start-ups by entrepreneurs just planning to create a conventional new venture, who also need to become aware of the opportunities that more sustainable business practices have to offer. A widespread sustainability orientation in start-ups could speed up the overall process of sustainably restructuring of industry and commerce.

The basic hypothesis of our research project is that new business ventures are generally more open to new ideas because they lack an already existing organizational culture; therefore, it should be easier to introduce sustainable thinking into new ventures than into established enterprises.

This chapter reports on the results of an empirical study of start-up processes. Start-up processes of conventional and of sustainability-oriented start-ups are analysed in order to discover how they differ. It is also an aim of the analysis to identify the triggers that lead to the implementation of more sustainable business practices in the new 'green' business ventures. The results of the analysis will serve as a basis for the development of services designed to support start-ups in adopting sustainable business practices.

Research Design and Method

In order to discover starting points for ecological and social intervention in new businesses, the start-up scene in Germany was analysed.[5] Start-up literature provided data about the institutions and actors active in this field (Federal Ministry of Economics and Technology 2000; DIHT 2000). These sources, however, offered no insight into the details of start-up processes. Neither did they help to distinguish between eco-start-ups and conventional start-ups so that we could discover what their specific features were.

In our empirical study we tried to achieve a detailed description of start-up-processes and the differences within these processes between the two types of firm. We carried out personal interviews with two groups involved in the start-up-process: commencing entrepreneurs and business advisers who offered a consulting service for start-ups. In order to obtain thorough insights we carried out 11 interviews with business advisers and ten interviews with start-up entrepreneurs. The interviewees were located throughout Germany. Table 9.1 details the industries, the length of time in existence and the numbers of current employees and founders involved in the start-ups that were visited.

Table 9.1   Category of industry, length of time in existence, number of current employees and founders in the examined start-ups

Industry	Years of Existence	Number of Employees	Number of Founders
Carpentry	1	8	1
Carpentry	1	–	5
Paint contracting	2	2	1
Car sales and garage services	3	15	2
Car sales and garage services	8	25	2
Manufacture of electrical engineering equipment	4	12	1
Semi-finished/finished materials producer	4	4	2
Wholesale distribution of domestic appliances	5	3	2
Wholesale distribution of solar power appliances	1	1	6
Software service provider	3	–	4

---

5   The restriction of the analysis to Germany might lead to specific results that cannot be generalized to other countries because of specific administrative circumstances in the German legal and economic framework of start-ups. But as a first step on this rarely investigated field we believe this restriction is acceptable.

To avoid misconceptions with our interviewees, we used the term 'ecology' rather than 'sustainability' in the interviews (see fn. 3). As a consequence, the following results refer primarily to ecological contexts within start-up processes.

Results

THE START-UP PROCESS

The start-up process covers a period of time which is hard to specify. The onset and the end of the process are not well defined and, in descriptive literature, the scope is delineated differently. The process of new venture creation is consistently characterized as a complex event in which varied planning and preparation activities are necessary and decisions need to be taken (Hisrich and Peters 1998; Szyperski and Nathusius 1999).

In general, start-up processes in the sample studied differed widely, especially in the amount of time spent on preparation. While some entrepreneurs required only a few months, others needed years for preparation activities. The reasons for these differences were varied and depended on individual circumstances. In one example, a team of founders created a start-up venture in the field of computer-based geographical information systems. As the equipment investment was affordable and they already had a first firm order, they were able to start their new venture within months. In another case of a carpentry start-up, the entrepreneur wanted to include a wood gasification technique in order to create a closed-circuit production process. The development of this technique took several years and led to a total preparation time of eight years.

What seems to be similar with most entrepreneurs is that they do not change their business ideas to any large extent in the course of the start-up process. They may decide to adapt the legal form of their enterprise and financing structures according to tax advantages, and alter minor operating procedures, but they do not vary their basic business idea. Once they have developed a picture of their future business venture, they are determined to pursue it.

A very problematic phase in most start-up processes is the first months of transacting business. At this time entrepreneurs are exposed to a heavy workload and often fail to execute important management tasks such as strategic planning and control. Financial difficulties are often a consequence and indicate that corrective action is necessary. Sometimes, though, it is too late to make the necessary changes. The reason for this phenomenon is that, in most cases, entrepreneurs operate alone or in pairs and have to deal with every incidental course of action themselves. In many cases, entrepreneurs are just not able to cope with the pressures in respect of time and business administration skills. One of the business advisers described this type of situation as follows:

> ... They are simply eaten up by their daily routines and are no longer able to think about strategic planning and orientation for the future.

Many of the entrepreneurs and advisers concluded that the weight of information and the heavy workload force start-up entrepreneurs to concentrate on essentials. They considered attempts to take ecological issues into account as an additional burden within the start-up process:

> ... this would be too much, in my opinion, because it is already a very demanding project.

> ... at this moment, you've got enough on your mind; you cannot think about these factors additionally.

These assessments correspond to the findings of Palmer (2000) who analysed a group of proactive SMEs and found that, apart from financial resources, time resources were the most important obstacle to making more progress towards environmental management. This is even more the case in start-up enterprises.

However, a few entrepreneurs took a different view and accepted that it was possible to implement ecological thinking into the start-up process.

At first glance, the start-up process seems to be filled with conditions that impede sustainable intervention. Entrepreneurs need access to information that will support the implementation of more sustainable business practices, and which can be easily applied during the start-up process. Otherwise, they will not put sustainability into practice during this crucial period.

BUSINESS ADVISERS TO START-UPS

Start-up business ventures are also affected by the advisers who work with them. There is a wide range of advising individuals and institutions that play a role in start-up processes. These include Chambers of Industry and Commerce, Chambers of Crafts, employers' associations, start-up fairs, start-up centres, banks, Deutsche Ausgleichsbank (the business start-up promotion agency of the German Federal Government), start-up consultants, accountants, lawyers, employment offices, start-up competitions, universities, business angels, venture capitalists, and start-up forums and clubs on the Internet.

In addition, start-up entrepreneurs often consult their own personal networks for information. These include family members and friends, as well as former employers, colleagues and business contacts.

Whether the new venture will work in a more sustainable manner could depend on how advisers assess and put forward ideas regarding more sustainable business practices. In the study, the business advisers were asked how they acted as partners of start-up entrepreneurs and how they assessed the opportunities for implementing ecological aspects during the start-up process.

Most of the advisers described their start-up service as a series of discussions with the entrepreneur. In these discussions advisers usually provided assistance in the development of the start-up concept. In addition, they dealt with figures such as expected expenses, cash flow, liquidity and anticipated profitability. Important issues in the discussions were often about financing and public financial support, as well as marketing.

Ecology plays, at most, a subordinate role in start-up consulting. The advisers emphasized that considerations of ecological issues depend very much on the industry in which the new venture is based. They only considered ecological aspects as relevant in connection with obvious demands of the market, cost savings and legal requirements. According to the advisers, most of the start-up entrepreneurs only took sustainable business practices into account as a means of distinguishing themselves from their competitors. This was usually done by expanding the range of products with ecologically 'friendly' products.

The business advisers saw the implementation of ecological considerations for a new firm as difficult when there was no immediate financial return or advantage associated with these activities. In small start-ups they even assessed an ecological orientation as dangerous, because of the possible additional financial burden that it imposed. The vast majority of the advisers obviously equated ecological business practices with increased costs. In many cases, the advisers considered the ecological alignment of products and services as being innovative. Therefore, their introduction to the market would take longer and could be burdened with added costs and greater risks. As a consequence, advisers reported being more wary with ecologically-oriented start-ups.

Some of the business advisers agreed that introduction of ecological issues into start-up consulting services was possible. Most, though, had not thought of doing so in the past.

In general, business advisers who are in a position to influence the strategic orientation of new enterprises tend to reduce new venture planning to a limited set of management issues. As a result, they only dealt with well-known, proven, conventional matters (such as financing, marketing and operations). If advisers were prepared to make environmental issues a regular part of their start-up consulting services, more new business enterprises might adopt a proactive approach to sustainable business practices.

ECOLOGICAL ORIENTATIONS IN START-UP PRACTICE

In practice, start-ups differ widely in their ecological orientation. There are green start-ups that consistently align all operating procedures, services and products according to environmental needs, as well as conventional start-ups with no ecological considerations at all.

We identified three broadly different sets of views that fell along different points of this continuum (see Table 9.2).

Table 9.2   Different categories of ecological orientation amongst start-up enterprises

Industry	Years of Existence	Number of Employees	Number of Founders
Carpentry	1	8	1
Carpentry	1	–	5
Paint contracting	2	2	1
Car sales and garage services	3	15	2
Car sales and garage services	8	25	2
Manufacture of electrical engineering equipment	4	12	1
Semi-finished/finished materials producer	4	4	2
Wholesale distribution of domestic appliances	5	3	2
Wholesale distribution of solar power appliances	1	1	6
Software service provider	3	–	4

The following sections give a comprehensive description of each group of start-ups, and show how and why start-ups differ in the environmental alignment of their new ventures.

Eco-dedicated start-ups   In eco-dedicated start-ups, environmentally friendly activities are undertaken in products, services and/or operational procedures. The entrepreneurs in this group are interested in techniques and materials that offer opportunities to be environmentally sound in their field. Their strategy is deliberately brought into line with environmental needs. In one case in our sample, a team of entrepreneurs was determined to develop a sustainable thermoplastic material out of renewable raw material for technical applications. Eventually, they developed a material that met high quality standards and was feasible for injection-moulded applications. With this new material it became possible to replace plastics in the plastics processing industry.

One reason for the adoption of sustainable business practices is the recognition of opportunities in the market. Start-up entrepreneurs in this group in particular see a favourable trend in their respective sectors for ecological orientations. They either think that they will be able to compete as a so-called ecopreneur in the conventional market or believe that they will become competitive as a result of developments in the market (such as rising prices or legal requirements).

They also identified a number of barriers to sustainability. When initial technical developments are necessary to achieve a higher level of environmentally sound procedures or products, financial support is reported to be especially difficult. In these cases, funding is essential to meet the costs of technical developments and to win recognition of new products or services in the conventional market. Moreover, in the early stages of business transactions, the new goods and services do not reach the necessary volumes to achieve competitive prices. As a consequence, expensive green goods and services have to compete with cheaper conventional products, and this in turn prevents higher demand from developing. After two years of continued existence, the above-mentioned producers of the sustainable material are still trying to gain recognition in the conventional plastics processing industry and they are still lack high-volume orders.

A very noticeable difference between the three groups is to be seen in the attitudes of the respective start-up entrepreneurs. Eco-dedicated entrepreneurs differed from the other two groups in the significance they attached to ecological issues. Their high level of environmental consciousness was reflected in expressed opinions and attitudes. They consistently alluded to their responsibility for the environment and its conservation for following generations:

> ... above all, for the following generation, we have to take care. If we want to leave something to them, we now have to think of something.

> Ecology is absolutely important.

All the individuals in this group pointed out that their environmental awareness had been developed since childhood from within their families. Their interest in ecological topics led to an active gathering of information particularly related to their area of business operations. As a result, their knowledge about how to act in the new venture in order to improve their environmental performance was much greater than in the two other groups.

Ecological considerations played an important role from the very outset and remained an integral part of each of their businesses. But, despite their environmentally friendly attitudes, these entrepreneurs were still aware of the limits of ecological issues as a business start-up tool. In the interviews, they repeatedly pointed to the necessity to focus on business essentials within the start-up process:

> ... first of all, in the start-up process, it is important to have a goal and get through. ... If one can, somehow, consider environmental issues as applicable to the products or services, one ought to do so.

> ... everyone should consider environmental issues within the start-up process ... but the ones who are not in the position to do so, should just leave it. Because, if they desperately tried, they would not survive.

Starting a new business venture with an extensive ecological orientation is not easy and often even more difficult than starting a conventional business enterprise. It is only the firm convictions of the entrepreneurial individual that leads to this kind of endeavour. As these individuals are the most important factor in creating a sustainable new venture, starting points for intervention are limited. It might therefore be promising to encourage and support those ecologically thinking individuals in converting their convictions into sustainable start-ups. Eco-dedicated start-ups take higher risks and face more market resistance than conventional start-ups and thus need special advisory and financial support.

Eco-open start-ups   In eco-open start-ups, goods, services and operational procedures are not designed according to environmental needs. Entrepreneurs in this group only deal with selected environmental issues. They either enlarge their range of products/services with environmentally acceptable features in order to target an additional customer segment or solve ecological problems with special measures. But eco-open start-up entrepreneurs often reject the adoption of more eco-friendly measures because of assumed higher costs:

> *... economic considerations are more relevant than saying I have to think ecologically in the first place. Because mostly this is more expensive.*

Entrepreneurs in this group expect additional measures not to fit easily with existing operating procedures. In general, they assess the feasibility of environmental improvement in business practices as being limited. Moreover, they tend not to anticipate market opportunities that would encourage them to opt for more environmentally sound business practices.

For example, a wholesale electrical appliance trader in our study offered a so-called 'eco-line' in its range of white goods, in addition to conventional goods. These products saved energy and water. The disposal of used products was secured by contracts with waste disposal companies that were required to take and dispose of these appliances. But the entrepreneur considered the introduction of further eco-friendly measures to be impractical.

As with the eco-dedicated entrepreneurs, eco-open entrepreneurs attached importance to environmental issues. Some start-up entrepreneurs even ranked their environmental awareness as high. They talked about responsibility for the environment and the necessity to maintain resources for future generations. Although they knew something about environmental topics, they did not communicate these issues as strongly as entrepreneurs in the first group; their ecological knowledge seemed to be restricted to their immediate field of work.

Analysis of the start-up processes in this group shows that there is no consistent importance attached to ecological considerations. According to these entrepreneurs, the implementation of environmentally sound business practices in the start-up process depends primarily on the industry in which the new venture will operate. As a consequence, ecological measures only appear selectively during start-up. As one entrepreneur in this group stated:

> ... in my opinion, the topic ecology doesn't play an important role for business founders, at least as long as you cannot make use of it in the industry. Business issues have to be considered first.

For this group, the impetus to include environmental measures is often external (for example, pressure from customers and suppliers). In one case, a customer suggested that the roof of the business premises was suitable for installation of solar panels. This suggestion and subsequent financial support by a public programme led to the use of solar energy in the start-up.

Asked why they did not consider ecological issues in the start-up process to a greater extent, the eco-open entrepreneurs often answered that they had not thought of it. Furthermore, they complained that there was a lack of information on this subject:

> ... it really wasn't mentioned anywhere.

This seems to confirm the findings of Schaper (2002) who analysed Western Australian pharmacies in order to find out whether there are factors which can be used to predict the level of environmentally responsible business behaviour amongst SMEs. In a range of nine possible factors he found that only two variables had a significant relationship with the level of environmental performance: time resources and the level of environmental information available to business owners.

The group of eco-open start-ups seems to be a promising target for implementing more eco-friendly measures in new business ventures. They are, at least partially, open to environmental issues and are prepared to accept suggestions for more sustainable business practices.

Eco-reluctant start-ups   Start-ups that are assigned to this group deal with environmental issues only when external requirements (especially regulations or the specific demands of customers) force them to do so. These entrepreneurs deal with questions of ecological conservation when they realize that they have a problem, such as when they come into conflict with environmental authorities.

In comparison with the two other groups, eco-reluctant start-up entrepreneurs made hardly any statements on the importance of ecological issues. In one case, the entrepreneur refused to answer the question about his personal opinion on this topic. In his opinion, environmental requirements and the problems they presented through the authorities were simply harassments. For these entrepreneurs, other issues, such as job creation, the order book and cost savings, were much more important than environmental issues:

> *... before we think about ecology we should think about how we can get more industrial plants to our region, in which people can work.*

> *... What is important to me is that I have to see how to get work. This is most important to me. If you can combine this with ecology then it is okay. But I'm not one who can try things only along this path, because this will not be enough; you cannot exist on it.*

Ecological considerations only occur arbitrarily at isolated points in time, when there is contact with authorities that force the entrepreneurs to act. In these cases, conservation measures are assessed as additional burdens within the start-up process. However, the eco-reluctant entrepreneurs do not completely object to eco-friendly business practices. Like their fellow entrepreneurs in the second group, some of them reported that they would have done more, if they had only thought of it.

Since eco-reluctant start-up entrepreneurs do not believe that it is necessary to operate in a more sustainable manner, it is probably difficult to find starting points for sustainable intervention in this group. Information about possible measures and financial support for specific environmental conservation measures might help them reach at least a minimal standard of performance. Overall, legal requirements appear to be the major means of forcing these entrepreneurs to adopt more ecologically sound business practices.

Conclusion

At the beginning of this project, it was assumed that all start-ups were fundamentally open to adopting sustainable business practices. However, the results show that it is not so easy. There are still several barriers to sustainability in the start-up process. Some of the key issues facing new entrepreneurs are as follows:

1. In our sample, several entrepreneurs in the eco-open, as well as in the eco-reluctant, start-up groups complained about a lack of information. Providing more information directly to business founders will clearly help in the adoption of more sustainable business practices.

2. The level of knowledge that business advisers have about ecological issues, and their willingness to discuss this with their clients, is also important in creating sustainable new ventures. It is necessary to focus in particular on business advisers who come into contact with entrepreneurs at an early stage of the start-up process.

3. Many start-up entrepreneurs are not fully aware of the potential market opportunities that might exist for environmentally friendly businesses. Therefore, it is necessary to draw their attention to successful best-practice examples in their respective industries. Start-ups might be more willing to follow successful examples than established business enterprises.

As many of the interviewees (both business advisers and entrepreneurs) pointed out, ecological considerations in the start-up process depend on the industry in which the new venture operates, since, obviously, different industries have different impacts on the environment. However, our analysis also shows that the approach to ecological issues can even vary considerably within the same industry. For example, in our study the two carpentry start-ups differed widely in their ecological approaches. One of them was classified as an eco-dedicated start-up and the other as an eco-reluctant start-up. This indicates that, apart from the industry itself, the attitude of the entrepreneur is important in determining whether or not ecological operating measures are put into practice. In our analysis, the so-called gap between the environmental attitudes of the entrepreneur and the environmental behaviour of his/her small firm (Tilley 1999) was only observed in the group of eco-open start-ups. Here, some entrepreneurs stated that their environmental awareness was high, but this attitude did not result in more 'green' business practices. In the other two groups, the level of environmental performance of the start-ups broadly corresponded with the environmental attitudes of the entrepreneurs.

Finally, the role of public funding in promoting sustainable enterprises is often overlooked. It was clear in the study that finance was an ongoing problem for start-ups, especially for green firms that encountered extra costs due to their commitment to sustainable business practices. It seems reasonable that government funding schemes for new firm ventures should make extra allowance for such projects, especially since (on the other side of the ledger) they help reduce the overall cost of environmental protection and clean-up.

To sum up: although the results of our study are not representative, they provide an insight into the intricacies associated with sustainable considerations in business start-up processes in Germany. These are starting points for ecological intervention in the entrepreneurial process aimed at creating an increasingly sustainable business culture.

However, much remains to be done to develop greater sustainability in the field of start-up entrepreneurship. This project and its results are just a preliminary step along that road.

References

Anderson, T.L. and Leal, D.R. (1997) *Enviro-Capitalists. Doing Good While Doing Well*, Rowman & Littlefield Publishers, Inc., Boston, MA.

Belz, F. and Strannegård, L. (1997) *International Business Environmental BarometerCappelen*, Akademisk Forlag, Oslo.

Deutscher Industrie- und Handelstag (DIHT) (2000) *Existenzgründung. Die wichtigsten Bausteine für das eigene Unternehmen,*W. Siewert, Bonn.

Dyllick, T. and Hamschmidt, J. (2000) *Wirksamkeit und Leistungen von Umweltmanagementsystemen. Eine Untersuchung von ISO-14.001-zertifizierten Unternehmen in der Schweiz*, VDF Hoschulverlag, Zürich.

Federal Ministry of Economics and Technology of Germany (2000) *Starthilfe. Der erfolgreiche Weg in die Selbständigkeit*, PID Arbeiten für Wissenschaft und Öffentlichkeit, Berlin.

Freimann, J. and Schwedes, R. (2000) 'EMAS Experiences in German Companies: A Survey on Recent Empirical Studies', *Eco-Management and Auditing*, Vol. 7, pp. 99–105.

Freimann, J. and Walther, M. (2002) 'The Impacts of Corporate Environmental Management Systems', *Greener Management International*, Vol. 36, pp. 91–103.

Hisrich, Robert D. and Peters, M.P (1998) *Entrepreneurship* (4th edn), Irwin McGraw-Hill, Boston, MA.

Isaak, R. (1999) *Green Logic: Ecopreneurship, Theory and Ethics*, Kumarian Press, Sheffield.

Morrow, D. and Rondinelli, D. (2002) 'Adopting Corporate Environmental Management Systems: Motivations and Results of ISO 14001 and EMAS Certification', *European Management Journal*, Vol. 20, No. 2, pp. 159–171.

Palmer, J. (2000) 'Helping SMEs Improve Environmental Management' in R. Hillary (ed.) *Small and Medium-Sized Enterprises and the Environment*, Greenleaf, Sheffield, pp. 325–342.

Schaper, M. (2002) 'Small Firms and Environmental Management', *International Small Business Journal*, Vol. 20, No. 3, pp. 235–249.

Szyperski, N. and Nathusius K. (1999) *Probleme der Unternehmensgründung: Eine betriebswirtschaftliche Analyse unternehmerischer Startbedingungen*, Josef Eul Verlag, Lohmar.

Tilley, F. (1999) 'The Gap Between the Environmental Attitudes and the Environmental Behaviour of Small Firms', *Business Strategy and the Environment*, Vol. 8, pp. 238–248.

10

How Venture Capital Can Help Build Ecopreneurship

Anastasia R. O'Rourke

ABSTRACT

A key factor in the growth of all new companies is their access to finance. This chapter introduces the concepts and mechanisms of venture capital – a key source of finance for new and high-growth ventures. What types of ecopreneurial companies have managed to attract venture capital and what sorts of companies are created as a result? The chapter first provides an explanation about the typical processes of venture capital investments, and then defines what an environmental or cleantech venture is, giving an overview of some of the patterns of VC investment into environmental ventures in North America between 1999 and 2006. Following this, a process-based model for the uptake of sustainability practices beyond investing in cleantech companies is presented. The chapter concludes by discussing why venture capitalists (VCs) might be convinced to do so.

Venture Capital: A Problem and Solution for Entrepreneurs

Until recently, investing in environmental enterprises has been considered by many VCs as a high-risk, low-return proposition – not a very attractive investing profile (EFC9 1998; Steen and Frankel 2003). In the first edition of this book, we wrote that environmental or sustainable ventures faced the problem that many investors appeared blind to opportunities within the sector, and that it was regarded largely as a niche investing activity. In the 1990s the image of 'environmental venture' in the VC community suffered from an apparent focus on 'end-of-pipe'[1] technologies whose markets were largely regulation-driven and fragmented.

---

1   'End-of-pipe' refers to methods and technologies that treat, reduce or otherwise remove emissions of pollutants after they have formed, using add-on measures. 'End-of-pipe' methods

Recently, the intersection of environmental technologies and venture capitalists has seen a dramatic shift. Environmental technologies have been reframed as 'cleantech' and promoted as 'the next wave of industrial innovation' (Parker and O'Rourke 2006). While 'environmental technologies' are often thought of as regulatory mandated solutions to environmental problems such as pollution, cleantech innovations offer more upstream, preventive, efficiency-driven solutions. One venture capitalist actively investing in the area has described it thus:

> On one side, cleantech is really about resource efficiency and productivity in supply – how to manufacture and produce to save energy, water, materials, etc. On the other side, these technologies are enhancing the bottom line of customers. (Propper de Callejon 2006)

Several macro-drivers have also underscored this shift in attitude. From high and volatile oil prices and concerns over energy security and supply, through to the commodity boom felt worldwide, efficiency in the use of resources has become a key concern for industry and policy-makers alike. Concerns over large-scale environmental issues such as climate change and the growth of carbon markets have also prompted a boom in green product marketing and consumer demand. New ventures seeking to serve these markets with their environmental or cleantech innovations are proliferating and attracting entrepreneurs.

Some of these ventures are attracting investment capital and producing rates of growth that have surprised many. Since 2004, investments in such cleantech ventures by venture capitalists has hit the mainstream, so much so that it is now regularly described as the third largest venture investing category behind software and biotechnology (Kho 2005). North American and European venture investing in cleantech has seen huge growth – from US$2.5 billion invested in 2005 to $5.8 billion invested in 2007 (Cleantech Venture Network 2007). High-profile venture capitalists, such as Kleiner Perkins Caufield Byers (2007) are proclaiming that it could be 'the largest economic opportunity of the 21st century. It is an unprecedented challenge that demands great innovation, speed and scale.' Others have even begun to call it a bubble ready to burst (Lux Research 2007; Kanellos 2007; Day 2007).

---

are often contrasted to 'cleaner production' or 'pollution prevention', which seeks to identify areas, processes and activities that create excessive waste products or pollutants in order to reduce or prevent them through alteration or eliminating a process (EPA 2008).

Despite the recent hype, venture capital[2] is both a potential solution for the development of sustainable business practices and a potential problem. Many highly *un*sustainable activities have been financed by VCs, while environmental ventures – until recently – were largely underfinanced. Even once financed, VCs can also put new ventures under great pressure to generate revenues early, fast and to a high degree, so that they do not have the time, energy or expertise to undertake other process-oriented sustainable business practices. In addition, there are still financing gaps for companies, especially those at very early stages or in emerging technologies. This results in some highly environmentally beneficial products or services failing to reach their full market and environmental potential (Chertow 2001; O'Rourke 2006). Despite this, VCs do have the potential capacity to catalyse sustainable business practices, both in *what* they finance and *how* they go about financing it.

The Nature of Venture Capital

Accessing finance can make or break any entrepreneurial venture, especially in its early days. Indeed, a lack of capital is often cited as one of the key barriers to growth by start-up ventures, and is often also blamed for their failure (Brander, Amit and Antweiler 2002).

Venture capital is an important source of capital for unlisted ventures at various stages in their growth. These are investors who both understand the risks of early stage companies and possess the know-how to overcome them (Bygrave and Timmons 1992). There is no strict regulatory definition of venture capital – unlike banking or insurance – but, generally speaking, venture-capital firms provide privately held entrepreneurial firms with equity, and sometimes debt or other hybrid forms of financing. Willingness to make equity investments in early-stage companies is a defining characteristic of VCs (Brander, Amit and Antweiler 2002).

Beyond the actual functional role venture capitalists play in the economy, they are also high-profile bell-weathers for change. When they embrace a new sector or technology – as they did with biotech, the Internet, nanotech, social networking and now cleantech – many commentators on social and industrial

---

2   In some regions such as Europe, the terms venture capital (VC) and private equity (PE) are often used interchangeably. In others (such as the United States and Australia), VC is thought to be distinct from PE which focuses on later-stage companies, buy-outs and debt. Here, the term 'VC' refers to equity investments into unlisted and high-growth companies.

change take note, as do other investors and large firms whose markets intersect whatever is the 'hot' sector. Thus, their influence extends beyond the actual amounts invested, companies created and returns generated.

A defining feature of VCs is that they are professionally managed funds and, as such, they act as mediators in a value chain sitting between entrepreneurs and larger pools of capital. There are also different players within each venture-capital fund. Limited partners are investors into the venture-capital fund who usually contribute most of the capital, whilst so-called general partners (the venture-capital fund managers) contribute only a small portion of the investment capital. General partners typically charge a management fee of 2–3 per cent of the funds under management. Venture-capital funds usually have a set time period (usually several years) and will often have a geographic, sector and/or stage focus.

Another feature of venture-capital investment that distinguishes it from other investment practices is the relatively high risks taken. Because VCs' investment decisions occur in an environment of 'imperfect information, entrepreneurial visions and educated guesses' (von Burg and Kenney 2004, p. 1139), their investing strategies are not always going to work. For example, Zider (1998) claims that usually only one in ten venture-capital investments are highly successful. But that one investment in the fund is sometimes so 'wildly' successful that it can make up for the other nine who either failed or grew only moderately.[3]

Although there are some differences, the venture-capital investment process tends to follow the pattern outlined in Figure 10.1.

Because VCs seek a return through long-term capital gain rather than through immediate and regular payments, they are exposed to the risk of bankruptcy and low liquidity. As a result, they seek to invest in companies that have the ability to grow quickly, address large markets and thus have a chance of producing higher than average returns. VCs usually try to minimize their risks by spreading investing into a diverse portfolio of companies, co-investing with other venture-capital funds in syndicates, managing several funds simultaneously, collecting market intelligence on an ongoing basis,

---

3   The US National Venture Capital Association (NVCA) estimates that some 40 per cent of venture-backed companies in the United States fail; 40 per cent return moderate amounts of capital; and 20 per cent produce high returns (NVCA 2008).

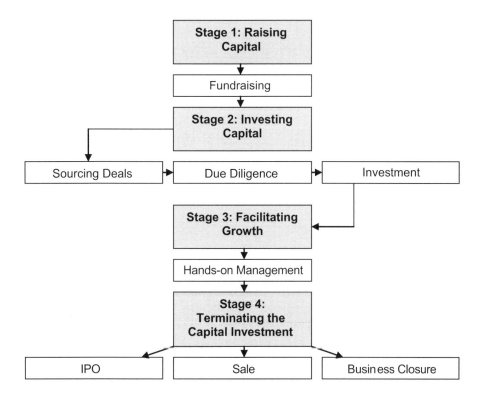

Figure 10.1   Stages of venture-capital growth and exit

and protecting themselves with a series of legal covenants in their investing agreements with the venture (NAVCA 2003).

Two main venture-capital strategies can be observed when it comes to sector- and stage-focused funds (Norton and Tenenbaum 1993; Sahlman, 1990). One strategy is to diversify the portfolio across stages and/or sectors in a *generalist* fund to cushion from any macro-drivers that might affect the investee companies. A second strategy is to *specialize* in a particular stage/sector so as to exploit technical expertise, industry knowledge and networks (Bygrave 1987).

As intermediaries with expectations to deliver returns, VCs face pressure to find and pick good deals. One of the core skills of a venture-capital firm is thus to pick companies with growth potential, then to actively create the conditions for growth in those businesses (Gorman and Sahlman 1989). Although VCs typically receive hundreds of unsolicited business plans from entrepreneurs every year, they also actively seek out prospective deals using trade fairs, venture fairs and their formal and informal networks. Prior to 2004, several environmental entrepreneurs attributed their lack of financing success to being unable to access such networks (Randjelovic, O'Rourke and Osatto 2003; Diefendorf 2001). This has changed with the advent of several dedicated fora for new cleantech/environmental ventures to make pitches to investors, and with the general increase in popularity in the space.

A number of different criteria are used by VCs when screening potential deals. Criteria will vary across venture-capital firms over time and will also sometimes be tacit. However, studies have shown that the following factors are often important considerations: source of the referral; size of the investment; industry sector; investor preference; geographic location; stage of financing (that is, early- or late-stage); state of the market; potential for the product/ service to have immediate and global application; expected returns; perceived risk; price and percentage of equity; and the quality of the management team (NAVCA 2003; AVCAL 2002; Zider 1998). Many studies have found that the most important decision criterion is the perceived quality of the management team and/or entrepreneur, followed by product and market characteristics, and then expected financial outcomes (Manigart and Sapenzia 2000).

VCs are time-constrained, which also affects how many and what stage of companies they can invest in. If they have raised a larger fund, they will be more likely to invest in later-stage, larger deals rather than many smaller ones. As a result, each capital investment made by a North American fund is typically in the millions, and funding gaps for very early-stage companies exist today, including for cleantech and environmental ventures.

Only about 10 per cent of all business plans make it beyond an initial screen into a process of more intensive due diligence (Gompers and Lerner 2001). In this process, ventures are assessed on their performance, risk profile, finance, technologies, management, staff, markets and potential for high returns. It is at this stage that VCs sometimes consider environmental risks, such as the possibility of accidents or liability stemming from environmental exposures. Environmental due diligence, if performed, is more likely to be done in a later-stage, more established company with an operating history. Start-up companies, in contrast, are unlikely to carry any historical environmental burdens.

Before any investment is made, an intensive process of structuring and negotiating the deal ensues. Issues to be addressed at this stage include the price (how much capital the company receives and the percentage of equity shares the VC gets in return) and protective settlements of the agreement (the use of different types of stocks and liquidation clauses in the event of business failure).

Once they have invested, VCs can make active use of their ownership status in ventures to both reduce risk and add value to the venture. VCs may participate in the company's key decisions and will often sit on its board of directors. They often provide (or bring in) expertise in fields such as product or service development, fundraising, market development recruitment and financial and strategic planning of the venture (Gorman and Sahlman 1989; Gompers and Lerner 2001). In effect, they try to influence the market outcome in favour of their investment (von Burg and Kenney 2004). It is this quality of 'hands-on management' could potentially be significant for fostering more sustainable growth amongst new companies.

On the other hand, for entrepreneurs, the process of seeking capital can be problematic and difficult (Sapenzia and Gupta 1994; Sheppard and Zacharakis 2001). The entrepreneurs must recruit the investor, and, conversely, the investor must sufficiently understand and value the firm's innovation and team. VCs can also hinder the growth of a venture if they offer the wrong strategic input or impose problematic constraints. Thus, conflicts of interest sometimes emerge due to infrequent communication, the technical complexity of innovations and differing levels of knowledge, and differences in planning horizons and time to pay-off (Sapenzia 1992; Bygrave and Timmons 1992).

VCs help to grow new ventures, but they eventually seek to 'exit' the investment (that is, sell the shares), usually in three to seven years (NAVCA 2002). VCs' success thus fundamentally rests on the firm's success and the ability to exit at a high valuation. VCs can exit their investment by one of four ways: via an initial public offering (IPO), sale to another private investor, sale to a strategic corporate buyer (that is, via a merger or acquisition) or 'write-off' (if the firm is liquidated, or the VCs do not expect to be able to exit by the time they have to close the fund). VCs usually invest with a particular exit strategy in mind (although perhaps not a write-off). Over the last 25 years in the United States, almost 3,000 firms financed by venture funds have gone public; however, mergers and acquisitions actually represent the most common type of successful exit (NAVCA 2003).

If capital gains are realized (and exits achieved), gains are typically divided up so that 80 per cent goes to the limited partners (alongside the principal) and 20 per cent to the general partners. The performance of venture-capital funds is rarely publicly reported; the only public data available reports funds in aggregate. Part of the reason is that returns are hard to measure, given that the funds, and the investee companies, often do not have a market price. Nonetheless, a typical 'venture-grade' return for a fund is in the order of a 15–30 per cent internal rate of return.

As intermediaries, the job of VCs is ultimately to maximize returns to the fund by exiting their investments, and this might not correlate with the firm's long-run earnings or chances of survival. Some authors have thus questioned whether the VC's success is synonymous with the longer-term economic success of the firm (Mason and Harrison 2002; Sapienza 1992; Baum and Silverman 2004). Likewise, it could also be questioned whether a successful venture-capital investment is the same thing as creating a successful sustainable company from an environmental perspective.

Connecting Environment and Venture Capital via Cleantech

VCs face a different task compared to other actors in the financial services sector engaging with environmental issues and sustainability. The ability and willingness of VCs to invest in smaller, higher-risk ventures pushes them towards the most innovative end of the sustainable business spectrum. Like other 'socially responsible investors' (SRI),[4] VCs investing in cleantech ventures use various positive and negative filters to select their investments. However, there are several major differences between SRI and cleantech venture capital.

First, most SRI funds are mutual funds and are limited to investing in publicly traded companies. SRIs tend to screen such companies on their relative management of environmental and social issues, rather than on the products or technologies they sell (O'Rourke 2002). The universe of 'pure play' cleantech or environmental companies has certainly been growing, but still remains small. These companies are also in the small to mid-cap size group. Typically, larger companies are the consumers or purchasers of clean technologies rather than primary producers. Some may also engage in cleantech and environmental markets via joint ventures, acquisitions or in-house R&D, but such activities will only constitute a small part of their overall revenues.

---

4   Socially responsible investing takes into account social responsibility and environmental sustainability criteria alongside conventional financial criteria. The three main strategies for socially responsible investors include screening, shareholder advocacy and community investing.

Second, VCs fundamentally invest on the basis of the anticipated future – rather than the past or current – performance of a firm. In contrast, the social and environmental assessments undertaken by SRI investors are mainly limited to the past or current performance of firms, even if they argue that performance in these realms is a good indicator for potentially positive future performance of the company's shares. The future orientation of a VC is especially true of investment into early-stage ventures, where the venture may consist of an idea, plus a plan and small team assembled to develop it (Randjelovic, O'Rourke and Osatto 2003). The market for the product may or may not exist, final design and materials may not be decided, manufacturing process not located, supply chains not yet organized, and distribution and sales not yet established. All of these factors will eventually have considerable effect on the environmental 'footprint' of the product or service offered, but it is impossible to define this in advance. Likewise, without an established management team, labour force or location, the venture's social impacts at this stage remain unknown.

An investor who is targeting the environmental or cleantech sector faces the challenge of defining a 'cleantech', 'greentech', 'environmental' or 'sustainable' business from the outset. These terms, though now widely used, are neither standardized nor lacking in contention. Despite several attempts (OECD 1999), a precise definition of the 'environmental industry' has always been difficult to agree because environmental issues span all industries and sectors (ELI 1998). Moreover, a technology's environmental performance is best understood over its whole 'life cycle' – that is, from the raw materials inputs, to processing, to distribution, use and disposal (Graedel and Allenby 2003). Companies may or may not realize they are in fact cleantech or have an environmental benefit; and, even if they do, might choose not to market their products using their green credentials. Sifting and screening environmental claims and impacts can be a complex procedure.

In 2002 organizations such as the Cleantech Venture Network and Clean Edge created and promoted the idea of 'cleantech' to their network of VCs and service providers. The cleantech label was coined in part to disassociate them from the image of 'high-risk/low-returns' that environmental venture investing had become to hold with these investors. Presentation after presentation emphasized the financial/economic dimension of cleantech over the environmental one, and often efforts were made to distinguish cleantech as *not* being the same thing as environmental technology (Parker and O'Rourke 2006; Markower 2006). These groups defined as cleantech those technologies that principally promised efficiency or economic productivity gains, and only secondarily created environmental benefits (such as reduced material, energy or water inputs, or the reduction of waste outputs).[5] This broader definition enabled many more technology firms to be counted under the umbrella of cleantech, and made the segment seem large and diverse.

The upswing in investments reported (Cleantech Venture Network 2007) coincided with several macro-drivers – such as increased power and fuel prices, and concern over energy security – attracting more investors and entrepreneurs into the space as well as increased media attention.

Investors active in cleantech can be classified by the degree of their orientation towards cleantech (as stated on their website and/or prospectus). *Specialists in cleantech* are those that mandate all the investments in their fund to be towards cleantech (or related terminology). *Partial specialists in cleantech* are fund managers who list cleantech (and related terminology) as one area of investment interest amongst others. Finally, *generalist funds* are managers who do not list cleantech or any other related terms as an area of interest; these funds either focus on other sectors or are generalist funds that have made opportunistic investments in cleantech companies.

In effect, these categories suggest that green or sustainable VCs can be described principally by what they invest *in*, not necessarily what they *do*. The model of venture capital itself is assumed to work in the same way as for any sector, whether it be IT, agriculture, biotech or semiconductors.

A Process Model of Sustainable Venture Capital

Case-work and interviews reveal that there is more to the story of venture capital and the environment than just the types and numbers of deals made in cleantech or environmental technologies. By taking a process-oriented view of venture capital, it is possible to identify a number of ways in which sustainability practices could be adopted by VCs and other stakeholders in the venture-capital process, following the main stages described in Figure 10.1.

When *fundraising* from limited partners, VCs articulate various portfolio strategies in their prospectus, which will mandate the types of investments they

---

5   The Cleantech Venture Network defines it as: 'Cleantech is any knowledge-based product or service that improves operational performance, productivity or efficiency; while reducing costs, inputs, energy consumption, waste or pollution' (Parker and O'Rourke 2006).

will look for after the fund is raised. Specialists in cleantech are limited to the definition of cleantech and categories that they give in their fund prospectus. Our research indicates that there are now approximately 85 specialist cleantech venture-capital funds that are investing in North American companies.[6] They range from smaller (US$10–20 million) funds such as SJF Ventures and Commons Capital to larger (US$250–500 million) funds such as Braemar Energy Ventures, Rockport Capital, DFJ Element, US Renewables and the Swiss Re/TCW Clean Energy Fund. Nearly all of these larger funds have been raised between 2005 and 2007, reflecting increasing institutional investor demand and interest in the category.

In North America, for example, the largest group of venture-capital investors in cleantech (as measured by the number of deals done and total US dollars invested) have in fact been the generalist investor funds. An examination of venture-capital funds I undertook indicates that only 7 per cent of total disclosed investors specialized in cleantech, and they were responsible for 9 per cent of all funds invested; partial specialists in cleantech accounted for 12 per cent of total disclosed investors (15 per cent of all funds invested); and generalist funds represented 73 per cent of investors (56 per cent of all funds invested). Some 8 per cent of funds did not provide sufficient information to determine their investment orientations.

Even though few do so today, VCs could actively market the environmental dimension of their portfolio and ongoing monitoring practices to LP investors. There is a growing demand for such work amongst the increasing numbers of institutional and individual investors asking for more accountable and sustainable investments.[7] Effectively communicating the environmental benefits created by the investments over time could help the LPs' own communication of what environmental benefits their investments are creating.

In the venture-capital *deal-sourcing* process, the rise of several cleantech- and environment-focused investing and business networks has helped ecopreneurs find capital.[8] In addition, several initiatives in cleantech- and/or socially-oriented business plan competitions have begun to raise the profile of such ventures to

---

6   Not all of these funds use the terminology of 'cleantech'; some call it clean energy, renewable energy, or greentech instead. The common theme is that they all limit their investments from the fund to this field.

7   See for example, the signatories of the UN Principles for Responsible Investment (http://www.unpri.org) and signatory investors for the Carbon Disclosure Project (http://www.cdproject.net).

8   Networks such as Investors Circle, the Cleantech Venture Network, CSI Cleantech, and World Resources Institute's New Ventures, are all active in the North American market.

investors and potential entrepreneurs alike. By providing leadership on social
and environmental criteria, such competitions educate their audience and raise
the profile of environmental entrepreneurship.

Likewise, VCs could integrate environmental and/or social indicators into
existing *screening criteria*. They could seek to expand their geographic locations into
emerging markets and consider financing ventures at an earlier stage and for lesser
amounts, helping to reduce the gap in financing which still occurs. Some specialist
funds have been raised to invest primarily in emerging markets and sustainable
practices – for example, E & Co, the Acumen Fund and Plebys International.

In the same way that environmental and social aspects are increasingly
integrated into due diligence assessments of mergers and acquisitions (M&A),
VCs in their *due diligence* could look more closely at environmental and social
issues, such as changes to markets due to regulatory interventions and potential
liabilities or extra costs arising from environmental emissions and exposures.
More proactively still, they could seek to ensure that the venture's management
has the capability to undertake ongoing eco-efficiency measures and ensure
stakeholder support for the venture.

In the *negotiation of the final investment deal*, investors could use the results of
environmental and social assessments. Some cleantech VCs have also found that
this negotiation stage is the best time to ensure that best practice in corporate
governance and environmental sustainability reporting structure is instituted.

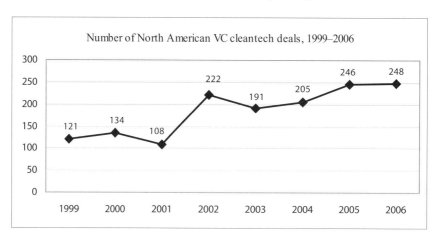

Figure 10.2   Number of North American cleantech venture-capital deals,
1999–2006

Source: Cleantech Venture Network (2007).

Some of the cleantech/environmental VCs already in existence have expanded their *hands-on management* role with ventures to include environmental and social expertise. For example, assistance has been given for investee ventures to go 'beyond compliance' as they grow, by incorporating eco-efficiency and pollution prevention techniques into the design of products and production processes; providing advice about the sourcing of materials, the choice of suppliers and the location of facilities; and creating integrated environmental management systems and reporting protocols. The idea here is that even cleantech companies have environmental impacts that need to be managed. The design stage is the most efficient time to consider the potential environmental footprint of a venture's products and operations in order to prevent future liabilities. In addition, VCs could work to gather stakeholder and customer support for the venture through their own networks. By doing so, the investors would effectively be helping to develop the market for the good or service, which in some cases does not yet exist.

There are still a large portion of venture-capital investments yet to be *exited*. Finding a suitable exit avenue for a sustainable cleantech venture should become increasingly viable as companies and investors look for exposure to this growth industry. Certainly, the recent high levels of public market interest in cleantech companies (as evidenced by the many indexes and exchange traded funds launched between 2005 and 2007) indicates investor demand for the sector. There have also been many cleantech mergers and acquisitions reported, with some well-known conglomerates such as ABB, Air Products and Chemicals, Danaher, General Electric, Honeywell, ITT and Siemens being the acquirers (SVB Alliant 2007). One study counted at least 540 cleantech M&A transactions for 2005 and 2006, most of which were for energy generation companies, followed by water and wastewater, and recycling and waste companies (SVB Alliant 2007). These figures, combined with data on initial public offerings in the cleantech space, indicate future possible exit avenues for existing cleantech portfolio companies of venture-capital funds. It is possible that SRI funds could help to build the financial markets for publicly listed cleantech companies, so long as these companies pass SRI's screens of superior environmental and social management. Exactly how much their environmental or sustainable performance will be valued by the purchaser remains to be seen.

The possible involvement of VCs in sustainable business ventures can be summarized by the four main levels of approach that VCs could use as part of their business strategy, listed below:

1. Make investments that deliberately target enterprises and technologies which deliver sustainable (positive environmental, social and financial)

products and avoid investing in clearly damaging technologies and practices.

2. Practise 'hands-on' management to guide companies in adding strategic environmental advantage and preventing the potential negative environmental and social impacts of new ventures.

3. Work to develop market, regulatory and stakeholder support for environmental/cleantech products and services.

4. Generate financially, environmentally, socially and organizationally sustainable rates of return on investment.

Conclusion: Why Would VCs Take a Leading Role?

Whether they know it or not, all VCs are already engaged with sustainable development. VCs often invest in environmentally or socially *un*sustainable companies, and also sometimes push for unsustainable growth rates in order to increase the perceived worth of the company and their own capital gain. In addition, their recent apparent blindness to environmental challenges and opportunities has resulted in the sector remaining underinvested for many years.

As this chapter has indicated, between 2002 and 2007 hundreds of VCs have piled into cleantech. However, despite the increasing number of specialist funds in cleantech, the majority of venture-capital investments still continue to come from generalist funds or investors who do not have any particular strategy for the sector. This fact alone suggests that the companies are viable in their own right and are not being sponsored by a non-financial ethic of environmental and/or social responsibility.

Likewise, any type of VC could develop more sustainable hands-on management practices across their portfolios, and not only in their cleantech investees. The question to ask is: why would VCs be interested in doing this pre- and post-investment sustainability work? Even if they are personally motivated to contribute to more sustainable development in their role as financiers, they are still under pressure from investors and also investee companies to make profitable investments. Sometimes there are trade-offs: it is not always a 'win–win' scenario as is so often posited (see, for example, Dyllick and Hockerts

2002; Esty and Winston 2006). Undertaking the interventions suggested above will take an investment of time, money, and specialized skill by VCs or the consultants they might hire.

VCs need to be convinced of the specific and measurable 'business case' for sustainability and eco-efficiency measures. Depending on what level VCs choose to engage with sustainability (see the four approaches listed above), different business-case arguments could be sought. For example, a VC looking to invest in targeted environmental or cleantech ventures (level 1) will assess the venture on its ability to capture new markets, differentiate its product and protect its reputation or brand as being environmental, cleantech or sustainable. A VC which focuses more on 'hands-on management' (level 2) will look for potential risk reductions, cost savings, increased efficiencies and maintaining the social licence to operate. These VCs need not just be dedicated or convinced of the 'cause' of sustainable development, and ventures located in any sector can realize such gains. VCs entering into the development of new markets (level 3) will work on untapped markets and look towards product differentiation. Finally, VCs which are looking for sustainable returns on investment (level 4) could benefit from increasing access to capital (in its fundraising and exiting stage) due to larger shifts occurring in the financial services sector towards more sustainable investments. Measuring and communicating these positive sustainability attributes will be key to all levels.

Aside from the business case, some authors claim that the larger driver for creating a viable capital market for sustainable and environmentally responsible industry innovation lies in regulation (see, for example, Diefendorf 2001; Stack 2007). The cleantech industry is at present particularly reliant on regulation, given that many sources of environmental capital remain underpriced or unpriced by the market.

The development of sustainable VC practices could also benefit from a regulatory stimulus. Previous government strategies to develop the modern venture-capital industry have used tax incentives, government guarantees and co-funding investments, especially at the seed-funding stage (Mangiart and Sapienza 2000; Chertow, 2001). Likewise, regulatory reforms could remove (and, in some countries, already have removed) subsidies for clearly unsustainable ventures, provide tax incentives for sustainable venture investments, and demand a higher level of environmental and social standards in existing venture-capital investments. Increased disclosure rules for LP investors in venture capital could also be instigated, similar to those made to the Pension

Fund Act[9] in the UK that helped stimulate mainstream investor interest in SRI. Since pension or retirement funds are currently the main investors in venture-capital funds, such changes could ultimately increase demand for sustainable venture-capital practices and sustainability-oriented IPOs.

The role of business researchers in this process is also important. Research evidence is needed to generate careful assessments of whether and when it is profitable to invest in the emerging cleantech business sector; and whether and when it is worth start up companies investing in corporate sustainability practices. Evaluating venture-capital practices that result in unsustainable development can also keep the sustainability debate in the financial services sector animated. The next step will then be to study the effects of the positive engagement by VCs with sustainability, by using measures of environmental, social *and* financial performance to see whether such efforts catalyse the widespread growth of sustainable entrepreneurial ventures.

References

Australian Venture Capital Association (AVCAL) (2002) *Winning Australian Venture Capital*, Australian Venture Capital Association Ltd, at: http://www. avcal.com.au (accessed 6 April 2003).

Baum, J. and Silverman, B. (2004) 'Picking Winners or Building Them? Alliance, Intellectual, and Human Capital as Selection Criteria in Venture Financing and Performance of Biotechnology Startups', *Journal of Business Venturing*, No. 19, pp. 411–436.

Brander, J., Amit, R. and Antweiler, W. (2002) 'Venture-Capital Syndication: Improved Venture Selection vs. the Value-Added Hypothesis', *Journal of Economics & Management Strategy*, Vol. 11, No. 3, pp. 423–452.

Bygrave, W. (1987) 'Syndicated Investments by Venture Capital Firms: A Networking Perspective', *Journal of Business Venturing*, Vol. 2, No. 2, pp. 139–154.

Bygrave, W. and Timmons, J. (1992) *Venture Capital at the Crossroads*, Harvard Business School Press: Boston, MA.

Chertow, M. (2001) 'The "Gap" in Commercializing Environmental Technology', paper presented at the American Association for the Advancement of Science Annual Meeting, San Francisco, CA.

---

9   Under this legislation, pension funds must declare the extent to which social, environmental or ethical considerations are taken into account in the selection, retention and realization of investments (Section 35, 1995 Pensions Act, UK).

Cleantech Venture Network (2007) *Investment Monitor: 15*, Cleantech Venture Network, Ann Arbor, MI. Available at: http://www.cleantech.com (accessed 1 March 2008).

Day, R. (2007) 'Cleantech Bubble Watch, Part 2', *Always On*, at: http://alwayson.goingon.com/permalink/post/14187 (accessed 1 March 1 2008).

Diefendorf, S. (2001) *Venture Capital and the Environmental Industry*, EFC9, Alameda, CA.

EFC 9 (1998) *Financing Environmental Technology*. EFC 9, Alameda, CA.

Dyllick, T. and Hockerts, K. (2002) 'Beyond the Business Case for Corporate Sustainability', *Business Strategy and the Environment*, No. 11, pp 130–141.

Environmental Law Institute (ELI) (1998) *Barriers to Environmental Technology, Innovation and Use,* Environmental Law Institute, Washington, DC.

Environmental Protection Authority (EPA) (2008) *Terms of Environment: Glossary, Abbreviations and Acronyms*, Environmental Protection Authority, Washington, DC. Available at: http://www.epa.gov/OCEPAterms (accessed 1 March 2008).

Esty, D. and Winston, A. (2006) *Green to Gold*, Yale University Press, New Haven, CT.

Gompers, P.A. and Lerner, J. (2001) *The Money of Invention: How Venture Capital Creates New Wealth*, Harvard Business School Press, Cambridge, MA.

Gorman, M. and Sahlman, W. (1989) 'What Do Venture Capitalists Do?', *Journal of Business Venturing*, No. 4, pp. 231–248.

Graedel, T.E. and Allenby, B. (2003) *Industrial Ecology* (2nd edn), Pearson Education Inc., Upper Saddle River, NJ.

Kanellos, M. (2007) 'Perspective: Is Cleantech a Bubble?', *CNET News*, 6 March, at: http://www.news.com/Is-clean-tech-a-bubble/2010-11392_3-6164565.html (accessed 15 March 2007).

Kho, J. (2005) 'Cleantech Funds Seen at $10 Billion', *The Red Herring*, 23 October, at: http://www.redherring.com/Home/14133 (accessed 15 March 2007).

Kleiner Perkins Caufield Byers (2007) *Initiatives: Greentech*, at: http://www.kpcb.com/initiatives/greentech/index.html (accessed 1 March 2008).

Lux Research (2007) *The Cleantech Report,* Lux Research, New York.

Mangiart, S. and Sapienza, H. (2000) 'Venture Capital and Growth' in D. Sexton and H. Landstöm (eds) *The Blackwell Handbook of Entrepreneurship*, Blackwell Publishers, Oxford, pp. 240–258.

Markower, J. (2006) Interview, San Francisco, 25 May.

Mason, C. and Harrison, R. (2002) 'Is It Worth It? The Rates of Return from Informal Venture Capital Investments', *Journal of Business Venturing*, No. 17, pp. 211–236.

National Venture Capital Association (NVCA) (2008) *VC Industry Overview: 2007*, National Venture Capital Association, Washington, DC.

North American Venture Capital Association (NAVCA) (2002) *Industry Summary Statistics: 2002*, North American Venture Capital Association, Washington, DC.

North American Venture Capital Association (NAVCA) (2003) *Industry Summary Statistics 2003*, North American Venture Capital Association, Washington, DC.

Norton, E. and Tenenbaum, B. (1993) 'Specialization versus Diversification as a Venture Capital Investment Strategy', *Journal of Business Venturing*, No. 8, pp. 431–442.

Organization for Economic Cooperation and Development (OECD) (1999) *The Environmental Goods and Services Industry: Manual for Data Collection and Analysis*, EuroStat, OECD Publications Service, Paris.

O'Rourke, A. (2002) 'The Message and Methods of Ethical Investment', *Journal of Cleaner Production*, No. 11, pp. 683–693.

O'Rourke, A. (2006) 'Unearthing Cleantech: Venture Capital Investments into Cleantech Companies, 1999–2006', paper presented at The Academy of Management Conference 2006, Atlanta, GA.

Parker, N. and O'Rourke, A. (2006) *The Cleantech Venture Capital Report – 2006*, The Cleantech Venture Network, Ann Arbor, MI.

Propper de Callejon, D. (2006) Interview, New York, 20 June.

Randjelovic, J., O'Rourke, A. and Osatto, R. (2003) 'The Emergence of Green Venture Capital', *Business Strategy and the Environment*, Vol. 12, No. 4, pp. 240–253.

Sahlman, W. (1990) 'The Structure and Governance of Venture Capital Organizations', *Journal of Financial Economics*, Vol. 27, No. 2, pp. 473–521.

Sapienza, H. (1992) 'When Do Venture Capitalists Add Value?', *Journal of Business Venturing*, Vol. 7, No. 1, pp. 9–27.

Sapenzia, H. and Gupta, A. (1994) 'Impact of Agency Risks and Task Uncertainty on Venture Capitalists–CEO Interaction', *Academy of Management Journal*, Vol. 37, No. 6, pp. 1618–1632.

Sheppard, D. and Zacharakis, A. (2001) 'The Venture Capitalist–Entrepreneur Relationship: Control, Trust and Confidence in Cooperative Behavior', *Venture Capital*, Vol. 3, No. 2, pp. 129–149.

Stack, J. (2007) *Cleantech Venture Capital: How Public Policy has Stimulated Private Investment*, Environmental Entrepreneurs (E2) and The Cleantech Venture Network, Ann Arbor, MI.

Steen, J. and Frankel, P. (2003) 'The Flow of Venture Capital into Clean Technology Ventures', *Working Paper Series: The Center for the Study of Fiduciary Capitalism*, St Mary's College, Moraga, CA.

SVB Alliant (2007) *Earth Wind and Fire: A Cleantech Perspective*, SVB Alliant, Palo Alto, CA.

von Burg, U. and Kenney, M. (2004) 'Venture Capital and the Birth of the Local Area Networking Industry', *Research Policy*, No. 29, pp. 1135–1155.

Zacharakis, A.L. and Shepherd, D.A. (2001) 'The Nature of Information and Overconfidence on Venture Capitalists' Decision Making', *Journal of Business Venturing*, Vol. 16, No. 4, pp. 311–332.

Zider, B. (1998) 'How Venture Capital Works', *Harvard Business Review*, Vol. 76, No. 6, pp. 131–140.

11

Offsetting the Disadvantages of Smallness: Promoting Green Entrepreneurs through Industry Clusters

Elya Tagar and Chris Cocklin

ABSTRACT

The relatively recent emergence of the environment industry has generated significant enthusiasm in the policy and business arenas in Australia and elsewhere. Alongside the commercial promise of the young industry, though, individual entrepreneurs and small firms are faced with significant challenges as they attempt to commercialize emerging and often innovative technologies. Based on their alleged success in the technology and other industries around the world, industry clusters and networks have been suggested as tools for strengthening and promoting this emerging industry sector in Australia.

This chapter examines the characteristics of the environment industry in Australia and critically evaluates the role that clusters and networks can play in promoting this innovative but fragmented sector. Through an industry survey and three industry case studies, the chapter concludes that local networking is a crucial component at the early stages of a new business venture, but that its importance wanes as firms become more established and are able to create business linkages of their own. The implications for clustering policies are twofold. First, economic development officials should look positively at clusters and networks as a means to encourage and foster entrepreneurial activity in the sector. Second, in order to maintain relevance to entrepreneurs as their companies grow, and in order to attract and deliver value to already larger firms, such clusters should include active elements of interaction with extraregional players.

Introduction

Over the last decade, a new set of business opportunities has emerged as industry and communities attempt to deal with sustainability. The so-called environment industry refers to the collection of businesses that are attempting to capitalize on these opportunities, by providing a diverse range of goods and services to public- and private-sector clients and consumers. In Australia, a 2000 Environment Industry Action Agenda sought to provide an analysis of the Australian environment industry, develop a vision for it, identify opportunities and impediments to growth, and 'develop a set of strategies and actions to overcome impediments and maximise opportunities' (DISRE 2000, p. 17).

Recognizing the specific barriers associated with small firm size and the fragmented nature of the industry in Australia, the Action Agenda's final recommendation was to 'increase clustering, networking and partnership building within [the] environment industry ' (DISRE 2000, p. 53). This recommendation is consistent with a recent revival of interest in the concepts of industry clusters and networks in academic and regional development circles. In particular, industry clusters and networks are seen as a means of 'offsetting disadvantages of smallness' (Bureau of Industry Economics 1991, p. 19), helping individual entrepreneurs and small companies attain economies of scale and scope, without losing their autonomy, flexibility and responsiveness in rapidly evolving markets.

This chapter examines the characteristics of the environment industry in Australia and the barriers environmental entrepreneurs face in this innovative but fragmented sector. In order to evaluate the role that clusters and networks can play in promoting the industry, the chapter compares the benefits of clustering and networking, as described in the extensive literature on these topics, with the findings of a recent study into the environment industry in south-east Melbourne. The chapter concludes that local networking is a crucial component at the early stages of new business development, but that its importance wanes as firms become more established and are able to create business linkages of their own. We also discuss, briefly, the implications for clustering policy and the role of governments in fostering appropriate forms of clusters and networks.

Many of the 'companies' or 'firms' we refer to in this chapter are in fact quite small enterprises, sometimes consisting of an individual entrepreneur and possibly a few staff. As we argue here, it is these micro-companies, centred on individuals with technologies and services that they are seeking to commercialize, which in many senses stand to benefit most from clusters and networks.

Defining the 'Environment Industry'

The term 'environment industry' refers to a rapidly evolving and internally diverse sector or group of subsectors. Exact definition of the field is made difficult by its internal diversity, its recent emergence and rapid evolution, and by the overlap of environmental and non-environmental uses of identical products and services. Various definitions have emerged, but convergence around the following OECD definition seems to be evident in recent literature (see, for example, DISRE 2000; Department of State and Regional Development 2001; Douglas and Hill 2001; OECD 2001):

> *The environmental goods and services industry consists of activities which produce goods and services to measure, prevent, limit, minimize or correct environmental damage to water, air and soil, as well as problems related to waste, noise and eco-systems. This includes cleaner technologies, products and services that reduce environmental risk and minimize pollution and resource use. (OECD-Eurostat, 1999, p. 9)*

The diversity of products, processes, technologies and services that come under the environment industry umbrella is reflected in its fragmented nature and the fact that the industry is only slowly forging a common identity. In Australia, for example, the environment management area alone is represented by over 24 separate industry and professional associations (DSRD 2001). Indeed, this diversity has led to the remark that the environment industry is 'less a sector than an agglomeration of providers of many types of goods, services and technologies' (OECD 2001, p. 11).

The Environment Industry in Australia: Challenges and Barriers

Environment Business Australia (EBA n.d.) estimates the annual turnover for the Australian environment industry at A$16.7 billion, representing 2.7 per cent of GDP, and as employing 146,200 people in 5,640 companies (EBA 2002). Export earnings have been estimated at A$300 million (DISRE 2000), giving Australia a minute 0.04–0.06 per cent share of a global market that is estimated at US$500–750 billion (EBA 2002). The sector is identified as a high-growth area, with recent growth rates of 7 per cent (DISRE 2000). Industry stakeholders believe that significantly higher growth rates are feasible, setting A$40 billion annual turnover by 2011 as the sector's target (DISRE 2000). In order to achieve that goal, growth rates of 10 per cent in the domestic market and 20 per cent in export markets would be required (DISRE 2000). This ambitious target is set in the context of a widespread perception of 'rapid market growth' (Vickery and Iarrera 1996, p. 7), especially in developing countries (see also Astolfi et al. 2000; OECD 2001; Vernon 2001).

Like its counterparts in other countries (see, for example, Higgins 1996; Industry Canada 2002), the Australian environment industry is characterized by a large proportion of individual entrepreneurs, micro-businesses and SMEs, which represent 80 per cent of firms in the sector (Environment Business of Australia 2002). As in many other OECD countries, increased subcontracting, corporatization of government bodies and full privatization is changing the ownership structure of the sector, with significant growth in private ownership and a growing influence by competitive market forces. Other factors affecting the structure of the sector include the emergence and maturing of subsectors and markets, with the corresponding effects of emergence of new companies on the one hand and rationalization and consolidation on the other (see DSRD 2001; Industry Canada 2002; OECD-Eurostat 1999).

According to recent reports on the environment industry in Australia (ACIL 2000a, 2000b, 2000c; Astolfi et al. 2000; DSRD 2001; Douglas and Hill 2001; Genoff and de Leeuw 2000), which include significant input from industry representatives and leaders, the impediments to growth facing the industry stem from three main sources: government policy, market conditions and the nature and features of the industry itself. Government policy issues include trade and industry support mechanisms that are likely to be similar to those required by other emerging industry sectors. Issues specific to the environment industry are the internalization of environmental externalities in the pricing mechanism, the counterproductive nature of subsidies that favour competing products (such as a rebate on diesel) and the international image of Australia as a producer of solutions for environmental problems. While this chapter focuses on solutions relating to the organization of the industry itself, broader policy issues are likely to be critical in terms of the ability of individual entrepreneurs and the Australian environment industry as a whole to grow and compete in the global market.

In terms of impediments related to the nature and features of the environment industry itself, the repeated themes from the reports are small company size and the fragmented nature of the sector. As represented in Figure 11.1, this combination gives rise to a number of problems affecting the growth potential of the industry, especially in regard to exports. In our interviews, surveys and group workshops with industry representatives, small firm size in the industry

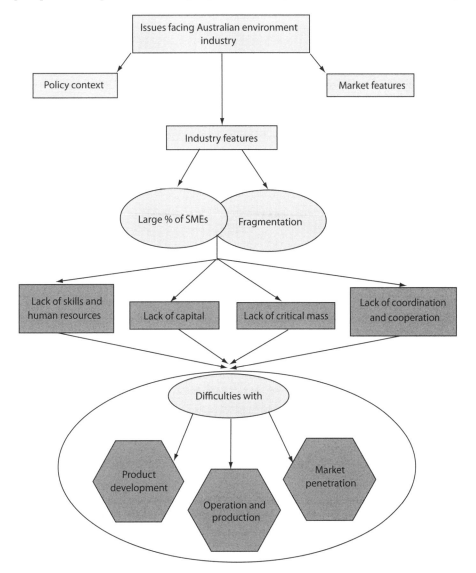

Figure 11.1   Issues facing the Australian environment industry

Sources: ACIL (2000a, 2000b, 2000c); Astolfi et al. (2000); Competitive Edge (2000); Douglas and Hill (2001); Genoff and de Leeuw (2000).

was repeatedly mentioned as a cause of limited access to capital, skills and human resources. Within the context of a fragmented industry, the studies suggest that a lack of coordination and cooperation restricts the ability of firms to pool resources to form the critical mass necessary for the innovation and production process, on the one hand, and marketing and sales, on the other. On the ground, those impediments lead to a range of specific problems faced by individual firms and by the industry as a whole at the product development, production and marketing stages (as listed in detail in Table 11.1).

Table 11.1   Specific impediments faced by entrepreneurs in the Australian environment industry

Product development
- Limited R&D funding, especially direct funding to companies as opposed to Cooperative Research Centres (CRCs)
- Technology rather than market-focused R&D
- Limited commercialization skills
- Limited room for innovation and experimentation
- Limited access to finance
- Limited access to, and uptake of, latest technology
- Limited information about market needs to inform product development
- Limited design skills
- Limited ability to move from single technologies to integrated products and packaged solutions

Operation and production
- Limited management skills
- Limited entrepreneurship, especially among executives of the mature sector of the industry
- Limited IT skills, especially in regards to e-commerce
- Limited ability to seek Environment Technology Verification (ETV)
- Limited production capacity

Market penetration
- Lack of knowledge about new market opportunities
- Lack of information about market-specific barriers, rules and regulations
- Limited ability to partner with local agents or firms
- Lack of effective marketing
- Limited or non-existent brand recognition and industry image
- Lack of industry vision

Sources: ACIL (2000a, 2000b, 2000c); Astolfi et al. (2000); Competitive Edge (2000); Douglas and Hill (2001); DSRD (2001); Genoff and de Leeuw (2000).

In light of these barriers, the DISRE (2000) sets out 18 recommendations aiming to promote industry growth. The final recommendation suggests that industry and governments look to 'increase clustering, networking and partnership building' within the sector (DISRE 2000, p. 53).

The potential usefulness of the recommendation to individual entrepreneurs and the industry as a whole is examined here against the background of the vast literature on clustering and industry networks, using case studies from the Australian industry to evaluate certain theoretical claims. These cases are based on a recent study carried out in south-east Melbourne.

The South-east Melbourne Study

The study was conducted in 2002 by the Monash Environment Institute, under the auspices of the Regional Business and the Environment (ReBATE) network. The work was undertaken in collaboration with three local city councils and several state government organizations (the Melbourne Development Board, the Department of Regional and State Development, EcoRecycle Victoria and the Victorian EPA).

The study area includes the seven south-east municipalities under the jurisdiction of the Melbourne Development Board (see Jenkin 2001). Until a national survey of the industry is undertaken, as proposed recently in an ABS Prospectus on a National Survey of the Environment Industry (Vernon 2001), it will be difficult to objectively ascertain the significance of any one region as a host of a proportionately significant number of companies in the sector. The choice of south-east Melbourne rested partly on a perception that exists amongst local economic development officials that a significant number of environmental companies operate in the region (Jenkin 2001), and partly on the presence of some major research institutions in the area, namely the Commonwealth Scientific and Industrial Research Organization (CSIRO) and Monash University, both of which conduct environmental R&D. In addition, the significant level of manufacturing, industrial activity and infrastructure in the region provides appropriate conditions for the development of the industry and makes the area a suitable choice for this study.

The research was based on a population of 270 companies producing environmental goods and services in the region, which were identified from a number of databases. The databases represent the efforts of a variety of local agencies to collate information about the environment industry at the local municipal, state and national (Commonwealth) levels. A survey was sent to all companies on the database, aiming to provide sufficient information on current activities, growth intentions and barriers to growth in order to allow a basic analysis of the industry and the potential usefulness of networking and greater collaboration with other local companies. The survey also aimed to gauge levels of interest in networking and collaboration, as well as any concerns that companies might have in relation to networks.

Responses were received from 49 firms, representing 18 per cent of the original business population. The survey findings were enhanced by qualitative data obtained via three detailed case studies. The case studies sought to evaluate the potential benefits of networking to a very small emerging company composed of a single entrepreneur (Company A); an established company with 12 employees that had been trading since 1989 and which had been controlled by the same owners since the 1970s (Company B); and a relatively well-established firm some 14 years old and employing 12 persons, with substantial export experience (Company C). The choice of companies rested on the presumption that the need for, and interest in, networking is likely to vary with a company's size and level of experience.

Offsetting the Disadvantage of Smallness: Networking and Clustering

In a review of the clustering concept, Saget notes that 'while the concept of clusters has aroused a great deal of interest in the economic literature, no single commonly accepted definition is available' (Saget 1997, p. 7). Indeed the terms 'clusters', 'networks' and 'industrial districts', referring to various forms of interfirm cooperation, suffer from considerable 'semantic ambiguity' (Paniccia 1998, p. 2). We have used the terms 'cluster' (and 'clustering') and 'network' ('networking') interchangeably in this chapter.

In examining the benefits of cooperation to individual entrepreneurs and firms, three main overlapping points emerge in the literature: benefits of shared resources (economies of scale or agglomeration economies), benefits of interaction and benefits of belonging to a greater identity (economies of scope). In examining the benefits beyond the confines of the individual firm, the thesis of 'flexible specialization' has been proposed by authors such as AnnaLee Saxenian (1990, p. 92; see also Baker 1995, p. 2 and Saxenian 1991), who argue that networks of SMEs enhance the economic performance of the region as a whole. Each of these is analysed in more detail below.

BENEFITS OF SHARED RESOURCES

Both empirical and theoretical studies demonstrate repeatedly how shared physical, financial and human resources can assist companies operating in formal or informal networks or clusters to reduce costs and utilize otherwise unattainable opportunities right across the value chain. The large proportion of individual entrepreneurs and SMEs in the sector, both nationally and within the south-east Melbourne respondent group, makes the economies of scale resulting from shared resources a particularly attractive opportunity for the environment industry.

Companies operating in clusters can share manufacturing and R&D equipment and facilities where sufficient product or process convergence exists. Shared R&D is particularly important to entrepreneurs and SMEs that are limited in their ability to invest in costly R&D infrastructure, especially in technologically sophisticated and rapidly evolving industries. Shared manufacturing facilities allow small companies to diversify and test new product-lines without investing in costly equipment (Doeringer and Terkla 1995; Enright and Roberts 2001; Folta and Baik 2001; Marceau 1999). The case study of Company A, an individual entrepreneur inventing and producing a variety of products made from recycled rubber, demonstrates the usefulness of networking in terms of R&D. The owner did not own substantial R&D or manufacturing equipment. Instead, R&D and manufacturing were undertaken in partnership with local companies and research laboratories, enabling the company to utilize a variety of specialized and costly equipment. 'If you know the people you can strike deals to get things done,' the owner stated about his ability to access equipment. While research laboratories charge around $150 per hour to use such equipment, through current formal and informal connections fostered over many years, he was able to use those resources for free: 'It don't cost me a cracker.' The importance of personal relationships was clear for this entrepreneur: 'I don't think anything can replace face-to-face contact.'

Clusters and networks can also help lower the cost of marketing through shared market intelligence and joint marketing ventures. Clearly, sufficient convergence in terms of target markets and clientele is required for joint marketing ventures. Where such convergence exists, the advantages of cooperation can come about by way of reduced costs as well as access to markets beyond the reach of many individual entrepreneurs and SMEs. Resource pooling may assist companies in marketing their products and services through hosting and sending common trade delegations, through common agents and partners in the export country, and through sharing bridging services such as interpreters and cultural experts (see, for example, Diesendorf 2001). Proponents of clustering also argue that operating within the broader context of a cluster allows small and specialized firms to benefit from economies of scope, by placing their product within a larger range of complementary products and services and providing the possibility of offering integrated solutions 'completely beyond the capacity of individual firms' (Bureau of Industry Economics 1991, p. 19). The issue of economies of scope is also discussed below in reference to the benefits of a greater identity.

In the survey conducted in south-east Melbourne, lack of effective marketing was the most frequently quoted barrier to growth, as well as the most frequently quoted barrier to entering new markets (51 per cent and 45 per cent of respondents respectively). In interviews with companies, it was also suggested that the costs and the expertise required for effective marketing were significant barriers to expansion in both domestic and export markets. The case study of Company B, a more established company engaged in the production of furniture from recycled plastic resins, demonstrated the need for marketing support. While the company was self-sufficient in terms of R&D and production, it lacked the managerial capacity, financial means and specialized skills for an effective marketing and sales department. This was best explained in the words of the owner: '… we don't have a sales force, we rely on relationships with clients.' This limitation was seen as a significant barrier to growth in the eyes of the owner-manager. She had been considering the possibility of sharing marketing efforts with complementary firms, and it is plausible that a formal cluster or network would encourage and help to facilitate such a process. 'I can see the value in face-to-face networking', she said, echoing the words of the owner of Company A, since 'it might help to get things done.'

Similarly, any help with becoming export-ready was important to both Company A and Company B. The owner of Company B neatly summarized the difficulties associated with exporting to Japan in the following way: '… six visits and they [only] take your business card'. The owner of Company A was similarly open about the challenges of exporting: '… that's one area where we've reached a stage where we've got to jump another level.'

Following on from the case above, the need for training and professional development can be identified, a need that clustering proponents suggest can also be shared in an industry cluster. Shared training can reduce the cost and create the possibility of improved skills in general areas such as marketing and e-commerce (see, for example, Scott 1998b), as well as in sector-specific areas such as environmental legislation or plastics recycling technologies. In the Melbourne survey, the second most frequently quoted barrier to growth was a lack of skilled staff (47 per cent of respondents). However, both the need for a local industry cluster or network and its ability to address the training issue are uncertain. In terms of general business skills, a number of programmes are currently offered by various local and state government agencies (see, for example, AusIndustry 2002 and DISRE 2002) and can be taken by companies as the need arises. In terms of specialized skills, it is likely that the wide array of product or process-related training needs would make it difficult to find sufficient synergies within the internally diverse environment industry. Notable exceptions are industry-wide issues such as environmental technology verification (ETV).

BENEFITS OF INTERACTION

Beyond the actual sharing of resources, proponents of clusters and networks point to the business benefits associated with the interaction of individuals within the same sector (see, for example, Capello 1999; Doeringer and Terkla 1995; LeVeen 2002; Uzzi 1996, 1997, 1999; von Hippel 1987). Face-to-face interaction within the framework of an industry cluster or network can provide business benefits through information and know-how exchanges, and through the facilitation of trust and relationship-building that help in 'decreasing the risk and uncertainty accompanying interfirm relationships' (Capello 1999, p. 7; see also Uzzi 1996, 1999). Interaction leading to 'subtle informational benefits' (Oakey, Kipling and Wildgust 2001, p. 401) and the 'collective learning process' (Staber 2001b, p. 538) can be of significant importance in rapidly evolving industries (see also Keeble and Wilkinson 1999; Longhi 1999; von Hippel 1987). Such interaction is particularly important in the innovation process, which is increasingly seen as an 'interactive process requiring intense traffic in facts, ideas and reputational information' rather than a simple linear process (Bureau of Industry Economics 1991, p. 16; see also Scott 1988, p. 15). The 'positive contribution of networking to the propensity to innovate' Roper (2001, p. 225) found in his empirical analysis of plant location in Ireland is echoed repeatedly in the literature (see Boekholt and Thuriaux 1999; Enright and Roberts 2001; Roelandt and den Hartog 1999; Porter 1990). In particular, the 'short feedback loop' (Enright 1998, p. 319), created through closer collaboration along the supply chain, is mentioned frequently as a source of faster and more efficient innovation, as buyers and suppliers cooperate to find solutions to specific and evolving needs.

A high proportion of companies in the Melbourne survey indicated that their main sources of information about business opportunities were personal networks and business referrals (83 per cent and 72 per cent, respectively). An increased level of interaction was likely to be beneficial in that respect, especially where companies had common markets or clients. As mentioned above, the entrepreneur who formed Company A was particularly interested in face-to-face networking, suggesting that it was a primary source of ideas, product innovation and refinement, market and industry intelligence, strategic partnerships and information of personal interest: 'It's imperative that you constantly talk to people, bounce ideas, listen to what they say.' When questioned about the actual value of getting together with others in the industry, his response was clearly positive: 'If you only got one idea out of a two-hour seminar it would be worthwhile.' The owner of Company B, while expressing concerns about time limitations, was also interested in the concept of networking, especially with strategic partners along the supply chain, such as architects and designers with environmental interests. Discussing the difficulties of forming useful business connections through the normal, or what Uzzi would call 'arm's length' (1997, p. 37) business relationships, the owner highlighted the benefits of face to face meetings: '… meeting [an architect] in a workshop might be more effective than knocking on their door.'

Interestingly, Company C, while seeing the benefit of face-to-face interaction, believed strategic partnerships were more likely to be found outside the geographic region. Company C produces technologically advanced and highly innovative systems for air pollution control, water and wastewater treatment and resource recovery. Though relatively small in size, it was more established than Companies A and B, and was already engaged in exports to a number of different countries. Its high level of specialization and its ability to interact with companies and individuals around Australia and overseas suggested that Company C stood to benefit less from, and depended less on, local networking. In the interview, the owner-manager was clear about the limited value he perceived in finding local partners: 'our networks are global … every day we get to the office and find a dozen emails from all over the world.'

BENEFITS OF BELONGING TO A GREATER IDENTITY

Cooperating within a geographic region can provide individual entrepreneurs and firms with a broader identity that can be utilized in marketing, attracting investment, lobbying for regional development and securing government assistance (Longhi 1999). As mentioned above, placing a small business within the context of an industry network can create economies of scope, extending the range of related products and services vertically (along the supply chain) and horizontally (across complementary products). Frequently mentioned examples of such economies of scope include wine regions in Australia and overseas, hi-tech clusters such as Silicon Valley, the industrial districts in Italy and the whisky industry in Scotland (see, for example, Folta and Baik 2001; Harrison 1997; LeVeen 2002; Paniccia 1998; Porter 1990; Saxenian 1990, 1991, 1994; Scott 1998a, 1998b). Noting the importance of image to the successful marketing of such regions, Enright (1998) argues that the creation of regional identity can be a powerful marketing and branding tool. Operating within the broader context of a cluster, it is argued, and placing their product within a larger range of complementary products and services, provides companies with the possibility of offering integrated solutions 'completely beyond the capacity of individual firms' (Bureau of Industry Economics 1991, p. 19).

Since marketing and attracting finance were amongst the most frequently mentioned barriers to business growth and expansion in the Melbourne business survey (51 per cent and 34 per cent of respondents, respectively), it is possible that operating within the context of a stronger identity would be of benefit to entrepreneurs in south-east Melbourne and similar regions. If companies can indeed cooperate to produce integrated solutions or offer a range of complementary products and services, it is possible that joint marketing could reduce costs, increase exposure and possibly attract investors to the region. Supporting that possibility is the fact that 82 per cent of survey respondents expressed interest in greater collaboration and partnerships, of which 68 per cent expressed interest in networking with 'firms with complementary products'. In order to evaluate the potential for a regional image in any given area, however, the existence of a comparatively high concentration of companies in the environment industry would need to be established – not every technology park will achieve the status of Silicon Valley! At the company level, the possibility of operating within a larger geographically-based entity was attractive to the smaller Companies A and B, while Company C was more interested in global networks and saw little advantage in creating a geographically-based identity.

REGIONAL BENEFITS

From a regional perspective, proponents of clusters and industrial districts argue that clusters and networks of SMEs provide the ideal setting for industrial success and comparative advantage based on 'quality, reliability and flexibility' (Baker 1995, p. 3; see also Saxenian 1990, 1994) rather than large investment and low wages. Analysing the superior performance of Silicon Valley over the similarly positioned Route 128 in the 1980s, Saxenian (1990, 1994) argues that the traditional model of vertical integration and internal diversification that gave 'stability and self reliance' to the 'small number of relatively integrated corporations' in Route 128 (Saxenian 1994, p. 3) also made the region less responsive, less adaptable and ultimately less competitive than the more dynamic Silicon Valley. Describing Silicon Valley as a region characterized by 'dense social networks' where 'companies compete intensely while … learning from one another about changing markets and technologies through informal communication and collaborative practices' (1994, pp. 2–3), Saxenian attributes its superior performance to the responsiveness and innovation that result from the region's 'flexible specialization' (1990, p.138). Saxenian draws parallels to the industrial districts of Italy and to 'networks of specialized small and medium-sized suppliers and contractors' (1990, p. 138) in Germany and Japan to conclude that 'Silicon Valley's decentralized industrial structure adapted successfully to the crisis of the semiconductor industry, while the large, vertically integrated firms of Route 128 appear to be paralysed by the decline of the minicomputer, and fast losing their edge' (1990, p. 141).

While it is beyond the scope of this chapter to evaluate the most appropriate model of regional economic development, the regional benefits identified in the literature do lend support to efforts by local authorities to increase the level of clustering and networking in their region. In reference to the environment industry in particular, local economies that display a greater ability to innovate and respond to changes in the rapidly evolving sector are likely to remain more competitive. The high level of small and very small businesses in the sector, the high proportion of new companies (nearly half of the companies that responded to the Melbourne survey were less than ten years old) and the highly innovative nature of some of the technologies in the industry indicate a vibrant entrepreneurial spirit in the sector. To the extent that clustering and networking can foster such entrepreneurial energy in its early stages, a region that adopts such policies is likely to benefit in the medium and long term.

Clustering: Risks and Potential Pitfalls

While the concepts of clustering and networking generate significant enthusiasm among some scholars, others urge caution in the adoption of clustering policies, warning against pitfalls and difficulties which are 'all too often neglected by enthusiasts who believe they have discovered the ultimate tool for economic development' (Boekholt and Thuriaux 1999, p. 391). Highlighting potential 'diseconomies of agglomeration' (Folta and Baik 2001, p. 3), critics argue that regional proximity and clustering can generate 'devastating competition' rather than productive cooperation (Florida and Kenney 1990, p. 69), that the costs of creating and maintaining functional networks can be prohibitive, that such networks can end up ineffective or, worse still, inward-looking and insular, and that industry in the region may suffer if networks of small firms are artificially encouraged over larger integrated corporations. While most authors do not rule out the use of clusters and networks in all circumstances, the evidence in the literature cautions against inappropriate or excessive cluster development (see, for example, Florida and Kenney 1991; Gulati and Gargiulo 1999; Gulati and Singh 1998; Paniccia 1998; Staber 2001a).

Clustering for Green Entrepreneurs: Assessing the Evidence

On balance, it is likely that clusters and networks can be useful in some circumstances, but ineffective in others. There is both a theoretical argument, established in the literature, and sufficient empirical evidence to indicate that, at least under some circumstances, clustering and networking can assist SMEs and the entrepreneurs who run them to overcome the disadvantages of smallness, through economies of scale and scope and through the benefits of interaction with other firms.

The high proportion of SMEs in the rapidly evolving and technologically sophisticated environment industry makes a good case for encouraging clustering through supportive policies for the sector. On the basis of the research presented above, it seems likely that an increased level of networking can indeed help entrepreneurs in the environment industry to overcome, in some ways, the very real barriers posed by their limited size and lack of resources. Principally, we believe that the economic potential of the sector as well as its positive social outcomes – which are generally unrewarded externalities – warrant a greater level of support from governments and local development officials.

However, the specialization and internal fragmentation within the sector reduce the likelihood that sufficient convergence will be found within any given region to provide the desired networking partners for each company. For example, from the research work in Melbourne, it appears that while both Company B and Company C fall under the 'environment industry' umbrella, they may have little by way of technology, product or customer synergies. As the companies grow and develop businesses connections outside the region, their need for, and interest in, local networks will probably diminish. At the early stages, however, the research suggests that local connections can be extremely useful and even crucial to business development.

The policy implications of such conclusions are significant. Local clusters and networks should be encouraged as a means for the support of individual entrepreneurs and small firms within the industry. Clearly, however, the inclusion of more established players is desirable in terms of the effectiveness and success of local clusters. In order to attract such players, remain relevant to small businesses as they expand and avoid the above-mentioned risks of insularity, we believe that local clusters must contain active elements of interaction with extraregional players. Unlike the case in less diverse, more established sectors such as the wine industry, it will be both difficult and undesirable to locate and maintain comprehensive environment industry value chains in any one geographical region.

It should be noted that while the benefits of cooperation may be more apparent in the case of individual entrepreneurs and small companies, larger firms and corporations are likely to benefit from interaction with small entrepreneurial players in the field. Supporting Saxenian's (1990, 1991, 1994) thesis that larger companies may suffer from stagnation and a limited ability to respond to rapidly changing markets, the studies in the environment industry mentioned above found that, despite the innovative nature of the industry overall, the more established subsectors such as waste management and water treatment do suffer from a lack of entrepreneurship (Table 11.1 above; also ACI, 2000a, 2000b, 2000c; Astolfi et al. 2000; Competitive Edge 2000; Department of State and Regional Development 2001). The history of some of those companies as large government bureaucracies may well explain some of the institutional inertia and limited entrepreneurial spirit identified in the studies. Regardless of the causes, however, it is likely that face-to-face interaction with innovative entrepreneurs and their companies within the framework of an industry cluster or network may be a useful tool to encourage innovative thinking and entrepreneurial spirit amongst the more established players within the industry.

The format and features of a cluster or network are clearly important factors in determining its potential benefit (see, for example, Markusen's (1996) typology of industrial districts). A costly, highly-structured and formal cluster imposed by well-meaning local development officials on an ill-prepared industry may well do more harm than good, and may even discourage cooperation by disillusioned companies. Instead, a more loosely facilitated informal network that can evolve over time may be a more appropriate model.

As the body of research and literature in this field improves, a clear, widely accepted taxonomy of clustering may emerge, relating the desired features of clusters or networks to specific regional and industry characteristics.[1] Such a development would provide a useful resource for both academic studies and local development officials, enabling a more sophisticated and detailed construction of appropriate clustering models for any given region. Until this point is reached, local initiatives should be informed by existing documented examples and theoretical work, adopting the most appropriate approach and tailoring it further to suit the circumstances and local entrepreneurs found in each region.

References

ACIL (2000a) *Environment Industry Action Agenda: Summary Record of the Second Stakeholder Workshop*, Sydney, p. 15.

ACIL (2000b*) Opportunities and Impediments: Environment Industry Action Agenda, A Paper for the First and Second Stakeholder Workshops*, Melbourne and Sydney, p. 6.

ACIL (2000c) *Environment Industry Action Agenda: Summary Record of the First Stakeholder Workshop*, Melbourne, p. 13.

Astolfi, F., Belt, R., Chan, C. and Male, B. (2000) 'Investing in Sustainability: A Discussion Paper to Assist the Development of an Environment Industry Action Agenda', Commonwealth of Australia Publication. Available at http://www.industry.gov.au/library/content_library/en1.pdf.

AusIndustry (2002) at: http://www.ausindustry.gov.au (accessed September 2002).

Baker, P. (1995) 'Small Firms, Industrial Districts and Power Asymmetries', *International Journal of Entrepreneurial Behaviour and Research*, Vol. 1, No. 1, pp. 8–25.

Boekholt, P. and Thuriaux, B. (1999) 'Public Policies to Facilitate Clustering: Background, Rationale and Policy Practices in International Perspective' in Organization for Economic Cooperation and Development, *Boosting Innovation: The Clusters Approach Conference Proceedings*, OECD, Paris, pp. 381–412.

---

1   A number of authors have attempted a typology of clusters or industrial districts – see, for example, Boekholt and Thuriaux (1999), Markusen (1996) and Paniccia (1998) – and those attempts go some way towards describing the features and logic behind different forms of clusters and networks. A notable example is provided by Ann Markusen (1996); however, like other early attempts, her system so far lacks the scope and sophistication to cover the wide variety of variables that development officials are likely to encounter in different regions, and there is little evidence that it or any other system is gaining wide currency in the literature.

Bureau of Industry Economics (1991) *Networks: A Third Form of Organisation*, Australian Government Publishing Service, Canberra.

Capello, R. (1999) 'Spatial Transfer of Knowledge in High Technology Milieux: Learning versus Collective Learning Processes', *Regional Studies*, Vol. 33, No. 4, pp. 353–365.

Competitive Edge (2000) *Draft Facilitator Report: Environment Industry Export Workshop*, Austrade, Brisbane, Sydney, Melbourne and Perth.

Department of Innovation, Industry and Regional Development (DISRD) (2002) 'Business Information – Guide to Business Programs and Services', at: http://home.vicnet.net.au/~entimp/nies/sitemap.html (accessed May 2002).

Department of State and Regional Development (2001) *Strategic Audit of Victoria's Environmental Management and Renewable Energy Industries*, DSRD, Melbourne.

Diesendorf (2001) 'Export Your Environmentally Sound Products to China', an email sent via Greenleap, 23 September.

Doeringer, P.B. and Terkla, D.G. (1995) 'Business Strategy and Cross-Industry Clusters', *Economic Development Quarterly*, Vol. 9, No. 3, pp. 225-237.

Douglas, M. and Hill, B. (2001) *Environment Industry Cluster Development: The South Australian Experience*, Department of Industry Science and Resources, Canberra.

Enright, M.J. and Roberts, B.H. (2001) 'Regional Clustering In Australia', *Australian Journal of Management*, Vol. 26 (Special Issue), pp. 65–85.

Enright, M.J. (1998) 'Regional Clusters and Firm Strategy' in A.D. Chandler, P. Hagstrom et al. (eds) *The Dynamic Firm: The Role of Technology, Strategy, Organization and Regions*, Oxford University Press, New York, pp. 315–342.

Environment Business Australia (EBA) (n.d.) at: http://www.environmentbusiness.com.au (accessed March 2010).

Environment Business Australia (2002) Presentation to Prime Minister's Science, Engineering And Innovation Council Working Group on the Environment Industry, 12 February at EBA webpage: http://www.environmentbusiness.com.au (accessed March 2010).

Florida, R. and Kenney, M. (1990) 'Silicon Valley and Route 128 Won't Save Us', *California Management Review*, Vol. 33, No. 1, pp. 68–84.

Florida, R., and Kenney, M. (1991) '"W(h)ither Flexible Specialisation" a Response to Saxenian', *California Management Review*, Vol. 34, No. 3, pp. 143–146.

Folta, T.B. and Baik, Y. (2001) 'The Evolution of Hot Spots and Blind Spots in the U.S. Biotechnology Industry', Research Paper, Purdue University Center for International Business Education and Research (CIBER) at:

http://www.krannert.purdue.edu/centers/ciber/publications/pdf/00-006Folta.doc (accessed March 2010).

Genoff, R. and de Leeuw, L. (2000) 'Background Discussion Paper to Environment Industry Cluster Development Report', Emerging Industries Occasional Papers, Department of Industry, Science and Resources, Canberra.

Gulati, R. and Gargiulo, M. (1999) 'Where Do Interorganizational Networks Come From?', *American Journal of Sociology*, Vol. 104, No. 5, pp. 1439–1493.

Gulati, R. and Singh, H. (1998) 'The Architecture of Cooperation: Managing Coordination Costs and Appropriation Concerns in Strategic Alliances', *Administrative Science Quarterly*, Vol. 43, No. 4, pp. 781–783.

Harrison, B. (1997) *Lean And Mean: The Changing Landscape of Corporate Power in the Age of Flexibility*, Guilford Press, New York.

Higgins, J. (1996) 'Canadian Perspective on the World Environment Industry', in Organization for Economic Cooperation and Development, *The Environment Industry: The Washington Meeting*, OECD, Paris and Washington, D.C, pp. 51–74.

Industry Canada (2002) 'Sector Competitiveness Frameworks Series, Environment Industry – Overview and Prospects', at: http://strategis.ic.gc.ca/SSG/ea01566e.html (accessed March 2002). The updated page can be found at: http://www.ic.gc.ca/eic/site/ea-ae.nsf/eng/h_ea02247.html (accessed March 2010).

Jenkin, J. (2001) Conversation about the level of environmental manufacturing in the Melbourne Development Board Region (John Jenkin is the development manager at the Melbourne Development Board, Caulfield.)

Keeble, D. and Wilkinson, F. (1999) 'Collective Learning and Knowledge Development in the Evolution of Regional Clusters of High Technology SMEs in Europe', *Regional Studies*, Vol. 33, No. 4, pp. 295–303.

LeVeen, J. (2002) 'Industry Cluster Literature Review', University of North Carolina, Department of City and Regional Planning. Available at: http://www.unc.edu/depts/dcrpweb/courses/261/leveen/litrev.htm#Conclusion (accessed August 2002). Alternative address: http://www.blackbusinessincubator.com/261/leveen/litrev.htm (accessed March 2010).

Longhi, C. (1999) 'Networks, Collective Learning and Technology Development in Innovative High Technology Regions: The Case of Sophia-Antipolis', *Regional Studies*, Vol. 33, No. 4, pp. 333–342.

Marceau, J. (1999) 'The Disappearing Trick: Clusters in the Australian Economy' in Organization for Economic Cooperation and Development, *Boosting Innovation: The Clusters Approach Conference Proceedings*, OECD, Paris, pp. 155–174.

Markusen, A. (1996) 'Sticky Places in Slippery Space: A Typology of Industrial Districts', *Economic Geography*, Vol. 72, pp. 293–313.

Oakey, R., Kipling, M. and Wildgust, S. (2001) 'Clustering among Firms in the Non-Broadcast Visual Communication (NBVC) Sector', *Regional Studies*, Vol. 35, No. 5, pp. 401–414.

Organization for Economic Cooperation and Development (1996) *The Environment Industry: The Washington Meeting*, OECD, Paris and Washington, DC.

Organization for Economic Cooperation and Development (2001) *Environmental Goods and Services: The Benefits of Further Global Trade Liberalization*, OECD, Paris.

Organization for Economic Cooperation and Development and Statistical Office of the European Communities (Eurostat) (1999) *The Environmental Goods And Services Industry: Manual For Data Collection And Analysis Statistical Office of the European Communities*, OECD, Paris.

Paniccia, I. (1998) 'One, a Hundred, Thousands of Industrial Districts: Organizational Variety in Local Networks of Small and Medium-sized Enterprises', *Organizational Studies*, Vol. 19, No. 4, pp. 667–699.

Porter, M. (1990) *The Competitive Advantage of Nations*, Basic Books, New York.

Roelandt, J.A. and den Hartog, P. (1999) 'Cluster Analysis and Cluster-Based Policy Making in OECD Countries: An Introduction to the Theme' in Organization for Economic Cooperation and Development, *Boosting Innovation: The Clusters Approach Conference Proceedings*, OECD, Paris, pp. 9–26.

Roper, S. (2001) 'Innovation, Networks and Plant Location: Some Evidence for Ireland', *Regional Studies*, Vol. 35, No. 3, pp. 215–228.

Saxenian, A. (1994) *Regional Advantage: Culture and Competition in Silicon Valley and Route 128*, Harvard University Press, Cambridge, MA.

Saxenian, A.L. (1990) 'Regional Networks and the Resurgence of Silicon Valley', *California Management Review*, Vol. 33, No. 1, pp. 89–103.

Saxenian, A.L. (1991) 'A Response to Richard Florida and Martin Kenney, "Silicon Valley and Route 128 Won't Save Us"', *California Management Review*, Vol. 34, No. 3, pp. 136–142.

Scott, A.J. (1988) *New Industrial Spaces: Flexible Production Organization and Regional Development in North America and Western Europe*, Pion, London.

Scott, A.J. (1998a) *Regions and the World Economy: The Coming Shape of Global Production, Competition, and Political Order*, Oxford University Press, New York.

Scott, A.J. (1998b) 'The Geographic Foundations of Industrial Performance' in A.D. Chandler, P. Hagstrom et al. (eds) *The Dynamic Firm: The Role of*

Technology, Strategy, Organization and Regions, Oxford University Press, New York, pp. 384–401.

Staber, U.H. (2001a) 'Spatial Proximity and Firm Survival in a Declining Industrial District: The Case of Knitwear Firms in Baden-Wurttemberg', *Regional Studies*, Vol. 35 (June), pp. 329–341.

Staber, U.H (2001b) 'The Structure of Networks in Industrial Districts', *International Journal of Urban and Regional Research*, Vol. 25 (September), pp. 537–52.

Uzzi, B. (1996) 'The Sources and Consequences of Embeddedness for the Economic Performance of Organizations: The Network Effect', *American Sociological Review*, Vol. 61, pp. 674–698.

Uzzi, B. (1997) 'Social Structure and Competition in Interfirm Networks: The Paradox of Embeddedness', *Administrative Science Quarterly*, Vol. 42, pp. 35–67.

Uzzi, B. (1999) 'Embeddedness in the Making of Financial Capital: How Social Relations and Networking Benefit Firms Seeking Financing', *American Sociological Review*, Vol. 64, pp. 481–505.

Vernon, B. (2001) *ABS Proposal for Discussion: A National Survey of the Environment Industry*, Australia Bureau of Statistics, Canberra.

Vickery, G. and Iarrera, M. (1996) 'Summary of the Environment Industry Expert Meeting' Washington, 13–14 October 1994, in Organization for Economic Cooperation and Development (1996) *The Environment Industry: The Washington Meeting*, OECD, Paris and Washington, DC, pp. 7–24.

Von Hippel, E. (1987) 'Cooperation between Rivals: Informal Know-How Trading', *Research Policy*, Vol. 16, No. 6, pp. 291–302.

12

Ecopreneurship, Corporate Citizenship and Sustainable Decision-making

David A. Holloway

ABSTRACT

This analytical chapter argues that changes to organizational values and business practices, envisaged by environmental entrepreneurs, should also encompass reforming the process of organizational decision-making to construct more 'robust' decision outcomes that enhance corporate performance. Effective internal governance and decision-making requires the commitment and involvement of the internal stakeholders – the 'social efficiency' of organizational employees. What is then required is an enhanced decision-making methodology labelled 'Organization Decision Enhancement' (ODE). The result is a collaboratively-oriented decision-making set of procedures.

Introduction

There are two streams of consciousness percolating into the global business sectors. The first is ecopreneurship and the associated concept of eco-efficiency (WBCSD 2008). The second is the more encompassing notion of corporate citizenship (United Nations 2008; Dunphy, Griffiths and Benn 2007). These developments should be viewed as part of a larger global concern about the issue of sustainable business practices in the modern era that incorporate growing corporate responsiveness to environmental and social sensitivities within society at large. Sustainability in business and the wider society (as well as the impacts of climate change) is now a mainstream concern.

This chapter extends these developments by positing that the reframing of organizational values, implied by these changes, should also encompass reforming the process of organizational decision-making (both strategic and tactical) to construct more 'robust' decision outcomes that enhance corporate performance. It questions and challenges the dominant paradigm that decision-making is the exclusive domain of privileged managerial positions within organizations, both large and small. The traditional 'command-and-control' management approach is no longer relevant within an entrepreneurial organization that embraces the embedded concepts and practices implied by corporate citizenship.

The organizing principle central to this chapter is in two parts. The first is that 'good' corporate governance does not guarantee 'good' organizational performance: it is a necessary, but not sufficient, condition. This is because corporate governance enacted at the senior management and board level that arises from the construction of 'best' decision outcomes is procedurally driven (focused on rules, guidelines and steps) whilst organizational performance is content-driven (the quality of the decision outcomes themselves within the larger competitive and economic context). The second part is that a collaboratively-oriented decision-making theory and methodology in which power, authority and responsibility is cascaded down through an organization will deliver epistemically more 'robust' decision options and outcomes, and enhance corporate performance.

The chapter has three parts. The first is focused on the reframing of organizational values that also encompass the internal stakeholders and lead to a reformation of organizational decision-making policies and practices. The second part details the phases involved procedurally in delivering such an enhanced decision-making methodology, labelled 'Organizational Decision Enhancement' (ODE). The final part analyses additional issues that are implied by such a depth and breadth of organizational change.

Reframing Organizational Values: A Sustainability Consciousness

The traditional organizational values encapsulated in the accounting reification of a focus on the 'bottom line' need to alter. The deeper notion of 'corporate citizenship' is slowly and increasingly being embraced in the mainstream business world by SMEs and larger corporations. The accounting literature now refers to this field as 'social and environmental accounting' (SEA) rather than the previous label of 'corporate social responsibly' that more clearly advocates the need for modern corporate bodies to report 'triple-bottom-line outcomes' (Unerman, Bebbington and O'Dwyer 2007).

There is a growing consciousness that corporations and other organizational bodies need to not only embrace concepts and the accompanying changes in the 'organizational mindset' associated with the notion of a 'licence to operate', but also re-evaluate internal governance and internal stakeholder issues. However, such a reorientation of organizational values is not easy. It cannot be dictated as a top-down change management process (Tourish and Hargie 2004). It has to be an inclusive process, both top-down and bottom-up. The aim is to move organizations beyond what Dunphy, Griffiths and Benn (2007) describe as second-wave corporations acting out of 'enlightened self interest' to third-wave organizations that are truly sustainable and sustaining: the advent of 'sustaining corporations'.

CORPORATE CITIZENSHIP

Corporate citizenship is also emerging and percolating through the global corporate consciousness (Dunphy, Griffiths and Benn 2007). There is now an established academic research discipline and a dedicated *Journal of Corporate Citizenship* as well as both popular and academic writings on the topic. The United Nations has published and is promoting its own ten-point Global Compact of Corporate Citizenship (United Nations 2008). These ten principles are grouped into four areas: human rights; labour standards; environment; and anti-corruption. These have been developed (politically) within the United Nations' larger global mandate and are not fully reflected in other published definitions of corporate citizenship. There is no current consensus about what exactly constitutes corporate citizenship. It is also often known and labelled widely as corporate social responsibility, or else as sustainable development, social and environmental accounting, triple-bottom-line reporting or sustainability (May, Cheney and Roper 2007; Unerman, Bebbington and O'Dwyer 2007).

The Corporate Citizen Research Unit (CCRU) at Deakin University in Australia has one of the better, more encompassing definitions for corporate citizenship:

> *Corporate citizenship is a recognition that a business, corporation or business-like organisation has social, cultural and environmental responsibilities to the community in which it seeks a licence to operate,*

as well as economic and financial ones to its shareholders or immediate stakeholders. Corporate citizenship involves an organisation coming to terms with the need for, often, radical internal and external changes, in order to better meet its responsibilities to all of its stakeholders (direct or indirect), in order to establish, and maintain, sustainable success for the organisation, and, as a result of that success, to achieve long term sustainable success for the community at large. (Sloan Work and Family Research Network n.d.)

This definition lacks a key element. There is no explicit role for a key internal stakeholder group: the staff or employees who are a key resource in any organization. It can be argued that this internal stakeholder group has been overlooked within the overall organizational reforms associated with these larger developments.

There are strong critiques of developments in this field. The Right, using a neoliberal economics framework, argues that this is a '... violation of the principles of free enterprise and a confusion of roles of the private, governmental and nonprofit sectors'. The Left argues that, at best, it is merely a public relations strategy and '... at worst, an illusion arising from an oxymoron – a misunderstanding of the social potential of the corporate form' (May, Cheney and Roper 2007, p. 3). Despite these deep critiques there is a continuing and expanding awareness of the principle and practices that have evolved over time.

ECO-EFFICIENCY

This is the quadrant of 'new' values in which those organizations, both small and large, with claims of an ecopreneurial business focus are located and evaluated. Voluntary environmental reports produced by these organizations relate eco-efficiency to the production of more goods and services using less energy and fewer natural resources, resulting in less waste and pollution. The World Business Council for Sustainable Development defines eco-efficiency as:

... the delivery of competitively priced goods and services that satisfy human needs and bring quality of life, while progressively reducing ecological impact and resource intensity throughout the product life-cycle, to a level at least in line with the earth's carrying capacity. (WBCSD 1996, p. 4)

The business examples provided by the WBCSD on its website primarily details cases of large organizations adopting some or all of the proposed elements of eco-efficiency in their business practices (WBCSD 2008). It may be an oversight, but there are no small businesses listed.

However, when it comes to voluntary reporting of environmental and social impacts, the motivational drivers are either to influence the organization's perceived legitimacy or to manage particular stakeholder groups in a positive way. The end result is that the organization in question is attempting to protect its customer base or market share and, at the same time, 'prove' its corporate citizenship credentials.

This does not explain the findings of a study of firms in New Zealand by Collins et al. (2007). Many small and medium-sized organizations do practise environmentally and socially responsible practices, but do not report this to the outside world. It appears that in this study at least these practices exist for ethical and other reasons rather than the self-interest of the organizations or their managers. One possible explanation for this is put forward by Roberts (2004), who argues that ethical behaviour in business is not as problematic as is often envisaged. It is more about exploring how ethical sensibility is often blunted by the individualistically-oriented predominance in the business world of traditional economic theories that emphasize narrow bottom-line and self-interested opportunism.

The Collins et al. (2007) study is a positive indication that eco-efficiency notions are permeating down through different organizations regardless of size; it also raises questions about the motivations behind the emergence of such practices.

SOCIAL EFFICIENCY

Sustainability developments should not be limited to eco-efficiency principles and environmental impact, but can also include social impacts. The term that could be posited is 'social efficiency' – a concept that requires both an internal and external stakeholder focus, even though most emphasis to date has been on voluntary reporting about an organization's interaction with, and associated impacts on, society at large. The aim has been to cover such issues as community relations, product safety, training and education, sponsorship, charitable donations and the employment of disadvantaged groups, amongst other things. However, most such reporting has been in relation to external, rather than internal, stakeholders (May, Cheney and Roper 2007; Unerman, Bebbington and O'Dwyer 2007; Dunphy, Griffiths and Benn 2007). Where there is an internal element, it tends to be limited to practices in relation to training regimes or employment opportunities for minority groups.

The future of truly sustainable entrepreneurial corporations lies in taking full advantage of the talent embedded in their workforces, by empowering them to be fully participative in internal decision-making processes. The development of this type of internal focus and critical internal stakeholder groups in addition to the current external social reporting would help move organizations from the Dunphy et al (2007) 'second wave' to 'third wave' corporations. Social-efficiency would then truly exist, incorporating significant internal and external stakeholder elements.

ACTIVE FOLLOWERSHIP

Such moves as outlined above require a radical rethinking of the vital role of 'followers' in organizations. There is a small but growing body of literature that advocates a recasting of the traditional role of followers (Chaleff 2003; Raelin 2003; Dixon and Westbrook 2003; Kelley 1992; Hollander 1992; Vanderslice 1988; Litzinger and Schaefer 1982). The call is to reconstruct the 'traditional' notion of 'follower', which tends to be a negative stereotype: typical followers supposedly display a passive and uncritical approach to work, as well as lacking initiative and a sense of responsibility for outcomes. Such followers merely perform assigned tasks given them and then stop awaiting the next task. Active followers, on the other hand, are able to think for themselves, either individually or collectively as required; they exhibit characteristics more often associated with risk-takers (and leaders); they are usually self-starters and problem-solvers; and they are rated highly by their peers and their nominal organizational superiors. These types of organizational 'actors' have discarded the pejorative 'follower' label: instead, they are, or attempt to be, equal and active participants in the decision-making process(es).

The result of such a transformation naturally impacts on the senior management role and also changes the leadership role. Senior managers, who are retained in this reframed organization structure, take on more of a 'mentor' or 'boundary rider' role in which they would have an equal decision-making role, but certainly not a privileged decision-making authority. However, they would normally act only as advisers or may be called upon when there is a decision-making impasse or an interpersonal dispute that remains unresolved.

The end result is not only enhanced corporate and internal governance, but also maximized opportunities to construct better and more positive corporate performance outcomes.

Entrepreneurship and Participative Decision-making

Entrepreneurship and the contested notions and nature of sustainability entrepreneurship, social entrepreneurship and ecopreneurship have been clearly explicated in earlier chapters of this book. It is not intended to canvass that depth of analysis again here. Instead, the focus of this section is to identify the elements of organizational culture and values within ecopreneurial ventures and the traits of ecopreneurs, that are relevant to a more collaborative and effective decision-making methodology.

Isaak, in Chapter 3 of this book, for example, identifies six strategies as a set of private-sector initiatives to foster and promote ecopreneurship and four public strategies to also foster the same outcome. His underlying purpose is to ensure that not only do new and exiting businesses take on and embrace sustainability, but that they do this successfully as a profitable and continuing business model. What he does not identify is the use of the talents and values of internal stakeholders (the employees) within decision-making processes, which can in fact help deliver such positive outcomes for entrepreneurial firms.

The 'greening' of businesses requires the development of organizational values that encompass internal 'social greening' to maximize the likelihood of success or what Linnanen refers to in his typology in Chapter 7 as the 'successful idealist': making money and making the world better. He also identifies three barriers to successful ecopreneurship, including the market-creation challenge and the finance barrier, although the most critical one is the ethical justification for existence. This means that ecopreneurs are highly motivated and committed to both their business and making the world a better place environmentally.

This personal commitment means that such value-led organizations recruit like-minded people as employees. Ecopreneurs also have a controlling ownership interest in their firms, which is often combined with an emotional dimension that is characterized by a mix of altruistic and self-interested behaviours (Mustakallio 2002). This does allow for the possibility of managing the firm in a way that promotes participative decision-making both ethically and as a pragmatic approach to maximizing decision-making processes and outcomes. In that scenario, sustainable decision-making becomes a viable tool for entrepreneurs.

Sustainable Decision-making: A New Paradigm

Existing organizations that adopt corporate citizenship, eco-efficiency and social efficiency values can generate significant changes within their own corporate culture. Newly established organizations (small, medium and large) that also take on these values are also adopting the same corporate culture. It is appropriate that corporate decision-making takes on a new dimension and paradigm that involves all internal stakeholders, not just managers. When this occurs, the result is a collaboratively-oriented set of decision-making procedures.

The ODE framework would also incorporate effective empowerment of the organizational workforce with accompanying delegation and devolution of decision-making power. Empowerment has to be genuine, and this means that there has to be effective delegation of authority and responsibilities to subordinates. Ironically, augmenting the power of subordinates, by having participation without effective delegation, can often increase the level *of control* over employees (Zorn, Page and Cheney 2000; Appelbaum, Herbert and Leroux 1999; Hardy and Leiba-Sullivan 1998). The organizational culture must provide for a climate that not only promotes open communication and active listening, but also encourages personal risk, trustworthy behaviour and initiative.

What is then required is a new decision-making methodology to operationalize such a move and change in organizational thinking and practice. The model proposed is Organizational Decision Enhancement (ODE), as depicted in Figure 12.1.

ODE Procedural Stages

The stages that ODE utilizes is not that different from other decision-making procedures used either individually or collectively – such as that of de Reuck, Schmidenberg and Klass (2002) – but is perhaps more refined and intellectually legitimate than the others. The main contributions of the adapted model are threefold in nature. The first is that the decision-making process is

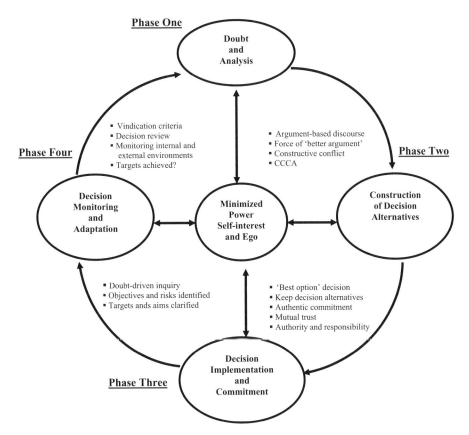

Figure 12.1   ODE procedural methodology

Source: Adapted from Cowan (2004) and de Reuck, Schmidenberg and Klass (2002, p. 141).

cascaded down through an organization: individual positional authority and responsibility is no longer predominant. The second is the use of the concept of constructive conflict and the third is the notion of continuous, conscious, collaborative adaptation. There are four main phases that are an essential part of an ongoing circular and recursive method, each of which is explained below.

PHASE ONE

The first phase of the adapted model commences in one of two ways. There is either a need to revisit previous decisions or a need to resolve a new scenario facing the organization. Both are driven by the Peircean notion of doubt-driven inquiry (Peirce 1931).

The initial analysis can be carried out in several ways, depending on the extent and seriousness of the decision. If the situation warrants a major review or decision, then the classical use of SWOT (identification of strengths, weaknesses, opportunities and threats) analysis can be used. Brainstorming; cognitive mapping and decision support software analytical mapping can also be utilized, but it could as easily be a simple group discussion of the current organizational conundrum. This can only work if information is shared openly and equally throughout the organization. As Wheatley has stated:

> ... if information is to function as a source of organizational vitality, we must abandon our dark clouds of control and trust in its need for free movement, even in our organizations. Information is necessary for new order, an order we do not impose, but order nonetheless. (Wheatley 1999, p. 97)

In the end, the objectives, targets, aims and risks are finally clarified to the satisfaction of the decision-making group. This first high-level phase can be short if the 'problem' is not a major one.

PHASE TWO

This requires the group members to draw upon their collective experience and problem-resolving capabilities, so as to enable the identification of a series of decision alternatives. This is a particular strength of ODE because it enables collective, as opposed to individual, creative forces to be unleashed.

During this phase the use of the Habermasian force of 'better argument' (Habermas 1987) comes to the fore. There is no silencing of voices. The communication channels between the group members uses 'constructive conflict' in which dissent, divergent views and alternative views are encouraged to help develop sets of decision options. Debate is open, vigorous and challenging. This group process applies a concept that is labelled as continuous, collaborative, conscious adaptation (CCCA).

PHASE THREE

The next phase requires the group to select the 'best option' decision without discarding any of the decision alternatives derived during the debating phase. The group decides on a set of agreed criteria to both rank and then evaluate (vindicate) the success or failure of the various decision options. These criteria can be any combination of quantitative and qualitative factors.

The procedure for such a 'best option' choice does not have to be through a total group consensus. It is sufficient for this to be accepted as a simple majority vote – if a vote becomes necessary. It is a fallacy to expect that there should be group consensus: in fact, such an expectation can lead to suboptimal decision-making. If there is not a consensus, however, it is important that the members of the group accept and commit to the decision option finally selected.

Embedded within this approach is the notion that the group also accepts responsibility for constructing the final decision outcome. This means that they accept a collective 'blame' for any negative or harmful results. This only works if it is agreed that the best learning occurs through the making of mistakes which subsequent decision-makers can avoid. A thoughtful degree of risk-taking is encouraged without fear and retribution. This requires mutual trust, mutual respect and openness.

PHASE FOUR

The implemented decision is monitored using the set of previously agreed criteria which effectively vindicates the 'best option' decision. This review is carried out by those group members who formed part of the minority view if there had not been an initial consensus on the final decision. In this way, the selected decision will be given the closest scrutiny.

Decisions, once reached and taken by the group, are settled only until confronted again by well-grounded doubt emerging from the decision verification processes. In other words, doubt in the form of failed expectations drives inquiry. It motivates a new process of inquiry to derive new, and more effective, decision outcomes. These new decisions then have to be evaluated as to whether they address the shortcomings of the prior decisions they will be replacing.

Thus, the 'best option' decision remains in force while ongoing, low-level monitoring of the internal and external environments is carried out. The final question(s) asked are whether the targets, aims and objectives have been achieved. If the answer is in the affirmative, then an organizational status quo remains in place unless an appropriate level of 'doubt' surfaces. If that happens, then the circular, recursive element of ODE methodology is activated and Phase One is recommenced.

Additional ODE Procedural Elements

There are also additional considerations that need to be taken into account in operationalizing a group decision-making methodology.

CONSTRUCTIVE CONFLICT

To be effective, debate needs to allow for the full and robust canvassing of issues and decision alternatives without being restrained by the niceties of striving at all costs for consensus and (false) calls for organizational unity and loyalty. Sonnenfeld (2002), in his study of boards of directors, argued that it is not rules and procedures that make groups robust into effective social systems, but the way people work together. Central to that is what he calls the fostering of a culture of 'open dissent':

> *Directors are, almost without exception, intelligent, accomplished, and comfortable with power. But if you put them in a group that discourages dissent, they nearly always start to conform. The ones that don't often self-select out … the highest performing companies have extremely contentious boards that regard dissent as an obligation and that treat no subject as undiscussable. (Sonnenfeld 2002, p. 112)*

The term 'constructive conflict', however, is preferred. Open dissent implies the possibility of mere negative thinking and argument without real contribution to a negotiated agreement and solution set. In contrast, constructive conflict requires that group members accept a charge to be proactive in the open debates and discussions. This means that each person, if 'dissenting', is obliged to come up with their own proposed decision alternatives. Such debate continues 'constructively' until an agreed position is reached. Of course, it is also possible that this is not truly *the* optimal decision – another differently constituted group of inquirers may well come up with a 'better' epistemic decision outcome – but, under these procedurally-driven conditions, it will be the best that this particular group can deliver.

CONTINUOUS CONSCIOUS COLLABORATIVE ADAPTATION (CCCA)

A number of elements are combined in the notion of CCCA. The first of these is the term 'continuous'. It takes into account the proposition that the world, both social and corporate, is a chaotic and turbulent environment and that the stability which previously existed no longer applies. As Entrekin and Court put it 'the 1970s was a relatively stable environment' (2001, p. 21). Now, uncertainty is everywhere. Business cycle times have also reduced significantly (Entrekin and Court 2001). As a result, decision-making processes must incorporate the need to *continually* be in motion. There is a need for 'continuous' monitoring of the internal and external environments.

The second – conscious adaptation – is an evolution of complexity theory and the concept of complex adaptive systems. Complexity theory explains system adaptation and survival through a process of non-thinking interaction amongst many individual 'agents' which, when aggregated, gives the 'whole' an ability to develop collective intelligence and learning capacity allowing for successful innovation and adaptation. The use of group creativity as envisaged by ODE theory enables both an *intelligent* and *conscious* process of adaptation and organizational learning that can go beyond mere survival. Through the use of 'conscious adaptation' it has the ability to respond proactively.

The last term that makes up CCCA is 'collaborative'. By using collaborative processes the collective whole is effectively greater than the sum of the individual actors. Greater mental processing power and attention is brought to bear on the situation. The aim of the group is to combine '… the elements of a conspectus of the problems and convictions that individuals have the opportunity to share, in a controversy or discussion' (Moscovici and Doise 1994, p. 72). This sociocognitive process identifies the differences between different points of view, then clarifies and integrates them at a higher level. The result is a transformation of individual views into a social representation of the group as part of a collective discussion and negotiation.

This collaborative process allows for two positive effects. Rigorous debate, controversy and constructive conflict help reshape individuals' arguments and representations to give a higher level of analysis to the organizational situation. The second enables the members of the group to internalize, allowing for enhanced commitment to, and acceptance of, the decision outcomes so constructed.

Conclusion

Sustainable decision-making is achievable by contemporary organizations, whether small, medium or large. The radical changes to corporate culture, leadership and management mindsets will already have been enacted by existing organizations embracing ecopreneurial and corporate citizenship principles and values. Newly established (primarily small) organizations would have fewer barriers and inertia to overcome in following a similar path and business model. It would be only a small further step to incorporate the additional changes that are conditional imperatives within the ODE decision-making methodology.

Truly entrepreneurial firms are not just ones that find new market niches, products or services. In some cases, the real sense of risk-taking, enterprise and innovation lies in developing new ways of working within the organization. As this chapter has attempted to point out, a focus on improved participative decision-making, alongside a commitment to sustainability in the long term, can often produce internally entrepreneurial firms that are both successful and green.

What is not advocated is the total democratization of decision-making. That is an unrealistic goal unlikely to be achieved in any organization. There will still need to be some differentiation of decision-making responsibility within each organization. These boundaries, however, need to be negotiated, and agreed to, by the respective actors and teams/groups within the organization, not merely determined in an arbitrary and top-down process.

If organizations are to reap the benefit from the existing high levels of knowledge/intellectual capital represented by their workforces – the internal stakeholders – then decision-making should not remain the exclusive domain of specific individuals or very small elite groups. Effectiveness and not efficiency (falsely perceived as timely) should be the aim of well-constructed decision outcomes. The adaptability and self-organizing capability of the workforce requires an inclusive, not exclusive, decision-making methodology to unlock and realize the future potential of the organization. The future awaits.

References

Appelbaum, S.H., Herbert, D. and Leroux, S. (1999) 'Empowerment: Power, Culture and Leadership – A Strategy or Fad for the Millennium?', *Journal of Workplace Learning*, Vol. 11, No. 7, pp. 233–277.
Collins, E., Lawrence, S., Pavlovich, K. and Ryan, C. (2007) 'Business Networks and the Uptake of Sustainability Practices in Small and Medium-Sized Enterprises: The Case of New Zealand', *Journal of Cleaner Production*, Vol. 15, Nos 8/9, pp. 729–740.

Chaleff, I. (2003) *The Courageous Follower: Standing up to and for our Leaders*, Berret-Koehler, San Francisco.

Cowan, N. (2004) *Corporate Governance: That Works!*, Prentice Hall, Singapore.

de Reuck, J., Schmidenberg, O. and Klass, D. (2002) 'General Decision Assurance Principles and Procedures for Strategic Planning', *International Journal of Management and Decision-Making*, Vol. 3, No. 2, pp. 139–150.

Dixon, I. and Westbrook, J. (2003) 'Followers Revealed', *Engineering Management Journal*, Vol. 15, No. 1, pp. 19–25.

Dunphy, D., Griffiths, A. and Benn, S. (2007) *Organizational Change for Corporate Sustainability* (2nd edn), Routledge, London.

Entrekin, L. and Court, M. (2001) *Human Resource Management Practice: Adaptation and Change in an Age of Globalization*, International Labour Office, Geneva.

Habermas, J. (1987) *The Theory of Communicative Action. Volume 2: Lifeworld and System: A Critique of Functionalist Reason*, Beacon Press, Boston, MA.

Hardy, C. and Leiba-Sullivan, S. (1998) 'The Power behind Empowerment: Implications for Research and Practice', *Human Relations*, Vol. 51, No. 4, pp. 451–483.

Hollander, E.P. (1992) 'Leadership, Followership, Self and Others', *Leadership Quarterly*, Vol. 3, No. 1, pp. 43–54.

Kelley, R.E. (1992) *The Power of Followership: How to Create Leaders People Want*, Bantam Doubleday, New York.

Litzinger, W. and Schaefer, T. (1982) 'Leadership through Followership', *Business Horizons* (September–October), pp. 78–81.

May, S., Cheney, G. and Roper, J. (eds) (2007) *The Debate over Corporate Social Responsibility*, Oxford University Press, Oxford.

Moscovici, S. and Doise, W. (1994) *Conflict and Consensus: A General Theory of Collective Decisions*, Sage, London.

Mustakallio, M.A. (2002) 'Contractual and Relational Governance in Family Firms: Effects on Strategic Decision-Making Quality and Firm Performance', doctoral dissertation 2002/2, Helsinki University of Technology, Institute of Strategy and International Business, Espoo, Finland.

Peirce, C.S. (1931) *Collected Papers – Volume 2*, Harvard University Press, Cambridge, MA.

Raelin, J.A. (2003) 'The Myth of Charismatic Leaders', *T+D*, Vol. 57, No. 3 (March), pp. 47–54.

Roberts, J. (2004) 'Agency Theory, Ethics and Corporate Governance', paper presented at the Corporate Governance and Ethics Conference, Sydney, 28–30 June.

Sloan Work and Family Research Network (n.d.), 'Glossary: Corporate Citizenship, Definitions of', at: http://wfnetwork.bc.edu/glossary_entry.php?term=Corporate%20Citizenship,%20Definition%28s%29%20of.

Sonnenfeld, J.A. (2002) 'What Makes Great Boards Great', *Harvard Business Review*, Vol. 8, No. 9, pp. 106–112.

Tourish, D. and Hargie, O. (2004) 'The Crisis of Management and the Role of Organizational Communication' in D. Tourish and O. Hargie (eds), *Key Issues in Organizational Communication*, Routledge, London, pp. 1–16.

Unerman, J., Bebbington, J. and O'Dwyer, B. (eds) (2007), *Sustainability Accounting and Accountability*, Routledge, London.

United Nations (2008) 'Global Compact on Corporate Citizenship', United Nations, New York, at: http://www.unglobalcompact.org (accessed 7 March 2008).

Vanderslice, V.J. (1988) 'Separating Leadership from Leaders: An Assessment of the Effect of Leader and Follower Roles in Organizations', *Human Relations*, Vol. 41, No. 9, pp. 677–696.

Wheatley, M.J. (1999) *Leadership and the New Science*, Berret-Koehler, San Francisco, CA.

World Business Council for Sustainable Development (1996) *Eco-efficient Leadership for Improved Economic and Environmental Performance*, WBCSD, Geneva.

World Business Council for Sustainable Development (2008) 'History of the WBCSD', WBCSD, Geneva, at: http://www.wbcsd.org (accessed on 7 April 2008).

Zorn, T.E., Page, D.J. and Cheney, G. (2000) 'Nuts about Change: Multiple Perspectives on Change-Oriented Communication in a Public Sector Organization', *Management Communication Quarterly*, Vol. 13, No. 4, pp. 515–566.

13

The Competitive Strategies of Ecopreneurs: Striving for Market Leadership by Promoting Sustainability

Holger Petersen

ABSTRACT

This chapter examines the importance and development of competitive advantages amongst ecopreneurial firms by examining 64 enterprises in Germany, Austria and Switzerland. The chosen enterprises fulfilled two prerequisites: they have made solutions for ecological problems to their core business, and they are also market leaders in special segments for ecological products or services.

Five factors were found to account for the competitive strategies of ecopreneurial firms: 'reputation', 'creativity', 'exclusivity', 'nearness to customers' and 'technical competence'. It appears that reputation and credibility are especially important for green businesses striving to develop a competitive market niche for themselves.

Introduction

Ecopreneurs are sometimes different to other entrepreneurs, but they also share some common characteristics. Like any successful business, ecopreneurial firms have to develop strategic advantages which they can use to survive in a competitive marketplace. Whilst there have been many theories about possible advantages, little empirical research has been done into the actual strategies that green firms use. This chapter provides an analysis of a recent study of 64 German, Austrian and Swiss enterprises, all of which have made solutions for ecological problems a part of their core business activities and all of which are market leaders in their particular niches. It describes the factors that these firms believe to be significant elements in their competitive strategy and then suggests a model which integrates these findings.

Background: Ecopreneurship in Central Europe

In Central European countries (broadly defined for the purposes of this chapter as Germany, Switzerland and Austria), entrepreneurs have been realizing green business ideas for about 80 years. This began as a reaction to the radical change in work practices and consumption during the industrialization era of the early twentieth century. Young people, especially from the cultured middle class, felt increasingly as if they were being treated like commodities and became concerned about their possible loss of contact with nature. Progressive European metropolises, like Vienna or Berlin, became the starting points of this first environmental movement. As a result of this movement, so-called 'life-reformers' and 'anthroposophs' founded their enterprises in the beginning of the twentieth century. Some of these enterprises, like Weleda (an international producer of health- and body-care products) and Voelkel (a German producer of organic juices) are market leaders today.

During the 1950s a German producer of baby food, Georg Hipp, followed them by promoting new methods of agriculture and became the greatest purchaser of organic fruits in the world (Hipp 2000). However, the real breakthrough for green entrepreneurs began with the second environmental movement in the 1970s. As a part of protests against conventional consumer goods, many people in Western Europe, Canada and the United States founded small business enterprises that concentrated on producing and selling simple items, such as food, cosmetics or clothes, on a more sustainable basis (Jungk and Müllert 1980). Some of them eventually grew quite large, such as Frans Bogaerts (founder of Ecover, a Belgian producer of cleaning products), Heinz Hess (founder of Hessnatur, a German mail-order house for clothing) and Anita Roddick (founder of The Body Shop, a British chain of body-care retailers). Although some of them expanded, most enterprises founded by these early ecopreneurs have remained small or medium-sized. Hipp, for example, employs round about 1,000 people, Hessnatur some 200 and Voelkel about 75 staff.

Over the last two decades many entrepreneurs have followed these pioneers. During the 1980s increasing sales by ecopreneurs, as well as increasing community protests against environmental damage, inspired some conventional entrepreneurs to change their production methods. Firms with existing established competencies in high quality standards, technical abilities and strong levels of internal corporate entrepreneurship used the opportunity to develop strategic advantages grounded in environmental factors. Firms such as Neumarkter Lammsbräu (a German beer producer), Rohner Textil (a Swiss producer of textiles), and Steinbeiss Temming (a German producer of writing paper) realized that they could gain a competitive advantage through green innovations, promoting new customer service ideas and adopting technical solutions that cut energy and waste costs.

As these developments indicate, ecopreneurship can take different forms. Ecopreneurial behaviour can be found in firms in different industries and countries, which can be run by very different individuals. Ecopreneurs are individualists, and each has his or her own unique business aims and vision. At the same time, they are also part of a general social change, which continuously generates new consumer needs and business opportunities out of the fact that environmental resources are limited.

How does an ecopreneur's way of doing business differ from that of conventional firms? Like every entrepreneur (Timmons 1986), an ecopreneur is concerned with introducing innovation, business growth and market success. One way of identifying the differences between conventional and green entrepreneurs is to examine the three dimensions of business suggested by Abell (1980):

- *Functions* – what are the benefits of the business's product or service for the customers?

- *Technology* – what methods, skills and instruments are used to realize the benefit?

- *Customer groups* – who is willing to pay an attractive price for the benefit?

On every dimension, the activity of a green entrepreneur will differ from that of a conventional one. With regard to functions, a conventional entrepreneur seeks to make profits by creating individual benefits for his or her customers. In contrast, an ecopreneur attempts to create public benefits as well as private ones: he or she cares about ecological sustainability, which is a public good. The ecopreneur's unique challenge is to extract private benefits out of a public good by promoting sustainability. Such private benefit can be attached to healthcare, wellness, status, economizing, ethical sense or something else. In this way, solutions for customers' problems must be combined with solutions to the so-called free-rider problem. Attractive additional benefits have to be attainable only for people who are willing to pay for them.

What does this mean for the technology dimension? Ecopreneurs are located in many different industries and use a variety of agricultural, chemical, biological and physical technologies that can range from low-tech to high-tech. There are thousands of possibilities – but there is one special demand: *production is part of the product or service*. To sell ecologically sustainable goods requires the ecopreneur to employ production methods that are either non-polluting or at least pollute at a low level. Organic agriculture is an example. A further challenge for entrepreneurs using such eco-efficient methods is to make the process transparent to the customer, so that they can identify the ecological advantage of purchasing products or services made with or using such technologies.

The third dimension relates to the firm's customers. Most ecopreneurial business ventures are, at their commencement, operating in advance of the mass market. Without a hard core of pioneer customers, they run the risk of effectively 'walking alone' and eventually failing. Like ecopreneurs themselves, such pioneer customers are not only curious and environment-conscious, but also convinced of their self-effectiveness, knowing that general progress is a result of many small individual steps. Many ecopreneurs have been active members of the first or second environmental movement discussed previously. As such, they started out in business with a personal network of like-minded people and with an affinity to their customers. Out of these roots they developed effective personal relationships with their customers, who shared their visions and ethical values. This community of pioneer customers provides four functions for the ecopreneurial business venture: they help generate sales income by purchasing the firm's products or services; they often give advice about how to improve products and services; they help spread knowledge of the new business to other customers by word of mouth (and may ultimately help develop a mass market); and they often provide a loyal base of solid customers that can help the firm survive if there are fluctuations or downturns in the broader markets they are competing in.

The Research Project

The purpose of this study was to provide a more detailed analysis of some of these successful ecopreneurial firms. Whilst there have been several case-study analyses of individual ecopreneurs and their firms, to date there has been little quantitative information about the characteristics of ecopreneurial firms and what helps give them a successful competitive advantage.

An initial selection was made of 126 firms from Germany, Austria and Switzerland from a variety of different sources, such as company information published on the Internet, lists of fair-trade exhibitors or suggestions by investment analysts. Each of the firms chosen produces or sells innovative products and services which help solve, or at least reduce, environmental problems as part of their core business activities. Moreover, each firm was perceived as occupying a leading or dominant role in its market position.

Of the 126 firms contacted, 64 (51 per cent) agreed to participate and were able to confirm that they held one of the largest (if not the largest) turnovers in their particular market segment. These respondents were then asked to complete a short questionnaire seeking information about:

- general firm demographics, including number of employees, turnover during the last financial year, and firm age;

- an estimate of their own market share and market position on a national, European and global level compared to their main competitors; and

- competitive advantages which are essential to their market success.

In each case, the questionnaire was completed by either the founder-entrepreneur or by a member of the firm's senior management team. In addition to the questionnaire, websites of the chosen companies were also examined to obtain additional information about the firms, their history, product/service offerings, founders and strategy.

Two-thirds of the respondents were based in the manufacturing sector and about one-third in the service sector. Some of the industries from which respondents were drawn included the organic food, clothing, body-care, renewable energy, packing,

furniture, building, tourism and services sectors (see Figure 13.1). Typical examples
included Enercon (a producer of wind turbines), Auro Naturfarben (natural paints),
Dennree (ecological food producer), Oschwald (carpets), Remei AG (cloth and
garments producer) and Konvekta (which produces a refrigerant free of greenhouse
gases). Firm sizes varied significantly, ranging from two to 15,000 employees, with
an average of 685 (however, the average was substantially distorted by a few firms
with more than 1,000 employees, and hence the median is a better descriptor of the
overall respondent set). The median firm size was 60 employees – that is, half of the
firms employed less than 60 people (see Figure 13.2).

Most firms were less than 20 years old: half of the participating organizations
were founded in 1985 or later (see Figure 13.3). Some 19 firms reported an age
of between 15 and 30 years, indicating that they had been founded in the 1970s
and 1980s, a time of increasing ecological awareness in Central Europe.

Many of the firms were also export-oriented; 36 respondents indicated
that they were exporting goods or services to other nations. Eleven companies

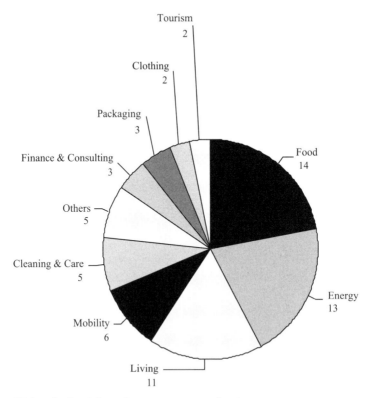

Figure 13.1   Industries of survey respondents

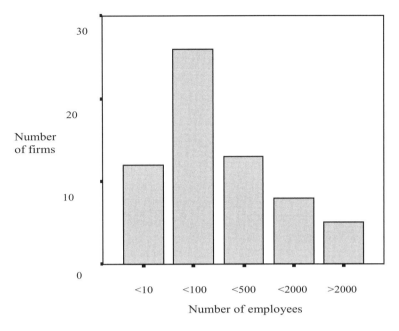

Figure 13.2   Sizes of respondent firms

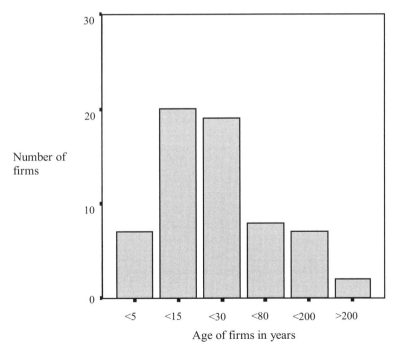

Figure 13.3   Age of respondent firms

claimed to occupy a leading position in their world market, whilst 15 stated that they were European market leaders in their respective niches. However, a number of firms occupied quite fragmented industries (such as car-sharing, tool-hire services or organic bakeries) where there still is no clearly defined national market, much less an international leader, and this made it difficult to assess the extent of their national or global market leadership.

Competitive Advantages

The analysis of the competitive advantages held by the firm was a key part of the questionnaire. Respondents were asked to evaluate the importance of a number of different issues, drawn from the existing literature (Schmitt 1997; Thürbach 1991). Twelve possible advantages were given: well-known brand names, low-prices, technological superiority, uniqueness of supply, credibility, comfortable access to supply, ability to set trends, good relationship with customers, reputation of the firm, ability to realize new product ideas, best ecological performance, and competent after-sales service. Respondents were then asked to rate the importance of each of these items in their market success (see Figure 13.4).

Competitive Advantage	Importance for Market Success (1 = not important; 6 = highly important)	
	Mean Score	Standard deviation
Credibility	5.2	1.1
Reputation of the company	5.0	1.1
Uniqueness of supply	4.8	1.3
Best ecological performance	4.6	1.4
Ability to set trends	4.6	1.4
Good relationship with customers	4.6	1.2
Competent after-sales services	4.5	1.4
Ability to realize new product ideas	4.5	1.3
Well-known brand names	4.2	1.6
Comfortable access to supply	4.0	1.4
Technological superiority	3.9	1.7
Low prices	2.8	1.6

Figure 13.4   Relative importance of different competitive advantages

According to these results, 'credibility' and 'reputation of the company' were the most important items for firms, followed by 'uniqueness of supply'. The analysis suggested that 'best ecological performance', 'ability to set trends', 'good relationship with customers', 'competent after-sales services' and the 'ability to realize new product ideas' were also relevant. 'Well-known brand names', 'comfortable access to supply' and 'technological superiority' had a lower level of relative importance. Although not provided here, analysis of the data also showed that (as might be expected) the importance of these last three items depended on the general characteristics of the firm: brand names, for example, were more important for larger firms than small ones. Interestingly, most of the ecopreneurial firms did not view the ability to compete on the basis of 'low prices' as relevant.

In order to reduce the number of items, a factor analysis was run on the data. Varimax rotated factor analysis was employed to determine if the answers could be reduced into common themes; items with a loading above 0.5 were retained (see Figure 13.5).

Five factors – 'reputation', 'creativity', 'exclusivity', 'nearness to customers' and 'technical competence' – collectively accounted for 78 per cent of the variance

	Loading				
	Factor 1	Factor 2	Factor 3	Factor 4	Factor 5
	'Reputation'	'Creativity'	'Exclusivity'	'Nearness to customers'	'Competence'
Reputation of the company	.903	.184	.069	.093	.150
Credibility	.820	-.099	.355	.207	.089
Well-known brand names	.697	.418	.006	-.283	-.005
Ability to set trends	.183	.898	-.016	.061	.176
Ability to realize product ideas	.047	.857	.227	.156	.105
Low prices	-.169	.020	-.833	.230	-.005
Uniqueness of supply	.070	.245	.782	.149	.078
Comfortable access to supply	-.073	.002	-.170	.865	.041
Good relationship with customers	.456	.242	.241	.608	-.119
Technological superiority	.027	.180	.100	-.083	.899
Competent after-sales services	.398	.190	-.016	.478	.609
Best ecological performance	.340	.477	.423	-.165	.218

Figure 13.5   Factor analysis of competitive advantage

in the data. Intriguingly, the question regarding '*best ecological performance*' was the only item which failed to load on to any factor.

As these data show, the most important perceived advantage of respondent firms appears to be issues relating to reputation. In other words, customers must feel confident about the credibility of the company, about the environmental advantages that it supplies and about the personal reputation of the ecopreneur at the helm of the firm (individuals, such Georg Hipp or Heinz Hess, mentioned previously). Reputation is an essential competitive tool, especially since many (if not most) customers cannot personally inspect and verify the ecological quality of a product and instead rely on information provided by the firm (Bech-Larsen and Grunert 2001).

Paths to Market Leadership

Although these findings are interesting, they represent just a statistical snapshot. How can they help provide suggestions about the way in which other ecopreneurs can also develop competitive advantages? This is an important issue for all 'green'-oriented entrepreneurs (Porter 1991). This section outlines some possible strategies on how to occupy and manage new business fields, for both new start-up green enterprises and established ones.

A competitive strategy begins with a business definition. As mentioned before, this definition outlines three dimensions: first, a set of supplied functions including useful, aesthetic or social benefits; second, a group of customers who are interested in these benefits; and, third, the technologies, skills and tools needed to realize them (Abell 1980). Every dimension enables an ecopreneur to develop competitive advantages. There are enterprises in a leading technological position, enterprises with excellent access and proximity to an attractive customer group and enterprises with the eminent ability to create products or services which provide benefits that customers are looking for (Treacy and Wiersema 1993).

Such competitive advantages are useful anchors for an ecopreneur for defining, developing and expanding his or her business gradually. If an entrepreneur is planning his strategy for the future, he can proceed from the dimension that is most significant to his business success (see Abell 1980). Possible paths are shown in Figure 13.6.

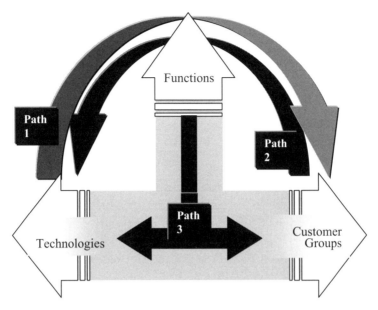

Figure 13.6   Three dimensions to defining the business venture

If an enterprise controls an ambitious *technology*, it may be reasonable to follow path 1. Firms on this path tend to first develop a new technology and only then focus on identifying the customer groups to which his or her products may appeal (Prahalad and Hamel 1990). Path 2 works in the reverse direction: some customers readily identify with, and buy from, a particular firm, and this can then serve as the basis from which new technologies and innovations are introduced into the market. Both of these paths are open to established firms.

However, ecopreneurs who are founding a start-up normally do not possess resources or competitive advantages such as a leading technology or privileged access to customers. They have to follow path 3. First, they have to find a gap in the market and develop a way of filling it (Kim and Mauborgne 2000). Turning the gap into a profitable niche often involves the creation of a new innovation, such as an eco-innovation, which serves a functional role. (Biolare, for example, was the first supplier of organic mushrooms in Germany, while Barnhouse simply started with an organic honey-crunch breakfast cereal.) Then, when the business is established, there is time to gradually expand the firm's activities by bringing in additional customers and technological innovations (Simon 1996). The founders of Farbglanz, for example, created the first non-polluting photo-laboratory with a direct mail-order service. Another example is Hubert Loick, a German maize farmer. He had a weakness for potato chips and crackers, and one day noticed some old maize crackers on his desk. The sticky residue inspired him to create a new kind of regenerative filling material for packing. In 1994 he took an opportunity to refine his crop and finally succeeded in commercializing an innovative packing material called FARM-fill. By the year 2000 his company, Hubert Loick VNR GmbH, had reached a turnover in excess of €1 million (Leendertse 2001).

Conclusion

Obviously, decisions about convenient strategies reflect many different factors, including the historical roots, experiences and personal aims of the decision-makers. This is especially true of enterprises that are driven by ecopreneurship, as they often develop unique strategies in correspondence with the individual background and interests of their founders and senior managers (Kuratko, Hornsby and Naffziger 1997; Ripsas 1999). There is no 'one best way' of developing and implementing a business strategy (Porter 1997). As the discussion in this chapter has shown, different competitive strategies can be employed, and they can focus on the functions, customers or technologies that help define the business.

Whilst this study only examined a small group of ecopreneurial firms, it does provide some interesting insights into the way in which such businesses operate at a strategic level. It is clear that marketing and branding issues, such as the firm's reputation, the creativity of the products or services that it offers and the exclusivity of its offerings are all perceived by the firms themselves to be important. Personal credibility is important for nearly every ecopreneur. Nevertheless, a successful competitive advantage cannot be solely created or maintained by just one individual. At some stage (typically once the firm has grown large enough), it becomes necessary to be able to transfer the spirit, skills, passion, decision-making and responsibility to a growing staff (Fischer 2000) – in other words, the ecopreneurial firm has to also become an intrapreneurial one. How to undertake this process would fill another chapter.

References

Abell, D.F. (1980) *Defining the Business: The Starting Point of Strategic Planning*, Prentice-Hall Englewood Cliffs, NJ.

Bech-Larsen, T., and Grunert, K.G. (2001) 'Konsumentscheidung bei Vertrauens-eigenschaften: Eine Untersuchung am Beispiel des Kaufes von ökologischen

Lebensmitteln in Deutschland und Dänemark', *Zeitschrift für Forschung und Praxis* (March), pp. 188–197.

Fischer, H. (2000) 'Globale Zukunftsmärkte für umweltschonende Produkte eines mittelständischen Unternehmens' *UmweltwirtschaftsForum* (March), pp. 26–29.

Hamel, G., and Prahalad, C.K. (1995) *'Wettlauf um die Zukunft''* Wien: Ueberreuther.

Hipp (2000) *Umwelterklärung – Werk Pfaffenhofen und Werk Gmunden*, Hipp, Pfaffenhofen.

Jungk, R. and Müllert, N.R. (1980) *Alternatives Leben*, Signal, Baden-Baden.

Kim, C. and Mauborgne, R. (2000) 'Knowing a Winning Business Idea When You See One', *Harvard Business Review* (September–October) pp. 129–138.

Kuratko, D.F., Hornsby, J.S. and Naffziger, D.W. (1997) 'An Examination of Owner's Goals in Sustaining Entrepreneurship', *Journal of Small Business Management*, Vol. 1, pp. 24–33.

Leendertse, J. (2001) 'Gelbe Kolben: Hubert Loick macht aus Mais Verpackungschips', *Wirtschaftswoche*, No. 27 (June), p. 78.

Petersen, H. (2003) *Ecopreneurship Und Wettbewerbsstrategie: Verbreitung Ökologischer Innovationen Auf Grundlage Von Wettbewerbsvorteilen* Marburg, Metropolis.

Porter, M.E. (1991) 'Towards a Dynamic Theory of Strategy', *Strategic Management Journal*, Vol. 12, pp. 95–117.

Porter, M.E. (1997) 'Nur Strategie sichert auf Dauer hohe Erträge', *Harvard Business Manager*, Vol. 3, pp. 42–58.

Prahalad, C.K. and Hamel, G. (1990) 'The Core Competence of the Corporation', *Harvard Business Review* (May–June), pp. 79–91.

Ripsas, S. (1999) 'Unternehmensgründung im Umweltschutz', Diskussionspapier des Wissenschaftszentrums, No. Po1-501, WZB, Berlin.

Schaltegger, S., and Petersen, H. (2001) ' Ecopreneurship: Konzept und Typologie'' Reihe: Analysen zum Rio Management Forum 2000, Luzern.

Schmitt, E. (1997) 'Strategien mittelständischer Welt- und Europamarktführer', Gabler, Wiesbaden.

Simon, H. (1996) *Die heimlichen Gewinner: Die Erfolgsstrategien unbekannter Weltmarktführer* [Hidden Champions], Campus, Frankfurt am Main.

Thürbach, R.-P. (1991) 'Mittelständisches Überlegenheitspotential sichern und ausbauen' in E. Jahn (ed.) *Auf der Suche nach Erfolgspotentialen*, Schäffer-Poeschel, Stuttgart, pp. 95–111.

Timmons, J. (1986) 'Growing Up Big' in D. Sexton and R. Smilor (eds) *The Art and Science of Entrepreneurship*, Ballinger, Cambridge, MA, pp. 153–167.

Treacy, M. and Wiersema, F. (1993) 'Drei Wege zur Marktführerschaft', *Harvard Business Manager*, Vol. 3, pp. 123–131.

Treacy, M., and Wiersema, F. (1995) *'Wege zur Spitze'*, Frankfurt am Main: Campus.

PART THREE
Cases

14

Entrepreneurship and Sustainable Tourism: The Global Gypsies Approach

Jim Macbeth and Yamini Narayanan

ABSTRACT

This chapter presents a case study of Global Gypsies, a four wheel drive (4WD[1]) vehicle tour company based in Western Australia. The firm is an example of a successful small-scale tourism enterprise that operates on the ethic of using the local physical, natural, social and cultural resources of a place to deliver the tourism product, while being meticulously attentive to the demands of environmental sustainability that touring through the fragile remote Australian ecosystem requires. This chapter examines the founding motives of the entrepreneurs, their initial and current product mix, and the steps they have taken to ensure their firm is also environmentally responsible.

---

1   Standard 4WD vehicles are not usually car-based vehicles and 4WD is not engaged on the highway. In addition, they will have a low-range gearbox, underside protective plates and extra ground clearance for more 'serious' off-road travel. Soft-roaders are usually based on a car or minivan chassis and have only a single-speed transfer case (that is, no low range) and, although they do have extra ground clearance and wheel travel, are not designed for serious off-road travel. AWD (all-wheel drive) often refers to cars, although most soft-roaders are also AWD.

Introduction

Maintaining a successful tourism business arguably means recognizing the four pillars of sustainable development: that is, environmental, social, cultural and economic factors. Therefore, besides needing to stay financially healthy, a tour business needs to be cognizant of its environment, the social context of its tours and the cultural context with which the tour interacts.

The Australian red desert is well known to many as 'the outback', travelling to which may be a physically and mentally highly confrontational experience. The vast expanses of arid desert, sand, bush, scrub[1] and wild grass, symbolize the collective Australian psyche and centrally occupy the Australian imagination. The sheer scale of the magnificent scenery dwarfs and overwhelms the visitor, while the remoteness and physical isolation, and the starkly beautiful environment, often inspires awe and surrender amongst visitors to the region. Global Gypsies have tapped into the market for this 'space'. Australia's rich natural heritage is also attracting a rising number of international visitors. Larson and Herr note:

> *Australia's unique natural environment is a critical element of its global tourism appeal and is regarded by tourism planning organizations as a key attribute that differentiates Australia from competing tourism destinations in the global market. (Larson and Herr 2007, p. 1)*

Contributing to sustainable tourism underlies the product mix of Global Gypsies, a small entrepreneurial tourism venture based in Perth, Western Australia. Besides environmentally responsible tours, the company also provides training for safari guides, four-wheel drivers and caravan owners. The fundamental ethic is the development of skills, knowledge and attitudes for safe and responsible practice by tour leaders and tourists alike. It is this approach that has helped make the company successful, since responsible tourism has become an important dynamic and is in demand from NGOs, government agencies and tourists alike.

Significantly, Global Gypsies is among the longest surviving small-scale 4WD tag-along tour operators in Western Australia; it was also the first 4WD company to have an environmental charter committed to protecting and conserving the landscape through which its guests travel. It has thereby achieved for itself a genuine respect from the 4WD community as being responsible, ethically-driven 4WD company with a keen understanding and knowledge of both the mechanics of 4WDing and the remote Australian outback.

---

1   'Scrub' is Australian slang for country with low bush, spinifex grass and small trees, located well outside settled areas.

Background

Global Gypsies Pty Ltd was born when two peripatetic pilgrims, Jeremy Perks and Jan Barrie, serendipitously met in Nairobi, Kenya, in 1993. Jeremy already had a successful partnership in an advertising agency and Jan ran a public relations firm. Both had a deep-seated desire to discard their well-paying secure lives in exchange for a satisfying lifestyle. Together, they quit their corporate careers and began a sojourn through Africa. During that expedition they decided to start their own wildlife safari tour business in Australia when they had completed their gypsy journey.

The couple arrived in Australia in the 1990s intending to create their own 4WD tour company, and planned to model it on the African safari experience. Jeremy spent several years working with a few 4WD tour companies in Western Australia as a tour guide and training and recruitment officer. At the time, he was a competent mechanic, had acquired extensive knowledge on the flora and fauna of the red desert outback, was a certified trainer and assessor, and was also qualified in remote-area first aid. Jan had worked in tourism, marketing and administration, and, between them, the pair had a wide set of complementary skills that could be used to create a new business venture.

Armed with this wealth of experience, Global Gypsies began trading in 1997. The couple intended to re-create the safari experience that was so successful in Africa. However, they discovered mistakes in their strategy almost immediately – Australia could not supply the cheap labour that was easily available in Africa, which meant that the pair had to streamline their tours such that several parts of it, like setting camp and pitching tents, were self-provided by the tourists.

Replicating African safari tours in Western Australia was not entirely feasible; however, the directors were committed to preserving both the quality and the uniqueness of the remote tourism experience. A series of improvisations led Jan and Jeremy to start the then commercially little-known concept of tag-along tours into the outback. In Jan's words, a tag-along tour is 'a tour into the outback where you self-drive your own or hired 4WD vehicle. [You] travel with others in a convoy and are led by an expert guide', usually Jeremy. These tours provide the safety of a group convoy while traversing remote areas, as well as a social component for all participants.

While tag-along tours have since become more commonplace, Global Gypsies managed to maintain some exclusivity by offering a unique feature – the presence of a safari hostess who provides high-quality and nutritious catering throughout the journey. This is the closest that the Gypsies have come to reproducing the African experience in Western Australia, and this sense of convenience and luxury in remote areas makes their tours very popular.

Wanderers at heart, it was clear to Jan and Jeremy early on that international travel would also eventually form an important part of the services that they had to provide. Here the Gypsies were planning to operate in a relatively familiar and well-established market; however, they found a unique way to deal with the challenges of growing their business into this niche.

Before finalizing local tours, Jan and Jeremy would usually take a reconnoitring trip to explore and familiarize themselves with the new territory. In contrast, for their new international tours, because of the high expense of international travel, the Gypsies found a way of reduce costs and time by extending an invitation to their customers to come and travel *with* them, to discover the new lands *with* them. While this was admittedly a risk in several ways, it led to the happy result of preserving the novelty and newness of the journey with none of the jadedness that one might associate with micro-managed travel programmes. According to Jan and Jeremy, every overseas trip organized by the Gypsies has thus been booked out within weeks of being announced.

In 2007, for example, the Gypsies conducted fully escorted tours to China, Botswana and Kenya, while in 2008 the firm offered journeys to Botswana and Kenya, along with two new trips in Borneo, and another in Greece. By featuring new explorations each year, the Gypsies capitalize on their strategy of keeping their experiences fresh for both their customers and themselves.

Today, the Gypsies management is still small, consisting of the two full-time directors, one part-time office administrator and six casual staff who are employed as required to assist with tours and training. They run approximately six extended 4WD tours to the outback each year; in addition, they coordinate several private-charter safaris within Australia, as well as a smaller number of international journeys. They also run a year-long array of training courses in 4WDing, caravan towing and safari-guide training. A final income stream is audiovisual materials: the firm produces and sells hundreds of caravan-training DVDs each year for caravan owners and drivers.

Industry Leadership Through Responsible Tours

Global Gypsies is now one of Western Australia's most successful 4WD tour companies and seeks to provide 'qualify, nature-based, soft-adventure, fully-escorted tours to remote areas in Australia and overseas' (GG Safari Guide Workshops n.d.). It has also expanded its training services by offering Western Australia's only safari-guide training programme (Safari Guide Workshops), the first caravan-towing training programme and accompanying caravan training DVD, as well as accredited recreational four-wheel driving tuition. All these programmes have a strong environmental focus. Global Gypsies is licensed by the state Department of Environment and Conservation and by the state government's transport management agency, Transport WA. It holds corporate memberships of Trackcare Western Australia, FACET (Forum for Advocating Cultural and Ecotourism, WA), TreadLightly and the Ecotourism Association of Australia.

Jan's and Jeremy's priority has been to remain a small company, and it is this focus, as well as their commitment to be guided by environmental concerns, which has enabled their business success. E.F. Schumacher, the father of environmental economics, argued in his classic *Small is Beautiful*:

> *We always need both freedom and order. We need the freedom of lots and lots of small, autonomous units, and at the same time, the orderliness of large-scale, possibly global, unity and coordination. (Schumacher 1973, p. 53)*

Schumacher believed that an emphasis on 'the small' would prioritize people over technology – technology would merely offer reasonable support within the local context.

The firm's ability to provide a pleasurable 4WD experience and a fundamental appreciation of nature in the remote Australian outback has earned Jan and Jeremy much respect amongst their clientele and the broader 4WD community. This has been coupled with their dedication to minimizing the tour's impact on the natural landscape. In 2004 Jeremy won the FACET Golden Guide of the Year Award (Tour Guide of the Year), which significantly increased the company's profile. Moreover, like other successful ecopreneurs in the ecotourism industry such as Bill Leverett, the founder of Dolphinwatch Hong Kong (Geneste 2005), both of the founding entrepreneurs genuinely take immense joy and pleasure in the tourism experience themselves. This has in turn assisted their business development.

Global Gypsies was the first and is still one of the few 4WD tour companies in the state to have an explicit policy on environmental preservation. This comprehensive environmental management policy covers five areas of concern while 4WDing in remote areas, including responsible 4WD practices, such as using only approved 4WD tracks and avoiding virginal land or reclaimed, reforested and revegetated areas. Ecological awareness is emphasized at every available opportunity during the tour. Specific instructions are provided on how to minimize damage to the environment should the 4WD get bogged,[2] for example, and in various situations such as while traversing lands controlled by the state Department of Environment and Conservation or within Aboriginal jurisdiction.

The policy carefully details the procedures for human and other waste disposal in the outback. It advises the clients to dig their 'bush toilets' at least 100 metres downwind from the campsite and to use only biodegradable toilet paper and it is emphatic that no waste be left behind in camping areas or thrown out of the vehicles – all waste that is not burnable must be carried to the next available town where it may be disposed off responsibly.

This concern is further extended in their third area, which covers ecologically responsible ways of managing their resource use. It advises the travellers to use biodegradable detergents and soaps, to refrain from using even these in lakes and ponds, and to take sufficient water supplies with them so that this precious resource in remote areas is not depleted. It also details instructions on using only provided wood to light campfires and to build one only of a size sufficient for cooking, so as not to damage the nearby bush. Jan notes that the campfires are a source of some dilemma in regard to their environmental protection principles. Ideally, they would not light fires at all, but they also have an obligation to provide their travellers with the 'complete' outback experience. Hence, the small fires are a concession to travellers who appreciate the campfires as a part of their outback camping experience.

Fourth, the policy also emphasizes that all 4WDs in each convoy comply with the vehicle's emissions standards and that all disposable fluids from the

---

2   'Bogged' is Australian slang for getting stuck, whether in sand, mud or other rough conditions. It can be a serious problem if the tide, for example, is coming in while bogged on a beach.

vehicles, such as engine oil, be stored so that they can be eventually disposed of according to prescribed procedures.

Lastly, the Gypsies' environmental policy includes another area that is vital to sustainability and sustainable tourism – the social and cultural aspects of the remote outback experience. The Gypsies commit themselves to researching the history, culture, and the local social and environmental landscape of tour areas as extensively as possible, so that they can provide their clients with a rich experience of the outdoors. They include local tour guides and speakers as much as possible, which not only promote traveller understanding, but also generate sustainable business opportunities and income to remote communities. This agenda also extols the clients to refrain from removing any rock, flowers or fossils from the area and to be particularly conscious to avoid harming local flora and fauna. However, the Gypsies are well aware of the efforts required to translate such knowledge into action, chief among these being the strategy of hands-on demonstration in order to illustrate more clearly the values and benefits.

Using Training and Research for Environmental and Commercial Advantage

Much debate also centres on the issue of 4WD tourism and, in particular, 4WD travel to remote and fragile ecological areas. Some critics have labelled 4WDs as 'vehicles of mass destruction' (Pepper 2007) because of fairly widespread concerns that 4WDs pose threats to native wildlife and flora, as well as damaging the lands they traverse. It certainly needs to be noted that the language of some of the popular online literature is quite disapproving and uncompromising in its dislike of 4WD travel (Pollard 2006).

Conducting responsible tours the Gypsy way also includes the provision of training programmes in responsible 4WD driving. The firm offers a one-day, nationally accredited 4WD training programme in partnership with Getabout 4WD Adventures from New South Wales. The course includes instruction not only for heavy 4WDs, but also for soft-roaders and AWDs. The course can also be enjoyed as a 'recreational' option for those clients who just want to learn how to enjoy the great outdoors without undergoing the accreditation process. Importantly, the course also warmly and unambiguously invites women to participate, which is a marked change in what has usually been a largely male-dominated tourism niche.

Shortly after Jan and Jeremy started their tag-along tour business in Western Australia, they made contact with staff at Murdoch University to discuss the possibility of cooperating in the provision of safari-guide training (that is, educating potential leaders of outback tours). This was a result of both observations of the level of outback tour guide standards and the advantage of the comprehensive African safari experience, where the tour guide profession is a highly respected one. With little or no financial incentive to run these courses, Jan and Jeremy organized these courses simply to use their own considerable background and experience to 'help the industry'.

Until they created the course, no such training was available other than what was being offered 'in-house' by some tour companies. A weekend workshop structure was adopted with sponsorship of a teaching venue by Murdoch University. These workshops now provide guidance in first aid, information on the natural landscape, track information, interpretation, basic 4WD mechanics and the fine and essential art of meaningful leadership. These workshops move from the classroom during the first afternoon to a touring situation with Jeremy instructing on the finer points of leading a tour as the vehicles make their way to a campsite some hours south of Perth. Camp is set and instruction continues through the hands-on process, including throughout and after meals. A second day is spent partly on breaking camp and some basic 4WD beach driving lessons, all with a deep environmental awareness.

Other training opportunities have also emerged over time. An essence of entrepreneurship is the ability to identify and successfully exploit new opportunities as they emerge, and the Gypsies have demonstrated a strong entrepreneurial flair in this regard. After having been in the business for several years, Jan and Jeremy noticed an interesting trend amongst their long-time customers – as they started to hit their mid-70s, they were exchanging their 4WDs for caravans. The market had started to mature. In 2005 the Gypsies branched out to undertake some caravan training, again based at Murdoch University and again using a weekend class and travel format. Association with such an established institution very quickly earned the Gypsies even greater credibility and the Caravan Industry Association agreed to align itself with the programme as a joint-venture exercise.

This led in turn to some other interesting outcomes. The caravan-training clients started to become their tour clients and vice versa. More importantly, for the benefit of customers who lived too far away to attend these programmes, a DVD was made to aid the wider communication of their training techniques nationwide. This project has been tremendously well received within the growing 4WD and caravanning community in Australia and internationally, and the DVD now has a high sales rate.

The firm has also helped to foster sustainability research in a number of practical ways. Research into sustainable tourism has increased dramatically in Australia in recent years, and in 2005 Global Gypsies was invited to become a member of the On Track Steering Committee. On Track was a three-year research project looking at the potential contributions and impacts of 4WD tourism in the Australian desert. It was part of the then Desert Knowledge Cooperative Research Centre, and the project was led by a team of researchers from four universities across Australia, including Murdoch. Global Gypsies has also contributed to this project by sponsoring researchers to join some of its tours and by facilitating survey work with people on the tours.

A Small Company: High and Low Impact Ethic

Destinations often get overrun by tours and tourists. Despite popular and persistent demands, Jan and Jeremy have stuck by their early decision to conduct only one tour per destination in a year. This is in stark contrast to larger 4WD tour operators that conduct several such tours in a single month. The Gypsies' decision minimizes their impact on the environment, and also makes the tour and the destination a very precious and fresh experience for both them and their customers. The Gypsies place immense value on savouring the experience and think nothing of driving along tracks at a leisurely pace and making several stops to marvel at wild flowers, or pausing to take in a spectacular view of a huge column of rocks. Experience and appreciation of nature thus become the essential agenda of the tour.

The ecopreneurial advantage of Global Gypsies comes from its inspired and imaginative approach of having a high impact on their customers and a low impact on the natural environment, thus satisfying one of the fundamental principles of sustainable tourism. The success of any business enterprise that seeks to be 'green' depends not only on the vision and dedication of its founders, but also on the attitudes towards environmental care in the local environment within which it is situated (Geneste 2005). To this extent, Global Gypsies has instinctively been particular about the approaches it uses to attract the kind of clientele that will have the most empathy with the Australian bush.

For instance, its tag-along tours with a catering service attract a sizeable number of female clients who generally accompany their husbands or partners. The safety of a convoy also encourages many female 4WDers to self-drive into the outback. Jeremy explains:

> Most outback tagalong tours are very much boys' weekends away, much rougher. We didn't want those kinds of tours. We always wanted a couple and people who are there to experience nature, the environment, rather than go bush-bashing and pushing their 4WD to the max. We use 4WD to get from A to B, not as an end in itself. We like to smell the roses along the way.

Global Gypsies has been emphatic about retaining 'the female element' from the outset. An essential part of its tours involves a 'Girlspeak' 4WD seminar in which Jeremy takes questions, comments and suggestions from his female clients on various aspects of 4WDing and offers elaborate explanations of the technical dimensions of driving and gear management. This focus on the 'softer side' has allowed the company to develop a female customer base who are cooperative in their efforts to enjoy the Australian bush while being responsible towards it.

Above all, such an ethic allows Jan and Jeremy to maintain their objective of remaining small. They are clear that it was their love for the Australian outback that made them consider their hobby as a business enterprise; however, they would not allow business priorities to dominate their own experience and perceptions of the outback beyond reasonable limits. Ironically, this has served as a valuable principle in creating a sustainable small business. Jan explains:

> It lets us maintain tight control of our finances so we always know where we stand. It lets us be flexible, we can take quick turns, make quick decisions depending on how we feel at the very last minute, all based on instinct ... these would take forever in a large business and actually compromise business interests. We work with instinct a lot, with people, when we are out there. It makes us feel more real, less calculative.

Moreover, because the company is of a small sustainable size, Jan and Jeremy can handpick employees who are ethically aligned with their work principles, and deliver an experience that is not compromised on quality. Jeremy defines quality thus:

> We feel we are really getting somewhere when there is a good sense of community in our convoy group; everyone is winding down to do

nothing but revel in nature. It is great when everyone in the group has been really touched by something they saw or felt on the way and that always happens. It's different if you are travelling alone, but if you are travelling in a group that experience of nature that we are talking about happens more quickly if the people have all bonded with each other. It rarely happens in big tours. For us, that is quality.

This attention to client fulfilment and satisfaction is combined with consideration for the natural environment. As explained earlier, Global Gypsies' guideline on ecological protection is followed as assiduously as possible to minimize the impact associated with 4WD travel. For instance, the travellers generally halt only at existing campsites and park their vehicles at least 100 metres away from water sites. While camping at virginal sites, the Gypsies are careful to use only open spaces and to limit the duration of the camp to no longer than an overnight stop.

Jan observes that being environmentally and socially responsible has suited their business model and the aim of remaining a sustainable business. She also believes that it possibly keeps customers loyal and supportive, and makes them 'feel good' about their decision to engage with the company. Jeremy argues, however, that there might even be a financial loss in being sustainable, since it puts less conscientious customers off. At the same time, Jeremy is not entirely convinced that these people are forever lost as customers and is hopeful that they will return to travel with him once they become wiser to the significance of the sustainability issues that responsible 4WDing considers. Jan explains their decision thus: 'Right now we do these things because we just feel that it is the right thing to do. But in future years, it may become mandatory. Maybe there will be legal ramifications if you don't.' Jeremy adds that on the whole, however, customers are becoming increasingly conscious of their impact on the remote ecology and are slowly beginning to seek reassurance that Global Gypsies is a green, certified company. Overall, the Gypsies' attention to the environment has given the company a level of credibility and respect that is invaluable to its business interests but difficult to objectively measure.

Conclusion

The Global Gypsies case study is an intriguing one because it illustrates how the business founders' passion for travelling can become a viable business enterprise; importantly, the green leanings of the directors have provided a unique opportunity to address some of the very valid concerns about heavy

4WD tourism into the relatively pristine areas of outback Australia. Global Gypsies has built a reputation for itself as a responsible, reputable company and has set a definitive standard for the ethical, green, cultural and technical approaches of 4WDing in general and 4WD tour companies in particular. Global Gypsies also provides an example of dedicated individuals who have taken the initiative in promoting values that celebrate an enjoyment of the beautiful natural resources in an aware and conscious manner.

Jan and Jeremy have important advice for new green entrepreneurs. They emphasize the need to thoroughly research the intended product or service to be delivered, as well as the market in which they intend to compete. The Gypsies did not have the resources to familiarize themselves with the market as well as they should have, and this posed some unanticipated challenges in the beginning.

Another important factor is to obtain sufficient start-up capital to meet both predicted and unexpected expenditures. Unforeseen problems can often damage firms operating on very thin financial margins, so access to sufficient finance is important until the firm is well established and cash flow is secure.

Finally, they also caution prospective entrepreneurs to 'not fall in love with your own ideas ... try and be practical about it'. Personal commitment is important, but not all personal passions can successfully translate into a viable new enterprise.

A key objective of Jan Barrie and Jeremy Perks has been to enjoy what they do while following their essentially green ethic. To date, they have been successful in this venture. The Global Gypsies approach thus offers itself as a useful model for ecopreneurship that amalgamates business and green ethics to the best interests of both.

References

Geneste, L. (2005) 'Hong Kong Dolphinwatch: The Evolution of an Ecopreneurial Business Venture' in M. Schaper (ed.) *Making Ecopreneurs: Developing Sustainable Entrepreneurship*, Ashgate, Aldershot, pp. 203–213.

GG Safari Guides Workshop (n.d.) *An Innovative Training Programme Presented by Global Gypsies*, Global Gypsies Pty Ltd Information and Workshop Pamphlet.

Larson, S. and Herr, A. (2007) 'Sustainable Tourism Development in Remote Regions? Questions Arising from Research in the North Kimberley, Australia, *Regional Environmental Change*. Available at: http://www.springerlink.com/content/m008w1710710151u/fulltext.pdf.

Pepper, R. (2007) 'The 4WD Debate', at: http://gpsvehiclenavigation.com/RMP/4WD-debate.php (accessed 3 March 2008).

Pollard, R. (2006) '4WD Users "Much More Dangerous"', *The Age*, 10 July, at: http://www.theage.com.au/news/national/4wd-users-much-more-dangerous/2006/07/09/1152383614616.html (accessed 3 March 2008).

Schumacher, E.F. (1973) *Small is Beautiful: A Study of Economics as if People Mattered,* Blond and Briggs, London.

15

Promoting Sustainability, Building Networks: A Green Entrepreneur in Mexico

Gabrielle Kruks-Wisner[1]

ABSTRACT

What do you do when your only source of income suddenly becomes illegal? The coastal community of Mazunte, Oaxaca, faced just this dilemma when the Mexican government banned the killing of sea turtles in 1990. The town's sole employer, a turtle slaughterhouse, closed its doors and the community was plunged into economic crisis. Since the early 1980s Hector Marcelli has promoted sustainable development in the region, seeking to balance a fragile ecosystem with the needs of the impoverished local population. It made little sense to Hector that Mazunte, a community so rich in natural resources, should live in poverty. He set to work with community members to develop environmentally sustainable alternatives to the turtle trade. Twelve years later, Mazunte and its environs are home to several thriving industries, including the manufacture of natural cosmetics, organic chocolate and peanut butter, and coastal ecotourism. Building on the success of this and other examples, Hector founded a national organization, Bioplaneta, to promote fair trade, organic agriculture and sustainable development across the country. Bioplaneta seeks to create fair-trade links between small producers and consumers, providing technical, diagnostic and financial assistance to over 40 small cooperatives. The Bioplaneta network has experienced impressive successes as well as challenges. These experiences highlight questions concerning the economic, social and environmental viability of fair-trade models and point to the important role that green entrepreneurs can play in the process of community revitalization.

1   This chapter was originally prepared as a study for the Environmental Initiative of Ashoka: Innovators for the Public. The author wishes to thank Ashoka for its support. Special thanks to Lauren Schutte for editing assistance and additional research.

Introduction

In the late 1980s the small town of Mazunte on the coast of Oaxaca, Mexico, became a battleground, the site of a classic 'jobs versus environment' showdown. The coast of Oaxaca is home to a number of species of turtle, including the rare leatherback turtle, and is the primary nesting ground of the olive ridley, Mexico's only non-endangered turtle. The construction of a turtle slaughterhouse in Mazunte quickly attracted the region's unemployed and landless, and sea turtles 'harvested' for their eggs, meat and shells rapidly became a staple of the local economy. Then, in 1990 after a protracted battle, the Mexican government banned the killing of sea turtles.

Many environmentalists welcomed the closing of the slaughterhouse following the 1990 ban. But Mazunte's very *raison d'être* ceased when the slaughterhouse closed, and the majority of the towns' residents found themselves out of a job. Hector Marcelli, an ecologist and community organizer in the region, recalled that 'people were very angry at that time. They were angry at the ecologists who took their jobs away.'[2]

To Hector it made little sense that Mazunte, a community so rich in natural resources, should suffer from underdevelopment and poverty. Since the early 1980s Hector has worked to promote sustainable development in the region, seeking to balance a fragile ecosystem with the needs of the impoverished local population. He began in 1983 by founding Ecosolar, an organization that sought to draw attention to the need for protection of Mexico's most ecologically fragile areas. Hector was a familiar face in Mazunte when he set to work alongside community members to develop environmentally sustainable alternatives to the turtle trade. He hoped to not only slow rural decline and urban migration, but also protect the environment by providing environmentally responsible models for economic development. He also hoped 'to show that environmentalism can be profitable'.

In 1999, after years of groundwork, Hector launched Bioplaneta, a non-profit organization promoting fair trade and sustainable development. Bioplaneta strives to provide real economic alternatives that benefit both rural communities and the environment. Today, Mazunte and its environs are home to a number of thriving alternative ecobusinesses, including a natural cosmetics

---

2 All quotes from Hector Marcelli derive from the author's personal conversations and interviews with him, carried in Mexico in March 2002. The conversations were held in Spanish and the translations are the author's own.

plant, organic chocolate and peanut-butter factories, and coastal ecotourism projects. Hector has expanded his model beyond Mazunte and Oaxaca, and currently operates in 12 states.

Hector's story in Mazunte and beyond is one of successful environmental entrepreneurship; he found promise in ruins while seeking to find new solutions to age-old problems of poverty, deprivation and environmental degradation. The following case study explores Hector's role in creating a thriving network of small businesses, as well as the role that community members themselves played, both as emerging entrepreneurs and as stewards of their environment. The study also considers some of the limits, structural and sociopolitical, that Hector and his partners in Bioplaneta face as they struggle in the context of Mexico's deepening rural crisis.

A Rural Crisis

Years before turning to the turtle trade, Mazunte lay in the heart of an active agricultural region. A system of price guarantees and subsidies ensured minimum income for small and medium producers, and promoted agricultural production in the region. Over the last 20 years, however, Mexican agriculture has declined. A combination of national development policies, trade liberalization, recession and declining prices for corn and coffee (two of Mexico's largest exports) has produced a crisis for small producers. After 20-plus years of neoliberal reform and adjustments, poverty rates have increased in Mexico, from 59 per cent in 1984 to 80 per cent in 1996. Almost half this number live in extreme poverty. In rural Mexico, 82 per cent of the population is classified as living in poverty and 55 per cent in extreme poverty (Wise 2003, p. 3).

Mexico began to liberalize its economy in the early 1980s, following an external debt crisis. Entry into the General Agreement on Tariffs and Trade (GATT) in 1986, the North American Free Trade Agreement (NAFTA) in 1994 and the Organization for Economic Cooperation and Development (OECD) in 1995 codified and accelerated the process of liberalization. The Mexican government reduced and/or eliminated agricultural tariffs and subsidies, in order to comply with trade agreements and attract foreign investment. Price guarantees for many products were eliminated. This had a devastating effect in rural areas, where the market was opened to competition from US and Canadian imports. At the same time, the price of export commodities such as corn and coffee declined internationally, further reducing profits to small and medium producers. Since 1994 corn and coffee have lost 27 and 58 per cent of their value, respectively (Wise 2003, p. 4).

In 1992 the government revised Mexico's land reform law, amending Article 27 of the constitution that guaranteed rural collective properties known as *ejidos*. Under the amendment, *ejido* land may now be privately leased or sold, opening the door to privatization and the reconcentration of land wealth. In the face of economic disaster, small farmers are abandoning the land to migrate to cities or to the United States. Massive urbanization reflects the decline of the rural sector: today only 25 per cent of the population lives in rural areas, compared to 57 per cent in 1950 (INEGI 2002).

Environmental Costs

Mexico is rich in diverse natural resources and boasts the fourth greatest biodiversity in the world (World Wildlife Fund 2002). However, the country also has the second fastest rate of deforestation, outstripped only by Brazil (Denniger and Minten 1996). Under pressure to relax environmental standards, the rate of deforestation, chemical contamination, erosion and biodiversity loss have all accelerated.

In many areas, small producers serve as unofficial stewards of their local environment, protecting the land and maintaining a wealth of traditional knowledge. Increased migration has taken a toll, as land is often abandoned or reconcentrated into large, commercial holdings. Other small producers are relegated to poor, erosion-prone areas, or practise slash-and-burn agriculture at great cost to the environment. Chemical-intensive monocropping by large agribusiness also contributes to watershed contamination and biodiversity loss.

It was in this context of economic and environmental crisis that the people of Mazunte sought alternatives to the turtle trade. And it was in the context of this crisis that Hector first conceived of Bioplaneta.

The Birth of the Bioplaneta Network

Hector first founded Ecosolar, the predecessor to Bioplaneta, out of love of the Oaxaca coast and environment. Ecosolar came into existence at a time in Mexico when environmental organizations were few and far between. Its purpose was to draw attention to environmental degradation on the coast and to champion the protection of ecological reserves. Hector is as committed to social equity as he is to the environment, and he quickly began to explore ways of promoting sustainable economic development as an alternative to destructive farming and resource extraction methods.

Early on, Hector realized that, without links between producers and consumers, the success of initiatives like Ecosolar's would be limited. 'For small producers to make it,' argues Hector, 'they need access to markets and effective distribution channels. Existing relationships between producers, technical facilitators, investors and consumers are too disorganized to take full advantage of the opportunities available.' Over the years Ecosolar's team had built up extensive links with producer associations, technical assistance organizations and business investors. Hector sought to recruit these individuals and organizations as members of a network that would share information and increase access to international markets. His starting principle was that any collaborative ventures must be beneficial to all parties.

Thus, Bioplaneta was born. The organization is an expanding arrangement of 'fair-trade' cooperatives, NGOs and distributors concerned with community development. The primary role of the Bioplaneta network is to create fair-trade links between small producers and consumers. Bioplaneta staff play a consulting role, providing technical, diagnostic and financial assistance. Today, the network includes 43 producer cooperatives, each consisting of five or more people, and an expanding group of technical partners including NGOs, universities and foundations. The organization has expanded from its origins in Oaxaca, and now works in 12 states.

Hector Marcelli: A Green Entrepreneur in Action

Hector Marcelli is a jack of all trades. A community organizer, an ecologist, an environmental engineer, and a market analyst – he is a self-taught expert in all of these fields. His curiosity and enthusiasm for problem-solving are the driving forces behind Bioplaneta.

Hector cut his activist teeth in the 1980s during a time of deepening crisis in Mexico's rural areas. His upbringing in a family that espoused Eastern spiritual philosophy allowed him to develop not only a deep connection with his environment, but also a commitment to the concept of 'impersonal service'. Hector's father stressed the importance of working for others out of love of giving, sharing and learning.

As a boy and young man, Hector spent a great deal of time exploring different areas of Mexico and developed a deep respect for the environment. In the early 1980s he worked as a community activist in Oaxaca, where he was able to combine his love of the environment with his passion for teaching. Although Hector's ties to Oaxaca remain strong, he has expanded his model and his work, and now oversees Bioplaneta projects in 12 states.

The success of Bioplaneta to date owes a great deal to Hector's personal dedication and commitment, as well as to his entrepreneurial qualities. In the true mark of a green entrepreneur, Hector was able to envision a thriving model of sustainable development in a region where official neglect and poverty have predominated. Bioplaneta is propelled by Hector's capacity for problem-solving, for galvanizing and involving community members, and for championing his ideas to local, national and international audiences.

A Tool for Small Producers

Bioplaneta supports small, worker-owned cooperatives in low-income communities. The cooperatives are located in ecologically important and fragile areas. Bioplaneta helps producers devise viable business plans that protect local resources and minimize environmental impact.

The Bioplaneta network, in Hector's words, is a 'tool' for small producers. Its staff serves as consultants to the producers, providing comprehensive support in every step of the process. Bioplaneta consists of two parts: Bioplaneta AC (*Asociación Civil*), a non-profit organization, and Bioplaneta SA (*Sociedad Anonima*), a for-profit business charged with marketing (see Figure 15.1). Within Bioplaneta AC, small producers and technical advisers work in close coordination. Bioplaneta SA searches for new markets and promotes the producers' products. The network of 43 cooperatives includes 27 producers of organic goods (such as cosmetics, chocolate, peanut butter, coffee and vanilla), seven ecotourism projects, four agro-ecology programmes (providing training and consulting in environmental services) and four artisan groups producing handicrafts.

The needs of each group of producers are unique, and Hector is quick to stress that there is no set template for Bioplaneta's work. Here, Hector's aptitude for creative problem-solving shines through, as he approaches each potential cooperative as a unique and exciting challenge. In each case, Bioplaneta staff begin by completing an examination of the cooperative in question. This

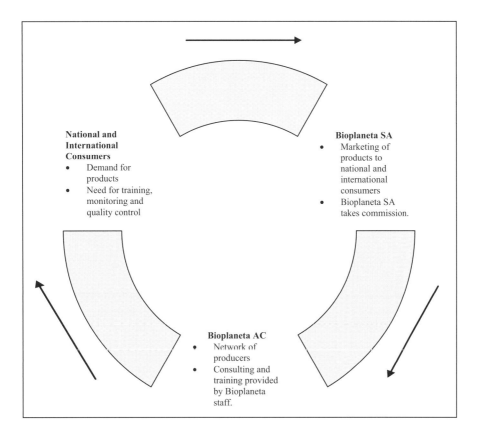

Figure 15.1   Bioplaneta organizational flow

diagnostic process considers the community, its needs and resources, as well as the cooperative's capacity for growth and its commitment to sustainable development. The diagnosis also takes into consideration the ecological impact of the cooperative, as well as the marketability of its products. After the diagnostic process is completed, Bioplaneta invites the group to sign an agreement, formally incorporating themselves into the network. The producers thereby become stakeholders in the organization, able to vote on its structure and leadership. The next step is to implement a production plan, providing training and assistance with the help of technical partners and other NGOs (see Figure 15.2).

Market-driven?

Bioplaneta SA takes on the task of marketing the wide range of Bioplaneta products. Marketing strategies are developed in cooperation with the producers.

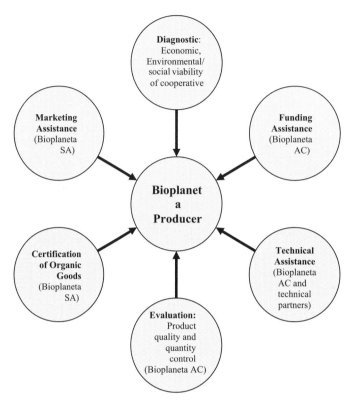

**Figure 15.2   The Bioplaneta consulting process: services provided to
                 Bioplaneta producers**

Bioplaneta staff help to connect producers to well-established international fair-trade networks, where consumers tend to buy in bulk. Hector estimates that 50 per cent of total sales are international. However, high transportation and transaction costs diminish the profitability of international sales. The national market consists of speciality stores and restaurants, corporate sales (for example, orders for company gift baskets) and direct sales via the cooperative's own stores and the Bioplaneta website. Internet sales remain low, however, as online sales are a relatively new phenomenon in Mexico. Marketing methods vary a great deal between the cooperatives. The producers of food goods – for example coffee, chocolate or vanilla – have tapped into a network of gourmet and health supermarkets and restaurants in Mexico. Artisans and handicraft producers, for their part, market their goods in craft fairs and markets near tourist centres.

Hector clarifies that, despite being for-profit, Bioplaneta SA is not market-driven. High start-up costs, transportation and transaction costs, and the price of organic and fair-trade certification have hurt the producers' profits. Moreover, small producers are pitted against large, multinational companies that enjoy the advantages of scale and access to technology and markets. Hector explains, 'We cannot be market-driven and still work for our producers. This is the problem with fair trade; the [market] conditions for it really do not exist yet.'

At the moment, the goal of the SA is simply to pay for its own operating costs in order to relieve some of the financial burden on Bioplaneta's non-profit arm. 'If we can get marketing to pay for itself,' Hector explains, 'we can concentrate more of our resources on training and assistance for the producers.' While Hector dreams that one day the SA will generate a surplus, this has not happened yet. Rather, profit margins for some of the producers are so slim that the SA often takes a commission of 1 per cent or less – not enough to cover its costs. Bioplaneta's commission varies depending on the profits of a given cooperative. Those which incur high transaction costs or suffer when international prices fall (coffee producers, for example) have very low profit margins. Other industries – for example, ecotourism or crafts – have higher profit margins and Bioplaneta takes a bigger commission – sometimes up to 10 per cent. In this way, the cooperatives cross-subsidize one another within the Bioplaneta network.

Mazunte Natural Cosmetics: A Success Story

The story of the Mazunte Natural Cosmetics factory, which emerged after the closing of the turtle slaughterhouse, is perhaps Bioplaneta's greatest success. In 1992, two years after the turtle ban, Hector and his colleagues in Ecosolar held an environment festival in Mazunte, in an attempt to highlight the dire situation of the town. International visitors attended the festival, and Mazunte caught the eye of Anita Roddick, founder of the British cosmetics company The Body Shop. Ms Roddick donated funds, equipment and formulas to a group of 15 women, with the idea that they produce a line of natural cosmetics.

Hector recalls that, when he first called a meeting to discuss Ms Roddick's proposal, many in the community felt ambivalent. It was an entirely new idea, unheard of in a town where most had been employed either in agriculture or in the turtle trade. Building from his long history and relationships in Mazunte, and helped by his natural skills as an organizer and teacher, Hector was able to convince a small group of women to try their hands at producing cosmetics. Today, the cooperative produces shampoo, conditioner, body oil and face cream, all made from organic, natural ingredients. Since their beginning in 1996 the women of Mazunte Natural Cosmetics have yielded a profit each year, through direct sales from their factory store, distribution through Bioplaneta, and through boutique sales throughout Mexico. The Body Shop purchases 5–8 per cent of their products each year, but the rest of the sales are independent. The cooperative divides the profits three ways: first, earnings are distributed among the members; second, a portion of earnings is set aside for reinvestment (these funds, for example, allowed the cooperative to purchase new land to construct tourist cabins); and, third, the remaining funds are used to support other social and environmental projects in the area.

While the success of the factory ultimately lies with the women who run it, Hector's contributions along the way are clear. From facilitating the first meetings with The Body Shop, to creating an ecological design for the factory building, and to assisting in increasingly ambitious marketing plans for the cosmetics, Hector is a constant catalyst for the cooperative's growth.

According to Bioplaneta's economic, environmental and social measures, Mazunte Natural Cosmetics is an unequivocal success. In economic terms, the cooperative has demonstrated that market demand for its products exists, and the women of the factory have exhibited strong administrative and business skills. From an environmental stance, the cooperative also scores high marks; the cosmetics are manufactured using only organic materials, and the factory cleans and recycles its waste water in a self-contained treatment plant. According to Hector, however, the social impact of the cooperative is the greatest triumph. The cosmetics factory has invested in other projects in the area, such as a neighbouring ecotourism project. In addition, the cosmetics cooperative has donated funds to help rebuild a local school destroyed by a hurricane.

A NETWORK OF NETWORKS

Bioplaneta emphasizes the need for a timely return on investment so that fragile new ventures will not founder. It ensures the survival of its newly emerging entrepreneurs by encouraging horizontal and vertical market integration, or, as Hector puts it, by building networks. Hector has always argued that producers would only see timely returns on their investments if they purchased inputs from one another, shared both their expertise and their earnings, and shrewdly marketed their finished products to targeted consumers.

Bioplaneta members have responded to the encouragement to build supply chains among themselves; they sell some US$100,000 worth of products annually to one another. Hector also fosters the establishment of networks through another mechanism. When members receive seed-money from Bioplaneta for a business, they are not asked to repay the donor. Instead, once they are operating in the black, their stakeholders must agree to give an equivalent amount – either in money or services – to another start-up fair-trade venture.

Mazunte Natural Cosmetics once again provides an example. Recognizing that they stood to gain from the economic development of the region as a whole, the women at Mazunte Natural Cosmetics have invested in other fair-trade and ecological projects in the area. La Ventanilla is a project a few kilometres down the coast that offers tours through a mangrove swamp and visits to a crocodile nursery. La Ventanilla intends to expand its business by opening a restaurant catering to ecotourists. The cosmetics cooperative has contributed funds for the construction of the restaurant. In part, this is a gesture of goodwill to their neighbours, but the cosmetics cooperative also hopes to benefit from an increase in ecotourism traffic in the area. In turn, La Ventanilla is paying off the value of its investment from the cosmetics factory by conducting tourism courses for the Tuxtlas Community Ecotourism Network. This network consists of projects in four villages that work together under Bioplaneta's umbrella.

When the Mazunte Natural Cosmetics factory won an international award for successful women's projects, it allotted the prize money to the chocolate confectioners of the San Rafael Toltepec Producers Union so that they could complete their own factory. Mazunte cosmetics has also contributed to several other Bioplaneta projects and demonstrated a sense of social responsibility by donating funds to help rebuild a local school destroyed by a hurricane.

Hector is thrilled to see the development of this strong, regional network. In another example, a group of six ecotourism projects stretching across Oaxaca from the mountains to the coast have joined forces. They share experience, promote one another's projects and, like the Oaxaca coastal network, are considering shared investment in a fleet of trucks. As Hector notes, 'You cannot force cooperation, but you can encourage it. People generally want to help each other, and they see that it works.'

It is the creation of grassroots networks more than anything that drives and motivates Hector at the helm of Bioplaneta. In this process, Hector often plays the role of facilitator, acting as the go-between among different cooperatives and groups. Groups of producers are encouraged to organize locally and to build connections with other groups regionally. Hector explains: 'Networks are what make us strong, as small groups working for change connect with one another. This is the positive side of globalization.'

ALTERNATIVE TRADE: MORE QUESTIONS THAN ANSWERS

Hector is proud to cite the achievements of the various Bioplaneta producers and cheerfully boasts of the development of regional networks. However, he is also realistic about the obstacles and limits encountered by his model. Economists and development practitioners alike have debated whether fair trade is economically sustainable. Others have questioned the environmental and social impacts of the model. The successes of, and challenges to, Bioplaneta highlight some of the most important issues facing the fair trade movement (Werner 2002).

Bioplaneta's producers operate in a relatively empty playing field, since the market for fair trade, organic goods and ecotourism remain largely undeveloped in Mexico. As the organization looks forward, it must consider that the fair-trade market is not without limits. Bioplaneta must contemplate whether a mushrooming growth in fair-trade industries might force prices down for its producers. Other questions arise concerning the environmental impact of fair trade. One or two projects in ecotourism, for example, have little impact. What will happen, however, if there is a market boom? How would Oaxaca or other fragile regions cope with such an increase in tourism, and what pressures would be placed on the land, resources and ecosystem?

Bioplaneta must also turn its attention to some serious sociopolitical concerns – namely that fair trade may create dependency on volatile, external markets and divert important focus from local needs. Bioplaneta promotes community-based development. Yet its cooperatives produce luxury goods and services, rarely intended for local consumption. As fewer people produce for local consumption, rural residents become more dependent on imports for basic needs, such as food. Bioplaneta's producers are also dependent on external markets and their fluctuations. Coffee producers, for example, have been hard hit by falling international prices. Although the fair-trade price for coffee is maintained at a 'just' or livable level, the competition from less expensive, non-fair-trade sources is fierce.

Hector is very aware of these and other critiques of fair trade, but sidesteps the issues by focusing on the larger goal of Bioplaneta – that is, the long-term sustainable development of rural communities. In fact, Hector argues that fair trade is not Bioplaneta's end-goal of, but a means towards economic and social transformation. The process of developing a fair-trade network, he believes, is more important than the end result. By building networks,

Bioplaneta encourages community development and strengthens civil-society organizations. It is this empowering process that Hector hopes will be the lasting legacy of Bioplaneta.

For Hector, a far greater threat to success comes from infighting within families and communities when residents who are not involved in the network see new enterprises flourishing and feel excluded. Church and political parties are another major threat. Hector explains that local officials often try to undermine emerging enterprises when they involve people from the political party that is not in power. In such instances, Hector finds himself playing a mediating role, seeking to educate community members about the wider social and environmental benefits of Bioplaneta's enterprises.

Conclusion: Spreading the Vision

Through his vision, energy, and skills, Hector has produced a sophisticated structure to promote both fair trade and community development. His creativity, his ability to conceive of new opportunities and his great skill in gathering both resources and support have enabled him to build a successful organization in a short number of years. Further, his natural skills as both a teacher and organizer have allowed him to play a pivotal role in establishing local, national and international networks. Hector believes that Bioplaneta's legacy will be more than a series of small enterprises. He believes that Bioplaneta will lead by example, inspiring others across the country and the globe to duplicate the model. In the long term, Hector hopes that the success of Bioplaneta's producers may influence national and international development policies and practices.

Reflecting the growing appeal of Bioplaneta's work in official circles, in 2002 the organization received two unprecedented grants from the federal government. The Ministry of Economics (Secretaría de Economía) gave US$170,000 and the Ministry of Social Development US$80,000 for the operating costs of the Bioplaneta network at the national level. Building on these relationships at the governmental level, Hector hopes in time to change the system so that, in response to the model pioneered by the Bioplaneta network, Mexican government policies will put the needs of network members at the forefront of its trade and development strategy. 'For the first time in the country's history, government is putting in money to support fair trade and organic commerce for communities to export,' Hector said. 'The politicians are seeing that the products seem successful, and they want to be in the photo.'

Hector harkens back to his upbringing as he explains his vision for Bioplaneta. His father was fond of saying that each person should contribute a 'grain of sand' towards the ideal of a more just world. Following this fatherly advice, Hector envisions Bioplaneta as stepping stone to the larger social change needed to address the fundamental problems of inequality, poverty and environmental damage in rural Mexico. 'We're not there yet,' Hector says of this change. 'We're still a long way off. People need to pick themselves up and do something. They need to get organized at the bottom, and then we will see change.'

References

Denniger, K. and Minten, B. (1996) *Poverty, Policies And Deforestation: The Case of Mexico*, The World Bank and International Food Policy Research Institute Washington, DC.

INEGI (Instituto Nacional de Estadística, Geografia e Informática de México) (2002) *Distribución de la Población por Tipo y Tamaño de Localidad*, 1950–2000, INEGI Mexico City.

Werner, D. (2002) 'Struggle for Sustainable Human and Environmental Well-Being on the Mexican Coast of Oaxaca', *Development in Practice*, Vol. 12, No. 1, pp. 71–78.

Wise, T. (ed.) (2003) *Confronting Globalization: Economic Integration and Popular Resistance in Mexico*, Kumarian Press, Bloomfield, CT.

World Wildlife Fund (2002) *Socioeconomic Root Causes of Biodiversity Loss*, World Wildlife Fund, Washington, DC.

16

Sustainable Harvest International: Expanding Ecopreneur Expertise

Jill A. Kammermeyer and Margaret J. Naumes

ABSTRACT

Creating local ecopreneurs is an ongoing process at Sustainable Harvest International (SHI), a small non-profit organization headquartered in Maine, USA. Founder and ecopreneur Florence Reed began with a commitment to save the rainforests by teaching sustainable agricultural techniques to local farmers in Central America. Her personal values and entrepreneurial willingness to take risks and create change led her to found SHI when she could not find another organization carrying out her mission. SHI operates through its local field trainers to encourage individual farmers to become ecopreneurial by implementing sustainable agro-forestry techniques, which in turn creates economic opportunity, evidenced by the variety of micro-projects that have been initiated. The field trainers, ecopreneurs with a strong personal commitment to the environment and their communities, build on SHI's training and resources to develop programs tailored to local needs. The creation of ecopreneurs has been furthered by SHI's self-view as an incubator to develop locally-based, ultimately independent organizations in affiliated countries. Sustainable Harvest International has been a significant force for environmental and economic change in the villages that it serves in Central America. Because of its integrated approach to environmental and economic needs, the impact on its participants will probably be long-lasting.

Introduction

Entrepreneurship has been the subject of discussion and definition going back to Jean Baptiste Say (1803) in the nineteenth century and Joseph Schumpeter

(1950) in the first half of the twentieth century. Say identified the entrepreneur's actions as creating value by shifting economic resources from low-yield activities to areas where they would be more productive. Schumpeter added the concept of innovation: entrepreneurs 'reform or revolutionize the pattern of production' (1950, p. 132). Subsequent writers have refined these definitions to include as entrepreneurs those who take advantage of change, as well as those who cause it. In essence, all entrepreneurs seek opportunities and then build on them.

According to Dees (1998, p. 3), social entrepreneurs are 'one species in the genus entrepreneur'. What sets social entrepreneurs apart from other entrepreneurs is their mission, which is focused on creating and sustaining social value. Whereas most entrepreneurs are often considered to be interested in creating economic value through new products or services, sales and profits, social entrepreneurs look for ways to make society a better place, not necessarily for themselves but for others. To accomplish that mission, they identify and pursue new opportunities and innovations, and are continually learning and adapting. They are apt to act on their beliefs, rather than consider constraints, particularly resources. They also have a strong sense of accountability to a wide range of constituencies (Dees, Emerson and Economy 2001). Much of the social entrepreneurship literature has been focused on non-profit organizations; however, there are well-known for-profit businesses that are also examples of social entrepreneurship (such as The Body Shop).

Green entrepreneurs, also known as ecopreneurs, are often found as social entrepreneurs whose focus is on sustainability and the adoption of environmentally sound business practices (Schaper 2002). Much of the emerging literature on ecopreneurship has focused on green entrepreneurs in the business sector. However, as in social entrepreneurship generally, there are important roles that can be played by ecopreneurs in the non-profit sector. This chapter describes Sustainable Harvest International (SHI), a young and growing non-profit organization. Its founder, Florence Reed, is an ecopreneur. SHI works through its agents in several Central American countries to encourage individual entrepreneurship and the creation of sustainable business organizations.

The Organization

Sustainable Harvest International is a non-profit organization based in mid-coast Maine, USA. Established in May 1997, its initial mission statement was spelt out in the following terms:

SHI provides farmers and communities in the tropics with long-term assistance implementing environmentally and economically sustainable technologies. Our mission is to reverse environmental degradation by helping rural inhabitants restore ecological stability and sustainable economic productivity to overexploited lands.

Since its foundation, SHI has helped more than 1,000 families and 84 schools in 91 communities in Honduras, Panamá, Belize and Nicaragua to plant more than 2,108,194 trees, build wood-conserving stoves, develop irrigation and composting systems, and build biogas digesters to provide fuel for cooking stoves. In Nicaragua alone, 60 families in six communities are scheduled to be added in the fiscal year 2008. Assistance is provided by locally-based SHI employees, formerly known as 'extensionists',[1] each of whom works intensively with families in a group of villages. The field trainer's role is to introduce new, sustainable land-use practices and agro-forestry techniques that can replace traditional 'slash-and-burn' agriculture. In some areas, for instance, field trainers have helped farmers develop rice paddies, which is a more efficient and environmentally sustainable agricultural practice.

SHI's efforts are intended to both improve the well-being of local communities and simultaneously protect rainforests from slash-and-burn agriculture. Tropical rainforests are found throughout the earth's equatorial zone and contain some of the planet's oldest ecosystems. It is estimated that they cover between 7 and 12 per cent of the earth's surface and are home to over 50 per cent of the world's species. Tropical rainforests are stratified in three to five layers: evergreen woody vegetation with a tall and typically closed upper canopy 30–50m above the ground; woody vines called lianas that can exceed 20cm in diameter; an understorey of seedlings and herbaceous plants; and an epiphyte community, such as orchids, that grows on the trunks and branches of larger trees. Such forests are also a rich source of biodiversity, new plant sources and numerous medicinal compounds.

One of the threats to the rainforest is slash-and-burn agriculture. Local farmers, seeking better land for growing crops, cut a section of forest and burn the fallen debris. The ashes enrich the soil, but the smoke adds to air pollution and, in a dry year, the fires sometimes spread widely. In some areas, the forest quickly regrows. Unfortunately, in other areas, the underlying layer of soil is

---

1   The term 'extensionist' is a common one used for employees that provide agricultural services and development organizations in Central America. At the end of fiscal year 2007, their title was changed to 'field trainers' to make their function clearer to contributors.

thin. Once the trees are cut, and the soil used for farming for a few years, the nutrients are lost and the land becomes vulnerable to soil erosion, which in turn can contribute to watershed degradation.

Agro-forestry, which includes planting varieties of trees that will enrich and stabilize the soil, and setting up nurseries to supply trees for planting are both key elements of SHI's programme. Depending on the country and the area, farmers might be encouraged to plant leucaena for firewood and mulch, hardwoods such as mahogany and cedar for timber, and shrubs such as cacao and coffee for cash crops.

Another important component of SHI's programme is the provision of long-term assistance. Field trainers only go into communities that have invited SHI to come and help, so as to ensure that they only form partnerships with people who share SHI's perception that ecological change is needed. The field trainer works with the farmers in a village for as long as necessary, to ensure that the farmers thoroughly understand and realize the benefit of the new techniques. SHI's involvement has expanded to include not only the sustainability measures referred to above, but also, at the request of the participants, help in finding appropriate markets, forming cooperatives and the provision of business assistance through micro-enterprise loan funds for women and community loan funds through its Rural Loan Fund Program.

Evolving Partnerships

SHI is organized along country lines. The organization originally worked with a local partner non-government organization (NGO) with a complementary mission: the Fundación Ecologista Hector Rodrigo Pastor Fasquelle (FEHRPF) in Honduras, EcoProyectos in Panama, Plenty International (Belize) Limited and the Fundación de Desarollo Sostenible (FUNDESO) in Nicaragua (see Table 16.1). Working with a NGO partner provided local connections and knowledge. The NGO partner also used the funds sent by SHI to take care of payroll and local expenses, saving SHI from having to deal with exchange rates and local administrative issues, but requiring a payment for these services.

Soon after its founding, Florence Reed began to envision a multistage model for fostering social entrepreneurs. Instead of simply operating one organization, she argued that SHI could in fact become an 'incubator' that set up operations in a country (Stage I), encouraged them to grow larger and become

Table 16.1   SHI partner organizations, 2003

Country	Honduras	Panama	Belize	Nicaragua
Partner	FEHRPF	EcoProyectos	Plenty International Limited	FUNDESO
Emphasis	Environmental protection and manages national park	Environmental protection	Village-based international development	Community development

more autonomous with a lead field trainer (Stage II), and then eventually graduate to an independent, affiliate status (Stage III). The multistage growth model has been implemented separately by each country to meet its unique needs. SHI has been successful in nurturing the formation of country NGOs to take on the responsibility and management of local operations. Three of the four programmes (Honduras, Nicaragua and Belize) have successfully legally incorporated as NGOs in their respective countries (see Table 16.2).

Table 16.2   SHI Central American organizational structure, 2008

Country	Honduras	Panama	Belize	Nicaragua
Affiliate/Partner Organization	FUCOHSO (FUndación COsecha SOstenible Honduras)	CEMAD (Centro de Estudios para el Medio Ambiente y el Desarrollo	Sustainable Harvest International – Belize (SHI-B)	FUNCOS (FUndación Nicaraguense COsecha Sostenible)
Status	Honduran NGO	Cooperating NGO	Belizean NGO	Nicaraguan NGO

A continuing element for SHI is a commitment to run a 'skeletal' organization, devoting as much of its revenues as possible to its mission. Its website (www. sustainableharvest.org) proudly states that 'we plant over 10 trees for every dollar donated to our program'. For fiscal year 2007, administrative expenses were 8 per cent of the total budget, with fundraising accounting for another 12 per cent. The SHI headquarters staff is deliberately lean, as of fiscal year 2007 consisting of founder and President Florence Reed, Executive Vice President Greg Field, Outreach Director Sarah Kennedy and Development Coordinator Christina Becherer. Program Director Greg Bowles and Central American Coordinator Mercedes Alvarez divide their time between the field and the United States.

The establishment of the position of Central American coordinator has allowed the president to devote more time to planning, administration and fundraising. The Central American coordinator is responsible for training, supervision and reporting from the field, and works closely with the field program director.

SHI's budget, along with its staff, has increased substantially over the ten years since its founding. During its first fiscal year, SHI raised $14,000 from 20 donors. In fiscal year 2007 the organization raised $1.1 million from more than 1,500 donors, primarily individuals, groups and small foundations; for two years, SHI has had a four-star (exceptional) rating from Charity Navigator, the largest evaluator of NGOs. Only 14 per cent of the organizations rated have received four stars for two years or more. Flo's personal contacts remain a core source of donors. Other revenue-generating activities include the website, speaking engagements, appeals through the organizational newsletter *La Cosecha*, and an annual fundraising dinner.

Another source of revenue is Smaller World Trips, operated by SHI, which bring interested parties and potential contributors to work with communities and see firsthand the results of SHI's work. When Smaller World Tours was launched in fiscal year 2005 the original intention was to increase cultural understanding and empower the global community to create a more equitable and sustainable world. Working side-by-side with local staff and families resulted in participants returning home with a strong connection to SHI's programmes. This connection is evidenced by the increasing percentage of travellers who become donors; rising from 42 per cent in financial year 2005 to 93 per cent by financial year 2007.

SHI is also engaged in several co-marketing agreements, including Grounds for Sharing/Thanksgiving Coffee (a supplier of fairly traded, shade-grown organic coffee), Robin's Chocolate, and Wicks 'n' More (a candle retailer). SHI has not received any funding from governments or large foundations because of the restrictions they impose: many foundations and governmental organizations emphasize short-term achievement of specific objectives, whereas Flo considers SHI's success to be based on flexible and integrative projects targeted to specific local needs.

Ecopreneurship in Action at Sustainable Harvest International

Ecopreneurship at SHI originates from the top. Florence Reed's interest in Central America became established in her years at university, where her varied activities included membership of the Committee on Central America, People for a Free South Africa and her role in founding an environmental group. Graduating in June 1990 with a double major in International Studies and Environmental Conservation, plus a minor in Spanish, she worked in a restaurant and babysat while waiting for a Peace Corps assignment. After intensive training in Spanish and agro-forestry in Costa Rica, which began in February 1991, she was assigned to Panama. It was here that she first saw the devastated countryside where the tropical forests had been cut down. Her Peace Corps job was to work with local farmers to plant trees. The trees helped to stabilize the soil, preventing further erosion and loss of water.

After her two years were up, Flo and a friend from the Corps investigated the possibility of setting up their own organization in Panama, to expand on the work they had been doing. They were forced to give up their ecopreneurship idea when the local company that employed them unexpectedly went out of business. In 1993 Flo came back to the United States where, as she put it, 'I wanted to find a job with an organization doing what I had planned on doing in Panama, but couldn't find any such organization' (quoted in Naumes and Kammermeyer 2002). She then worked for several non-profits over several years. One, whose mission was to plant trees around the world, hired her as the coordinator for Central American programmes. In that role, she developed plans for a tree-planting and training programme in Honduras. However, the executive director denied final approval of her project, telling her to focus on raising money instead. Frustrated with her inability to follow through on her environmental idealism, she resigned in April 1997. As Flo explained:

> I had been thinking for years about the possibility of starting an organization of my own. This was sort of the final straw for me, deciding that nobody else was actually doing what I wanted to be doing. And now I also felt that I had made a commitment to two Hondurans, who I had hired, and to a number of communities and farming families who we had made plans to work with. These people were counting on this to happen. (Quoted in Naumes and Kammermeyer 2002)

Initial funding providently arrived on the day she resigned, in the form of a cheque from a young man in Switzerland. He had met Flo a few weeks earlier in Panama, where she had shown him her work. Now, hearing her plans for the new organization, he sent her $6,000 as venture capital. Flo immediately sent half directly to Honduras, to provide about three months' pay for the extension agents that she had recruited while still an employee of the previous organization. She used the remaining half for other start-up expenses.

Sustainable Harvest International was incorporated as a not-for-profit organization in May 1997. The two Honduran field trainers worked with 16 communities in north-east Honduras, near the Guatemalan border. During the dry season, they helped farmers develop tree nurseries with over 100,000 seedlings of many tree species, which were transplanted to farms and community land during the rainy season. The trees were to provide watershed protection, erosion control, soil improvements and shade, as well as (eventually) firewood. The field trainers also taught programme participants to build wood-conserving stoves that used 80 per cent less firewood than the traditional process of cooking over an open fire.

The multistage model envisioned by Flo Reed was built around the work of the field trainers at the community level. As the number of communities and field trainers increased within a country, a lead field trainer would be appointed to coordinate local activities. All field trainers receive training from SHI, and 'best practices' are shared across country programmes as well as communities. The transition of a country's programme to a separate NGO would enable more effective locally-based programmes and fundraising. SHI continues to provide technical assistance and training, as well as some financial assistance.

Two aspects of this multistage approach are especially important in fostering ecopreneurship through the SHI framework. First, Flo always expected that SHI would continue to seek new opportunities. The creation of independent, ultimately self-sufficient country programmes would allow the parent organization (SHI) to free up resources that it could then invest in other new opportunities. Second, increased independence would allow the various country programmes to develop and try their own ideas. An example was the addition in Honduras of a field trainer specializing in rural micro-business. Although the rural loan programme was established by SHI, the micro-business position allowed communities to develop and implement ideas that could meet particular local needs. The farmers, who have adopted sustainable agricultural practices to replace slash and burn, are not interested in remaining at the subsistence farming level. Helping them develop cash crops and marketing opportunities both encourages them to continue their green activities and entices neighbours to explore the potential of adopting similar techniques.

Ecopreneurship is continually pushed at all levels of the organization. Programme decisions are made from the bottom up. Dinis Morales, a Nicaraguan field trainer, describes his experience, which is shared by other field trainers: 'In the short time I have been with the organization, I have noted (that) there is not a lot of bureaucracy. It is we, the extensionists, who decide together with the farmers the things to do' (SHI 2002, p. 8).[2]

There is no question that the success of ecopreneurship at the local level is heavily due to the background and enthusiasm of the field trainers. Virtually all of the field trainers were already interested in or actively practicing sustainable agriculture before joining SHI, as Morales exemplifies: 'I am currently working with Sustainable Harvest International on issues that I have been working with throughout my life: environmental and human sustainability, helping the poor *campesinos* increasing their incomes, and giving a new light to their vision' (SHI 2002, p. 8).

Several field trainers have degrees in agriculture, and all have received additional training through SHI and elsewhere. All were ecologically-oriented before they met Flo Reed; SHI has enabled them to become entrepreneurial as well, through their teaching and programme development. As an example, a field trainer in a Mayan village in Belize, in conjunction with his sister, started an agricultural programme of organic gardening in a local school. Students from the project also received a $3,000 grant from the Ministry of Agriculture, developed an organic production plot and found an ongoing commercial buyer for their entire crop.

Like the Belizean school children, some of the farmers themselves are now becoming entrepreneurs. They are actively seeking markets for surplus crops. In several areas, they are participating in growers' cooperatives or community loan programmes. Although these activities may be primarily based on economics, the result is that farmers remain committed to sustainable practices that in turn are good for the environment.

The farmers, in their quest for an increased standard of living, are green, if only as a consequence of their quest. They are analogous to Walley's and Taylor's (2002) 'opportunistic entrepreneurs' in the for-profit sector. The micro-projects that farmers have become involved with because of their association with SHI are varied. As of fiscal year 2007, projects included 1,900 tree nurseries, over 220 fish ponds, 60 biodigesters, more than 1,000 compost projects, 190 worm composting projects, 190 irrigation projects, 77 grain silos, 13 community seed banks, 6 mills, 140 animal husbandry projects and 160 schools with more than 7,000 class contacts per quarter.

---

2   All quotes from the field trainers and programme participants are translations throughout.

Panamanian field trainer Daysbeth Lopez sees her work with SHI as a way to give back to the community:

> I have lived in this area all my life, so my professional background and employment with SHI fit perfectly with what I wanted to do within my community. I truly appreciate the opportunity to offer what I have learned to the families of the place where I'm from. I help them with any difficulties they encounter in production using sustainable methods, soil management and protection of the environment. I want to thank SHI for what it does in Panama, and for giving me the opportunity to contribute to that. (SHI 2006, p. 9)

The Impact of SHI

Sustainable Harvest has grown substantially since its inception. In its first year, SHI served 16 communities with Flo Reed and two field trainers in Honduras.

Ten years later, SHI included 1,242 families working in over 80 communities with 36 in-country employees. In addition to the field trainers, three countries have microbusiness/finance coordinators and all programmes have administrative assistants, internalizing the services formerly provided by partners (see Table 16.3).

Table 16.3   SHI programme statistics, February 2008

Country	Honduras Affiliate	Panama Affiliate	Belize Affiliate	Nicaragua Affiliate
Years with SHI	10	9	8	7
Communities	42	9	16	14
Families	548	164	350	180
Country employees – field	10	4	7	7
Country employees – administration and field	3	1	1	3

The scope of SHI's services has expanded in response to meeting the participating farmers' needs. While some of their output is directly used to improve family nutrition, surpluses are often available for sale. With the field trainers' help, farmers have also planted crops specifically for market. SHI has helped to organize ten growers' cooperatives, to enable farmers to earn better prices for their products. SHI staff have also identified new customers and markets, including habanero peppers for Marie Sharps (a Belizean hot sauce company), Tabasco peppers in Honduras and organic cacao in Belize that is now supplied to the UK chocolate producer Green & Black's. SHI has also helped set up several women's collectives, primarily in Honduras, whose projects have included baking bread to sell locally, growing annatto to make into a paste for local cooks, and producing herbs that can be processed and sold as natural medicines. In addition, the number of community loan funds set up for its participants by SHI has grown from 15 to 23 in four years. As a result of the improved agricultural productivity and marketing efforts, family farm incomes of participants have increased by as much as 2,000 per cent.

The initial Central American coordinator, who had started with SHI as an extensionist in 1999, gave his view of SHI's growth:

> This (growth) was possible (because of) three aspects. (First,) the support that the families give to SHI extensionists and the different activities that SHI promotes in the communities. Second, the dedication of the extensionists (who) work hard, (putting in) overtime and holidays to carry out an excellent job. (Third,) the financial support that the people of (the) United States and other countries give to carry out activities. (SHI 2002, p. 3)

A measure of SHI's global impact is the several thousand requests for help that the organization has received. These come from many sources, including farmers and neighbouring communities who are not currently participating in SHI's local programmes. In addition, Flo Reed has received requests from individuals, communities and potential partner organizations from South America, Africa and Asia. In 2003 Flo and SHI were nominated for an environmental impact award from the World Association of Non-Government Organizations (WANGO). In recent years she has received an honorary doctorate for her work, along with many awards such as the Yves Rocher Women of the Earth award, Traditional Home's Classic Woman award and Etown's E-chievement award. Clearly, recognition of the impact of SHI's programmes has now extended well beyond Central America.

Future Challenges and Opportunities

Like many other entrepreneurial organizations, one of the significant issues raised by SHI's success is how to continue to grow while maintaining the mission. On one side, there is continued pressure from participating farmers for more support services. Although providing this is consistent with SHI's mission, expanding economic and marketing services creates some difficulties and costs for the organization. It requires changing staff skills at both the local and organizational level, since the focus until now has been primarily agricultural. In Honduras, the expanded services have required the addition of a specialist in rural micro-business, rather than expanding the role of the field trainers. The challenge is to meet this need without diverting too much attention from SHI's role as an ecopreneurial change agent.

An alternative way of expanding SHI would be to maintain its current range of services, and simply extend them to new geographic areas. Communities in other Central American countries, such as Guatemala and El Salvador, have already requested assistance; and there are also many other parts of the world where the rainforest is vulnerable to slash-and-burn agriculture and where SHI's expertise would be beneficial. Even within the countries currently serviced, there are many areas that do not have a field trainer. However, SHI's focus has continued to be on providing additional depth in the countries they already serve.

The major challenge for SHI, like many young organizations, continues to be revenue generation. As noted above, there are many more requests for SHI's services than resources available to meet them. The organization has successfully cut costs, most recently by moving its headquarters to rural Maine. (However, this can also give rise to some unforeseen problems. For example, since much of SHI's funds are raised through personal contact, revenues may be limited by the staff's ability to interact with current and potential donors.) The decision to concentrate on small donors amplifies the demands on staff members' time, and potentially raises the fundraising cost per donated dollar. SHI is engaged in some cause-related marketing, primarily through its website, but on a small scale. A big boost to their cause-related marketing was their participation in Stonyfield Farm's 'Bid with your Lid' programme, giving them exposure to Stonyfield's yoghurt customer base as well as a guaranteed minimum donation from the company.

The Stonyfield Farms promotion is an example of the synergies that could be developed with other, even for-profit, organizations with similar goals. Stonyfield has a long history of concern for healthy food and a healthy environment, pledging 10 per cent of its profits 'to organizations and products that work to protect and restore the earth' (www.Stonyfield.com/Earth Action). As green marketing increases in importance, ecopreneurs such as Samuel

Kaymen, one of the founders of Stonyfield Farms, look for innovation and synergies between and within the private and NGO sectors. Relationships can also be developed with the increasing number of ecology and sustainability programmes offered by schools and universities including Earth University (Costa Rica) which focuses on Central America.

Conclusion

Sustainable Harvest International has been a significant force for change in the villages that it serves in Central America. Although definitions of entrepreneurship are generally written with for-profit organizations in mind, SHI clearly meets Schaper's definition (2002, p. 27) of successful entrepreneurship: '(It) requires individuals and organisations to embrace a cohesive process of planning and idea development, the marshalling of resources, finance sourcing, the adoption of creative and innovative techniques and the taking of calculated risks.' Flo's commitment to her initial vision, even before start-up funding was available, is one of many instances where she has taken risks in the interest of her mission. From inception, SHI has had a plan for its continued growth and self-renewal. Its use of local field trainers, while perhaps building on traditional agricultural agent models, has led to innovation amongst farmers and villages.

An important balancing act for the organization has been the need to work intensively with each group of farmers over a long period of time and yet to find ways to expand its work, given scarce resources. The primary limitation on growth has been revenues; without an increase in revenue there can be no expansion of its mission. The multistage model for programme development within a country is innovative. It enables Flo Reed and SHI to remain entrepreneurial even as the organization grows in size and complexity. As country programmes mature, they are expected to become more self-sufficient, both in decision-making and fundraising. This process not only frees up funds to be invested in new areas and programmes, but also allows SHI to remain focused on the start-up and early growth phases that plant the seeds for local ecopreneurship. Decentralized decision-making also allows and encourages the field trainers to innovate so that they can meet the specific needs of their areas. Their work with farmers and schools is leading to radical change and greening in the agricultural technology of their villages.

SHI clearly exemplifies an organization that is concerned with the triple bottom line of social, environmental and economic impact. Its primary focus is, and has always been, protecting the environment, specifically the rainforests. To carry out this mission, it has needed to work with subsistence farmers to change their agricultural practices from slash and burn to sustainable agriculture. This change has had a profound impact on the farmers' standard of living. Even non-profit organizations have to be concerned with the economic bottom line. There must be sufficient revenues to cover the costs. However, for SHI the monetary results are merely the means to an end.

Currently, SHI's work is concentrated in four Central American countries which contain a relatively small part of the world's tropical rainforests. Even if the organization chooses not to expand out of this geographic region, SHI's model has excellent potential for adoption in other regions, both in terms of the use of locally-based field trainers and in terms of the multistage country model. In a for-profit organization, sharing technology or programmes would create competitors and would therefore be undesirable because it would reduce market share. There is some evidence that this is not a concern for non-profits, who in many cases appear to view imitation not as a threat, but as helping to further the social values embodied in their mission (Naumes, Kammermeyer and Naumes 2003). For ecopreneurs and other social entrepreneurs, it isn't market share that counts; it's 'social value share'. The more organizations that are working towards the same goal of sustainability, the more likely it is that sustainability will actually be achieved.

Regardless of its future direction, Sustainable Harvest International has created local ecopreneurs in Central America. Extensive training and decision-making authority have enabled the field trainers to confidently put their environmental ideals into practice. Consequently, local organizations are being created that can continue to find new ways of carrying out an ecological mission, even though the focus may shift somewhat towards economics (that is, raising living standards). On the individual level, farmers are likely to continue the use of sustainable agricultural techniques, as long as their standard of living improves. Kruger (1998, p. 174) sums up this challenge in the following way: 'Individuals need to perceive a prospective new course of action as a credible opportunity, which requires the opportunity to not just be viable, but be perceived as viable.'

One way of creating such perceptions is by delivering a higher family income, improved nutrition, and successful agricultural techniques for the families who participate in SHI programmes. This, in turn, provides an impetus for neighbours and colleagues to adopt similar agricultural practices, thus creating and sustaining ecological benefits without needing to be personally entrepreneurial. This view is supported by Schaper who argues that:

> By demonstrating the economic benefits that come from being greener, ecopreneurs act as a 'pull' factor that entices other firms to proactively go green, in contrast to the 'push' factors of government regulation and stakeholder or lobby-group pressure. (Schaper 2002, p. 27)

In response to its expanded role in creating sustainable communities by fostering ecopreneurship, SHI modified its mission statement in 2003:

> Sustainable Harvest International (SHI) is building a global network of local partners working toward environmental, economic and social sustainability. SHI facilitates long-term collaboration among trained local staff, farmers and communities to implement sustainable land-use practices that alleviate poverty by restoring ecological stability.

The organization's success in carrying out this mission and in establishing local ecopreneurship is perhaps best summarized in a quote from Nicaraguan participant, German Lira:

> I have the support of SHI with the work on my farm and am planting areas of my land with trees so that in the future I will not have to take trees from the forest for lumber. I also have started nurseries of cedar and mahogany with the objective of reforesting the area around my community's watershed so that the water sources will be protected for future generations (SHI 2007, p. 4).

References

Dees, J.G. (1998) 'The Meaning of Social Entrepreneurship', Center for the Advancement of Social Entrepreneurship, The Fuqua School of Business, Duke University, at: http://www.caseatduke.org/documents/dees_sedef.pdf.

Dees, J.G., Emerson, J. and Economy, P. (2001) *Enterprising Nonprofits: A Toolkit for Social Entrepreneurs*, John Wiley & Sons, Inc., New York.

Kruger, N. (1998) 'Encouraging the Identification of Environmental Opportunities.' *Journal of Organizational Change Management*, Vol. 11, No. 2, pp. 174–183.

Naumes, M.J., Kammermeyer, J.A. and Naumes, W. (2003). 'The Impact of Management Changes and Growth on Social Entrepreneurship in Not-For-Profit Organizations', paper presented at the annual meeting of the World Association for Case Method Research and Application (WACRA), Bordeaux, France, July 2003.

Naumes, M.J. and Kammermeyer, J.A. (2002) 'Sustainable Harvest International', *Case Research Journal*, Vol. 22 (Spring), pp. 47–70.

Say, J.B. (1803) *A Treatise on Political Economy; or, The production, Distribution and Consumption of Wealth*, Volume 2, Claxton, Remsen & Haggelfinger, Philadelphia. Fourth edn translated by C.R. Princep (1880).

Schaper, M. (2002) 'The Essence of Ecopreneurship', *Greener Management International*, Vol. 38 (Summer), pp. 26–30.

Schumpeter, J.A. (1950) *Capitalism, Socialism and Democracy* (3rd edn), Harper & Row, New York.

Stonyfield Farms (2008) at: http://www.stonyfield.com (accessed February 2008).

Sustainable Harvest International (2002) *The View from the Field: Annual Report Fiscal Year 2002*, SHI, Portsmouth, NH. www.sustainableharvest.org

Sustainable Harvest International (2006) *Planting Hope, Restoring Forests, Nourishing Communities: Annual Report Fiscal Year 2006*, SHI, Surry, ME. www.sustainableharvest.org

Sustainable Harvest International (2007) *Planting Hope, Restoring Forests, Nourishing Communities: Annual Report Fiscal Year 2007*, SHI, Surry, ME. www.sustainableharvest.org

Walley, E.E. and Taylor, D. (2002) 'Opportunists, Champions, Mavericks…? A Typology of Green Entrepreneurs', *Greener Management International*, Vol. 38 (Summer), pp. 31–43.

17

Sustainability Entrepreneurship: Organizational Innovation at *Native*Energy

Bradley D. Parrish

ABSTRACT

This chapter presents an empirical case study of successful sustainability entrepreneurship. Specifically, it considers the extent to which innovations in organizing, as opposed to innovations in technology, contribute to sustainable development. For the purposes of this chapter, 'organizing' is understood as 'both the prescribed frameworks and realized configurations of interaction' that constitute an enterprise's structures and processes (Ranson, Hinings and Greenwood 1980, p. 3). An in-depth case study of the design and development of *Native*Energy, a US-based company that is a leading example of successful sustainability entrepreneurship, is used to investigate this question. This case demonstrates that innovations in organizing can determine the nature, extent, and effectiveness of change for sustainable development, as well as who reaps the benefits it affords. But organizational design innovations can also create difficulty for entrepreneurs because those designs do not align with existing institutional arrangements. The chapter concludes by suggesting that the value of sustainability entrepreneurs lies in their role as social change agents who embrace the full range of means and ends for sustainable development.

Entrepreneurship and Sustainable Development

The importance of entrepreneurship to sustainable development is perhaps not immediately obvious because in common practice the means and ends of sustainable development are reduced to an 'enviro-tech' paradigm (see Parrish 2007). In this paradigm, the problem of sustainability is seen primarily as one of environmental degradation and its solution as the development of new technologies. This places scientists, technologists and inventors at the forefront of the quest for sustainable development. Private enterprise is valued primarily for its research and development function, which is financed by the prospect of commercializing new technologies. With the exception of a few high-tech start-ups in the environmental services sector, entrepreneurship plays no obvious role in this process.

However, the 'enviro-tech' paradigm is a misleading simplification of sustainable development. In reality, the ends embodied by the concept of sustainable development include not only continued human survival, with its emphasis on biophysical systems, but also meaningful improvements in the human experience of life on earth. As Elgin insightfully observes, 'If we do no more than work for a sustainable future, then we are in danger of creating a world in which living is little more than "only not dying"' (1994, p. 235). Sustainable development is as much about *developmentalism* as it is about *environmentalism* (Kottak 1999). Thus human progress, understood as a qualitative improvement in the experience of life on earth, is central to the concept. The 'enviro-tech' paradigm also emphasizes the physical artefacts of human activity (technology) to the exclusion of social artefacts, such as institutions and organizations. The critical role such social artefacts play in either exacerbating or ameliorating the biophysical and experiential challenges to sustainable development are increasingly recognized (Norgaard 1994; Western 2001). As depicted in Figure 17.1, a more complete understanding of sustainable development must extend the means and ends from the limits of the 'enviro-tech' paradigm, as represented by the lower-left quadrant, to include the full range of means and ends, as represented by the full spectrum of all four quadrants.

With this fuller understanding of sustainable development the importance of entrepreneurship becomes much more evident. While inventors of new technologies introduce novelty to the left side of the spectrum, entrepreneurs – innovators of human organization – introduce novelty to the right side. This diagram also demonstrates why social, environmental and sustainability entrepreneurship should not be conflated. Environmental entrepreneurs combine innovations in human organization with available technologies to address the biophysical challenges to sustainable development (lower quadrants of the spectrum). Social entrepreneurs combine innovations in human organization and technologies to directly improve human quality of life (upper quadrants of the spectrum). Sustainability entrepreneurship is unique in addressing the full spectrum of sustainable development within a

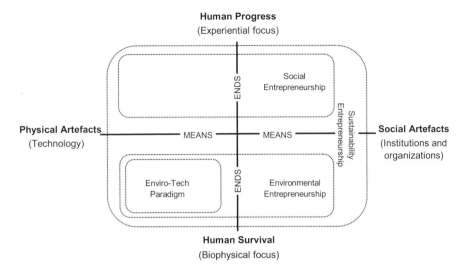

Figure 17.1   Means–ends paradigm for sustainable development
Source: Adapted from Parrish (2007).

single venture. The question is: to what extent do innovations in organizing, as opposed to innovations in technology, actually contribute to sustainable development?

In exploring this question, I use an in-depth case study of the design and development of *Native*Energy, a leading example of successful sustainability entrepreneurship, to investigate the importance of organizational innovations for advancing sustainable development. This study is based on a concept of entrepreneurship as a form of expertise (Sarasvathy 2001) or 'maturity' (Thorpe et al. 2006) in which the practical and mostly intuitive knowledge and abilities of entrepreneurs are used to co-produce new opportunities and new possibilities through skilful interpretation and interaction with changing social and ecological contexts (Dimov 2007; McMullen and Shepherd 2006; Sarason, Dean and Dillard 2006). The unfolding process of organizational design through which the founders of *Native*Energy constructed their enterprise is described in the next sections.[1] This is followed by an examination of how the entrepreneurs' innovative solutions to the challenges they faced impacted on their ability to contribute to sustainable development. The chapter concludes with a discussion of the value of sustainability entrepreneurship to sustainable development.

---

1   This case study is based on analysis of more than ten hours of multiple stakeholder interviews and over 70 pages of primary documents.

Introducing *Native*Energy

*Native*Energy is a private, for-profit, US-based enterprise that retails carbon offsets[2] and renewable energy credits to consumers and businesses, and finances the development of new renewable energy projects that are owned by Native Americans,[3] family farmers and local communities. The company pioneered a new business model that supports the construction of new renewable energy projects and the economic development of socially and economically marginalized communities. Founded in 2000, within seven years *Native*Energy had 15 employees based in the company's Vermont headquarters, while its operations spanned the entire United States, including projects with Alaskan Native villages. The company is recognized as a leader in the industry.[4] A recent study of carbon offset retailers from around the world ranked *Native*Energy among the top in the industry for quality of offsets and second in total number of offsets sold (Clean Air – Cool Planet 2006). The company's reputation has led to partnerships with leading 'ethical' brands, such as Ben & Jerry's, Clif Bar and Stonyfield Farm, and to the company being selected as the sole offsets provider for the production and promotion of Al Gore's film on climate change, *An Inconvenient Truth*. In August 2005 *Native*Energy became majority-owned by some of its Native American tribal partners. At that time, the company's governing board was changed to include a Native American representative in addition to two of the original founders, who remained as company CEO and vice president.

Tracing the Interactive Process of Enterprise Design

THE MAKING OF OPPORTUNITY

The US renewable energy market has historically been driven by regulation. This began to change during the 1990s as deregulation reforms in the energy industry and rising public awareness of air pollution and climate change issues

---

2   'Carbon offsets' are a reduction of CO_2 emissions from one activity equivalent to the emissions generated by another activity. These activities are said to be 'carbon-neutral' because there is no net increase in the carbon content of the atmosphere.

3   The term 'Native American' refers to the indigenous peoples of North America. Native Americans belong to a number of distinct historical and contemporary polities, often termed 'tribes'. Native American tribes have one of the highest rates of persistent poverty in the United States (Beale 1996).

4   As evidence of this, the company's co-founder and CEO was recently called to give expert testimony before the US Congress's select subcommittee on global warming and energy independence.

led to the emergence of consumer demand as a second significant market driver. New, private electric service providers (ESPs), such as Green Mountain Energy Company, entered the market to sell electricity branded as 'green'. As the market began to mature towards the end of the decade, however, the business model of Green Mountain Energy and other ESPs came under public attack by several national environmental groups who charged that consumers were paying a premium for repackaged 'green' energy that already existed. In other words, consumers who were paying price premiums to support the growth of renewable energy alternatives were not in fact contributing to new renewable energy production. Tom Boucher, one of the original founders of Green Mountain Energy, and some other long-time employees of the company were of a similar mind that the market had evolved to a point where much more could be done than simply marketing existing renewable energy. Boucher had spent most of his decades-long career in the energy industry, initially working for conventional energy providers before co-founding Green Mountain Energy to pursue opportunities in the newly deregulated energy markets. After watching the market's continued evolution, Boucher, several years on, felt that there were emerging opportunities to promote the expansion of renewable energy beyond the scope of what even Green Mountain Energy was offering.

At the time, industry insiders were beginning to consider decoupling the environmental attribute of renewable energy from the actual electricity produced as a real possibility (Holt and Bird 2005). Boucher was aware that electricity generation was responsible for only about one-third of the United States' total carbon dioxide emissions and saw potential in the idea of decoupling environmental attributes from physical units of electricity as a way of addressing the range of other activities that result in carbon emissions, such as driving automobiles or heating buildings. When, in May 2000, BP Amoco acquired a significant stake in Green Mountain Energy and the corporate offices moved from Vermont to Texas, this provided the impetus for Boucher and a number of colleagues to leave the company.

FORMING THE ENTERPRISE

Shortly after leaving Green Mountain Energy, Boucher was asked to help develop renewable energy production on Native American tribal lands. This sparked a new and sustained interest for him that would have profound implications for the venture to come. By August of that year Boucher had registered a new enterprise, *Native*Energy, as a private, for-profit company with the intention of building a business model around the idea of decoupling environmental

attributes from electricity and with a new-found interest in using these
opportunities to support Native American communities. Boucher was joined
in this exploratory venture by Tom Stoddard and two other colleagues from
Green Mountain Energy. Stoddard was a corporate lawyer whose interests in
environmental issues first found expression when he joined Green Mountain
Energy's in-house legal team. His decision to join *Native*Energy's founding
team provided an opportunity to place these interests more firmly at the centre
of his professional life. Stoddard and the others were aware that they were
attempting to enter an emerging market that was 'immature, poorly-defined
and of unknown size'. Yet, despite these great uncertainties, they felt compelled
to proceed, as Boucher explained:

> *The picture in my mind was so clear as to the opportunities with this
> evolving market I didn't really pause at stepping out of what I was
> doing and into this because I just felt the opportunity was there and
> someone had to get it going.*[5]

Over the next several months the group worked to devise a new business
model that would address the problems they saw with the existing industry
and embrace the potential they felt existed to make more meaningful
environmental and social contributions. The two biggest problems they saw
hampering the existing renewable energy market were, first, environmental
attributes coupled with physical electricity units were limited by electricity
distribution infrastructure. This meant that environmental attributes were
restricted to electricity consumption and only localized, regional markets
could be established. Second, sales of 'green' energy seldom resulted in the
creation of new renewable energy production. To help finance the construction
of new renewable energy projects suppliers needed long-term contracts for the
environmental attributes they produced (known generically as 'green tags'),
while buyers would agree to only short-term contracts due to the uncertainty
and expected long-term decline in the market price of green tags. The market
value of a single year's green tags were usually worth only about 1.5 per
cent of the project's overall cost. At this level, the environmental attributes of
renewable energy production were insufficient to support new production.
Instead, *Native*Energy's founders were specifically looking for a model that
would result in the construction of new renewable energy projects – the key
to the emerging, consumer-driven, voluntary market – that could be sold to a
national market and, in particular, would support smaller, local projects owned

---

5   All the quotes from Tom Boucher and Tom Stoddard are taken from the author's primary
    research transcripts.

by Native American tribes, family farmers or other economically marginalized communities.

The result of this intense, collaborative effort at idea generation and practical problem-solving was the formulation of a radically new 'forward streams' model unlike anything yet seen in the marketplace. This model was premised on a simple, but significant, innovation: aggregating the annual stream of green tags that a new renewable energy project would produce over the next 15 to 25 years and selling these upfront to consumers at their net present value. On the finance side, this gave developers what they needed: long-term contracts paid upfront. The present value of 15–25 year aggregated streams can account for 20 per cent of project costs, making the green tags an important source of funding for new projects. And since these tags were sold before the projects were built, this upfront income stream significantly reduced the financing costs of construction, making the whole project less expensive overall. On the marketing side, this gave consumers what they wanted: green tags that resulted in the creation of new renewable energy production and the associated additional environmental benefits (known in the industry as 'additionality'). By focusing on smaller-scale projects that would be uneconomic without this additional source of financing, *Native*Energy could make a real contribution to increasing the production of renewable energy. This also fit well with their interest in supporting Native American tribes, family farmers and other community-owned projects that tended to be too small to be economically viable without an additional income stream. Stoddard explained the rationale behind this model:

> We could be described simply as a retail seller of an intangible commodity. As it happens, that commodity can have greater or lesser environmental attributes associated with it. There are two or three dozen marketers who sort of stop there, and we, very deliberately from the beginning, wanted to go beyond that and leverage this intangible commodity as an opportunity to create other kinds of change besides environmental change. And to do that we sort of re-characterized it, if you will, created a new product out of it that does more than simply give more money to large corporate wind farms or the like, and actually enables customers to create real change by financing specific new projects. And then layering further on top of that, what do you do with this new financial tool to create new projects? It seemed to make sense to add on another layer of value, social value, and try to focus on projects in indigenous

communities and family farmer-owned projects that create sustainable
economic benefits for communities in need.

ENTERING THE MARKET

The group of entrepreneurs developed a business plan around this model and
went searching for investors. By the summer of 2001, however, they had yet to
obtain any significant financial support for their venture. Stoddard described
the challenges they faced in attempting to enter a new market with a new
business model:

> *You know, we were talking to investors that had never heard of green*
> *tags. And we were talking to them about this different kind of green*
> *tags. We had no customers; we had no website; we had no supply; we*
> *had nothing other than a concept, and a strange one at that. You know,*
> *you're selling something that doesn't exist to people who, when they*
> *buy it, they don't actually see it or touch it; even when the project does*
> *exist or comes into being, they don't get a tangible product. That's not*
> *an easy sell to a venture capitalist.*

Before any investment was secured, or a first sale could be made, lack of
income and conflicts of interest forced two of the four founders to step away
from the venture. This left Boucher and Stoddard as the only remaining
founders, along with an increasingly committed team of employees, to carry
on. Thus the decision was made to proceed without any external funding. As
Boucher explained:

> *So we finally said, 'enough of this'. Decided just to do it ... [But without*
> *funding] this has been a very painful five years based on having to*
> *basically create the earnings to pay for the operations when you're*
> *trying to start up and grow.*

In early November 2001, *Native*Energy entered the green tags market with
'WindBuilders', a single product offered exclusively over the company's website.
Because the company was specifically targeting the voluntary consumer market,
WindBuilders was initially offered as a membership programme in which
customers would sign up to offset 12 tons of carbon emissions by committing to
purchase green tags over the course of a year. As Boucher and Stoddard gained
experience in the marketplace, however, they discovered that customers were
wary of committing to ongoing financial obligations. Over time, they gradually

reduced the unit sizes on offer and shifted to a more sophisticated marketing approach that built on their unique business model.

In addition to decoupling environmental attributes from physical energy units, the *Native*Energy entrepreneurs further innovated in their marketing by recoupling these attributes to other products and associated activities that generate carbon emissions. They took one product, green tags, and created multiple brands to target specific market segments, such as CoolHome, CoolDriver, CoolBusiness, CoolTour and so on, even creating a CoolWedding certificate for carbon-neutral weddings. They then established relationships with well-known 'ethical' brands to couple the green tags with their products as small add-ons. For example, customers buying *Native*Energy offsets as gifts were given the option to include a free pint of Ben & Jerry's ice cream. This strategy in particular enabled Boucher and Stoddard to realize their goal of raising public awareness that lifestyle activities other than just electricity use are important sources of carbon emissions, while also helping them increase market penetration.

Selling to, and partnering with, established companies with strong ethical reputations became a central component of Boucher's and Stoddard's strategy to establish a presence in the market. In addition to creating brand awareness, the founders sought to build consumer trust by showing they had earned the trust of these well-respected leaders in ethical business. They had discovered early on that customers were sceptical of buying green tags from a for-profit business. They initially considered organizing as a non-profit entity, but felt that the level of financing the venture required could only reasonably be provided by private investment. Particularly because of this consumer scepticism, they take reputation and trust very seriously. One way of building this trust is by obtaining third-party verification of the quality of their green tags. However, the 'forward streams' model they developed was so unconventional for the industry that it could not be accommodated by most existing certification schemes. The need for strong partnerships with reputable companies was therefore even more pressing. As Andy Perkins, one of the early entrepreneurial collaborators explained, corporate customers are in a better position to appreciate the significance of *Native*Energy's unique products:

> *One of the strategies that's been very important for Tom [Boucher] is to deal with companies who actually understand the issues, and you have a much different conversation in a business sell. And they're willing to dig into the issues and want to do something for their own*

environmental reasons. [Then] when you put that list of companies in
front of someone and say, 'Well, these are the people, this is the kind of
company that does this', it builds some credibility and acceptance at the
consumer level as well.'

PARTNERING WITH TRIBES

Boucher and Stoddard initially had some trouble securing development
partners who were willing to work on tribal-owned wind projects. Native
Americans are US citizens, though Native American tribes recognized by the US
federal government retain sovereign status and are governed by independent
tribal governments. Tribal sovereignty is relegated to specific geographic areas
that are either remnants of a tribe's historical territory or, in some cases, are
even historically unrelated areas of often marginal land. The prospect of tribal
politics, an additional layer of bureaucracy, and the cultural differences that
come with working inside a sovereign tribal nation were enough to deter most
private developers. Because of this, Boucher and Stoddard had to settle for a
farmer-owned wind project in South Dakota for their first sale of green tags
in 2001. However, that project was delayed after some of the green tags had
already been sold. *Native*Energy had a legal obligation to replace those tags
with a new wind project, and so in April 2002 they took the opportunity to
negotiate an agreement with the Rosebud Sioux Nation, located on the border
between South Dakota and Nebraska. The project was for a single 750-kw wind
turbine to serve as a demonstration and capacity-building project for a group of
mid-western US tribes. This project was partially financed by a US Department
of Energy grant, but needed additional revenue to make construction of the
turbine economically viable.

This project brought the *Native*Energy entrepreneurs together with another
entrepreneurial group of opportunity seekers – officers of the Intertribal Council
on Utility Policy (COUP). This council was established as a collaborative effort
by five mid-western US tribes to explore opportunities in the energy industry.
By the late 1990s COUP had set its sights on the wind energy market, as it
estimated that wind on tribal reservations had the potential to produce enough
energy to power 50 million homes every year. Yet despite this potential, the
Native American communities were cautious about commercializing one of
their resources. As Bob Gough, Secretary of COUP, explained:

In fact I remember talking to some reporter and – we needed to ask
permission from the wind itself, to use the wind. It was done in

*ceremonies and prayer offerings and – and that just surprised them.
They were sure none of the other wind developers went and asked
the wind for permission. And I remember being amazed by that, and
surprised that they were surprised. Now it's surprising, right. Now you
have to ask EPA [Environmental Protection Agency] or FAA [Federal
Aviation Administration], or somebody.*

The project did go forward, and in 2003 the Rosebud turbine became
*Native*Energy's first tangible success in its effort to use the voluntary consumer
market to drive the construction of new renewable energy production.
Through this experience, Boucher and Stoddard established a relationship
with the Rosebud Sioux Tribe and the officers of COUP that was characterized
by mutual trust and deep respect; so much so that discussions soon turned to
the tribes taking an ownership stake in *Native*Energy. Boucher and Stoddard
were keen on the idea, as it was a natural extension of their own vision for
the company. However, practical realities again proved challenging. The tribes
with which *Native*Energy was working were some of the poorest in the nation,
and diverting tribal funds from social programmes for an equity investment
would be difficult.

Boucher and Stoddard again set to work to figure out how cash-poor tribes
could purchase a stake in their rapidly growing and cash-hungry company.
Together they devised another innovative financial mechanism to turn this
seemingly intractable situation into a mutually beneficial outcome for both
parties. The *Native*Energy entrepreneurs proposed a transfer of shares to
COUP to hold in trust for the tribes. These shares would be non-transferable
and subject to forfeiture if not purchased by the tribes within a set number of
years. To claim the shares, tribes could make tag-for-equity swaps. The plan
was that as new, tribal-owned wind projects were built, *Native*Energy would
make partial cash payments and partial equity payments for the green tags
produced. This would allow cash-poor tribes to buy into a vertically aligned
company, while still receiving some cash income streams for their green tags. At
the same time, it meant that *Native*Energy could reduce its cash-flow burden by
reducing its cost of goods. The goal of tribal ownership could be met, and both
sides were better off for it. In August 2005, using this purchasing mechanism,
*Native*Energy became majority-owned by Native Americans. Boucher reflected
on what this meant for the business he had worked so hard to build:

*I think it was a feeling that it was the right thing to do, but also, which
is a good thing, is that we think it's good business. We think it's a good*

*way to help differentiate ourselves from our competition. And this is
something we discussed openly with the tribes as we talked with them
that, you know, we're not simply at a social issue here, we're out to
create a strong, strong company, strong business, but one that supports
sustainable economic development for the tribes and others so that it's
very much a part of our mission. But we don't lose site of the business
aspects and it's because of that that it has a good future and it's why we
continue to promote the evolution of the company to be a tribal-owned,
eventually probably 100% tribal-owned operation.*

EXPANSION THROUGH CONSOLIDATION

*Native*Energy expanded to include green tags from sources other than wind,
such as farm methane abatement projects, as its sales continued to grow rapidly
within an increasingly sophisticated market. To cope with this rapid growth,
the founders gradually streamlined their approach by consolidating the vast
range of branded products into a smaller number of wide-ranging brands
and increasing their focus on corporate customers as the main drivers of this
growth. In their ever-present search for sources of cash to finance their growth,
Boucher and Stoddard decided to both revisit their search for private equity
investment and expand their income streams.

To attract private investment the company put together a new bid for
venture-capital investment. By August 2007 *Native*Energy was specifically
seeking investment from ethical investment funds and, in keeping with the
company ethos, from some of the wealthier Native American tribes that could
afford to invest in private equity. To expand income streams, the company
elected to add non-new-build (low additionality) green tags to its product line.
Although Boucher and Stoddard had resisted this move for a long time, they
eventually reconsidered this position because they felt they were excluding
themselves from too many revenue opportunities. They felt there was nothing
inherently wrong with lower-additionality green tags; they just were not as
beneficial as new-build tags. For this reason they continued to push the higher-
quality, new-build green tags by educating customers about the difference
between the two, while providing tags with lower additionality, if requested
by customers. Despite the usual assumption that growth must be bad for the
environment, Boucher and Stoddard felt that, because of their innovative
business model, growth at *Native*Energy is actually a good thing. As Boucher
explained:

Our growth is causing the right natural resources and new resources to be utilized and built, so I think growth is not bad in any way that it's normally considered in terms of business in manufacturing.

Opportunities and Challenges of Organizational Innovations

The entrepreneurs who founded *Native*Energy have built an enterprise that effectively contributes to environmental quality and the quality of life of disadvantaged communities. What enabled these entrepreneurs to make such meaningful and innovative contributions without introducing any new technological innovations? To explore this question, Table 17.1 examines three of *Native*Energy's organizational innovations and the direct effects they produced.

Table 17.1   Examples of *Native*Energy's organizational innovations

Organizational Innovation	Resulting Effects
'Forward streams' business model	• Supports the new construction of renewable energy projects with upfront payment covering up to 20 per cent of project costs • Provides customers with a mechanism to directly support growth of renewable energy production • Provides company with a market-based revenue stream and quality-based market differentiation
'Decouple-recouple' marketing approach	• Enables nationwide participation in the voluntary offsets market for green tag producers and customers • Expands public awareness of electricity-related emissions to include many other carbon-emitting activities • Gives the company increased market penetration
'Tags-for-equity' financing mechanism for tribal buy-in	• Provides cash-poor tribes with the opportunity to acquire an ownership stake in a vertically aligned company • Provides the company with investment for growth and relieves cash-flow stress by lowering the cost of goods • Adds additional value to green tags and provides additional market differentiation

These examples demonstrate the importance of innovations in organizational design for sustainable development. Although technology – in this case, renewable energy technology – was a critical component, it was the innovations in organizing that determined the nature, extent and effectiveness of change for sustainable development and, just as importantly, who reaped the benefits of the enhanced well-being it afforded. For *Native*Energy, the major challenges to be overcome were organizational and institutional constraints on the way in which energy is produced and used. Long-time *Native*Energy employee Billy Connelly explained:

> *We're in a position … to address the most significant problem of our time in an effective way because … we not only know what the problem is, we know what the solutions are. And, we're capable of implementing them.'*

What is significant about these innovations is that they are designed in a way so as to produce outcomes in which benefits to the environment, organizational stakeholders and the enterprise itself are mutually supportive and reinforce one another. While this is no easy achievement, considering the strong incentives for organizations to compartmentalize goals (Tilley and Parrish 2006), balancing the interests of the 'self' and the 'other' where the 'other' includes both social and environmental interests seems to be the hallmark of successful sustainability entrepreneurship (Parrish 2008; Schlange 2006; Young and Tilley 2006).[6] In fact, the synergies between these differing interests are often so strong that the entrepreneurs have difficulty identifying any one overriding rationale for their approach. Indeed, the overriding rationale seems to be precisely the synergy of the outcomes achieved as evidenced by Stoddard's reflection on *Native*Energy's unique business model and marketing approach:

> *On a personal level it is most definitely not simply another marketing tool. It happens to be a marketing tool, and an effective one. But I recall my feelings out at the Rosebud turbine dedication and seeing the people, seeing the communities – that was the proudest moment of my professional career, was seeing that that turbine was up and running and knowing that I'd helped play a material role in making that happen through NativeEnergy. It's very rewarding to me personally that it helps people in need, as well as the environment. You know, whether one outweighs the other I don't know.*

The ability of the entrepreneurs to obtain these results through bold, new organizational innovations reflects other research on entrepreneurship and

---

6   Parrish (2008) explores the unique cognitive design principles employed by successful sustainability entrepreneurs. It is this unique approach to problem-solving, termed 'perpetual reasoning', that enables sustainability entrepreneurs to accomplish this careful balancing act in organization design.

new organization formation which suggests that new enterprises tend to demonstrate greater innovations in organizing (Katz and Gartner 1988), and that these early developments are crucial to the long-term performance of the enterprise (Bamford, Dean and McDougall 1999; Boeker 1989; Eisenhardt and Schoonhoven 1990; Stinchcombe 1965). For example, Miles and Randolph found that 'choices made early in the development of organizations serve both to shape their enduring character and to constrain the range of options available to them in later stages of organizational life' (1980, p. 45).

But while organizational innovations provide new possibilities for building strong enterprises that make substantial inroads towards sustainable development, they can also create additional obstacles for entrepreneurs. As Aldrich and Fiol have suggested:

> ... among the many problems facing innovative entrepreneurs, their relative lack of legitimacy is especially critical, as both entrepreneurs and crucial stakeholders may not fully understand the nature of the new ventures, and their conformity to established institutional rules may still be in question. (Aldrich and Fiol 1994, p. 645)

In *Native*Energy's case, the business model was too innovative, too unlike anything else in the industry, to be eligible for quality certification by most existing third-party certifiers. Certification is an important source of credibility in this industry, and being excluded from this institutionalized mechanism for building trust could have been a fatal blow to a new and struggling enterprise. This suggests that organizational design innovations can create difficulty for sustainability entrepreneurs because those designs do not align with existing institutional arrangements. By their nature, institutions are geared towards conventional practices and are unable to accommodate innovative approaches, even when those innovations offer better solutions. However, in recognition of *Native*Energy's achievements, there are indications that the 'forward streams' model is emerging as a new standard for industry practice.

Conclusion

This case demonstrates the important role that entrepreneurs can play in advancing sustainable development. As innovators of human organization, entrepreneurs instigate changes in enterprises, markets, industries and other social institutions. *Native*Energy's entrepreneurs used their values, experience, vision and creativity to rethink accepted practices by developing an innovative business model, marketing approach and financing strategy that contributed to sustainable development by addressing pressing ecological and social concerns in a way that also satisfied the needs of the enterprise. Through these innovations they further contributed to the evolving dynamics of the renewable energy industry. When, like *Native*Energy's founders, entrepreneurs embrace the full range of means and ends for sustainable development, they can construct enterprises that survive and thrive by contributing to human well-being and the functioning of ecological systems. While these enterprises bring immediate benefits to the stakeholders and regional ecosystems in which their operations are based, they also contribute to restructuring larger human activity systems. The value of expert or 'mature' sustainability entrepreneurs rests not in their ability to build any particular type of enterprise, but in their ability to transcend the confines of present realities by producing new possibilities for realizing sustainable human development.

References

Aldrich, H.E. and Fiol, C.M. (1994) 'Fools Rush In? The Institutional Context of Industry Creation', *Academy of Management Review*, Vol. 19, No. 4, pp. 645–670.

Bamford, C.E., Dean, T.J. and McDougall, P.P. (1999) 'An Examination of the Impact of Initial Founding Conditions and Decision upon the Performance of New Bank Start-ups', *Journal of Business Venturing*, Vol. 15, pp. 253–277.

Beale, C.L. (1996) 'The Ethnic Dimensions of Persistent Poverty in Rural and Small-Town Areas' in L.L. Swanson (ed.) *Racial/Ethnic Minorities in Rural Areas: Progress and Stagnation, 1980–90*, Economic Research Services (USDA), Washington, DC.

Boeker, W. (1989) 'Strategic Change: The Effects of Founding and History', *Academy of Management Journal*, Vol. 32, No. 3, pp. 489–515.

Clean Air – Cool Planet. (2006) *A Consumer's Guide to Carbon Offsets*, Clean Air – Cool Planet, Portsmouth, NH.

Dimov, D. (2007) 'Beyond the Single-Person, Single-Insight Attribution in Understanding Entrepreneurial Opportunities', *Entrepreneurship Theory and Practice*, Vol. 31, No. 5, pp. 713–731.

Eisenhardt, K.M. and Schoonhoven, C.B. (1990) 'Organizational Growth: Linking Founding Team, Strategy, Environment, and Growth among U.S. Semiconductor Ventures, 1978–1988' *Administrative Science Quarterly*, Vol. 35, pp. 504–529.

Elgin, D. (1994) 'Building a Sustainable Species-Civilization: A Challenge of Culture and Consciousness', *Futures*, Vol. 26, No. 2, pp. 234–245.

Holt, E. and Bird, L. (2005) *Emerging Markets for Renewable Energy Certificates: Emerging Opportunities and Challenges*, National Renewable Energy Laboratory, Golden, CO.

Katz, D. and Gartner, W.B. (1988) 'Properties of Emerging Organizations', *Academy of Management Review*, Vol. 13, No. 3, pp. 429–441.

Kottak, C.P. (1999) 'The New Ecological Anthropology', *American Anthropologist*, Vol. 101, No. 1, pp. 23–35.

McMullen, J.S. and Shepherd, D.A. (2006) 'Entrepreneurial Action and the Role of Uncertainty in the Theory of the Entrepreneur', *Academy of Management Review*, Vol. 31, No. 1, pp. 132–152.

Miles, R.H. and Randolph, W.A. (1980) 'Influence of Organizational Learning Styles on Early Development' in J.R. Kimberly and R.H. Miles (eds) *The Organizational Life Cycle*, Jossey-Bass, San Francisco, CA.

Norgaard, R.B. (1994) *Development Betrayed: The End of Progress and a Coevolutionary Revisioning of the Future*, Routledge, New York.

Parrish, B.D. (2007) 'Designing the Sustainable Enterprise', *Futures*, Vol. 39, No. 7, pp. 846–860.

Parrish, B.D. (2008) 'Sustainability Entrepreneurship: Design Principles, Processes, and Paradigms', PhD thesis, University of Leeds, UK.

Ranson, S., Hinings B. and Greenwood, R. (1980) 'The Structuring of Organizational Structures', *Administrative Science Quarterly*, Vol. 25, No. 1, pp. 1–17.

Sarason, Y., Dean, T. and Dillard, J.F. (2006) 'Entrepreneurship as the Nexus of Individual and Opportunity: A Structuration View', *Journal of Business Venturing*, Vol. 21, pp. 286–305.

Sarasvathy, S.D. (2001) 'Causation and Effectuation: Toward a Theoretical Shift from Economic Inevitability to Entrepreneurial Contingency', *Academy of Management Review*, Vol. 26, No. 2, pp. 243–263.

Schlange, L.E. (2006) 'What Drives Sustainable Entrepreneurs?', *Applied Business and Entrepreneurship Association International Conference*, Kona, HI, USA, 16–20 November.

Stinchcombe, A.L. (1965) 'Social Structure and Organizations' in J.G. March (ed.) *Handbook of Organizations*, Rand McNally, Chicago, pp. 142–193.

Thorpe, R., Gold, J., Holt, R. and Clarke, J. (2006) 'Immaturity: The Constraining of Entrepreneurship', *International Small Business Journal*, Vol. 24, No. 3, pp. 232–250.

Tilley, F. and Parrish, B.D. (2006) 'From Poles to Wholes: Facilitating an Integrated Approach to Sustainable Entrepreneurship', *World Review of*

Entrepreneurship, Management and Sustainable Development, Vol. 2, No. 4, pp. 281–294.

Western, D. (2001) 'Human-Modified Ecosystems and Future Evolution', *Proceedings of the National Academy of Sciences of the United States of America*, Vol. 98, No. 10, pp. 5458–5465.

Young, W. and Tilley, F. (2006) 'Can Businesses Move Beyond Efficiency? The Shift Toward Effectiveness and Equity in the Corporate Sustainability Debate', *Business Strategy and the Environment*, Vol. 15, No. 6, pp. 402–415.

18

The Mimosa Project[1]

Kumba Jallow

ABSTRACT

This case study tracks the progress made by two 'green entrepreneurs' in setting up a small business venture near Leicester in the United Kingdom – the Mimosa Project – which aimed to be environmentally, as well as economically, successful. The case study charts the entrepreneurial processes involved and examines how individuals who show the characteristics of entrepreneurship develop and establish themselves and their business. In addition, the case study describes the processes involved in setting up and delivering an environmental service – garden waste collection for later composting – and the challenges for environmental management in the organization itself.

The business sought internal integrity by addressing environmental management issues, and wished to promote environmental issues by carrying out 'green' projects. The case also demonstrates that green entrepreneurs are in many ways similar to economic entrepreneurs, but may need additional resilience in order to balance the economic and environmental requirements of a green business. Although the entrepreneurs were successful in developing an organization that fulfilled their model, their long-term aims were not achieved, and the case examines the lessons to be learnt when two entrepreneurial personalities attempt to work together.

Introduction

The Mimosa Project was set up in 1998 by two individuals who wished to demonstrate that environmental and economic principles could sit side-by-side and be combined to create an effective organization which would be capable of delivering environmental projects, as well as being sustainable in the long term. Both of the people involved had experience in the business and the environmental fields to a greater or lesser degree, and both demonstrated

---

1 This chapter was originally published under the author's former name, Leigh Holland.

characteristics of entrepreneurial ability. The question was raised – could they work together in an effective way to deliver the proposed project?

Environmental Entrepreneurship in Action: Two People, One Goal

The two people involved in this case came together because of a desire to promote a 'greener' way of carrying on business and to demonstrate that economic and environmental goals could both be achieved. Both were of the mind that local enterprises could develop environmental solutions to local problems and that such enterprises had the potential for greater integration into local community affairs. In effect this follows Schumacher's (1973) 'small is beautiful' philosophy and is a more useful analysis for explaining the development of green entrepreneurial activity than the market-driven economic models (Burns 2001). It has also been recognized that entrepreneurial activity can help to achieve social objectives, especially where this is responsive to changes in societal demand for services and products (Austin, Stevenson and Wei-Skillern 2006) – in this interpretation, in demands for greener products and services. Different models of social entrepreneurship have been developed to explain the types or forms of entrepreneurial activity – these generally fit into three main types: not-for-profit organizations with business-style activities to finance their social operations; for-profit organizations which hope to show social benefits in their 'bottom line' (a dual or triple bottom line as discussed by Peredo and McLean 2005; Weerawardena and Mort 2005; Thompson and Doherty 2006); and partnerships of either or both types with other public organizations that are engaged in social activities (Dorado 2006). This range of forms is also echoed in the work of Dart (2004), who argues that social enterprises are business-like forms of traditional voluntary-sector organizations, Thompson and Doherty (2006) and Vega and Kidwell (2007) who also discuss the 'think global, act local' philosophy of green entrepreneurs. Dixon and Clifford (2007) also pick up on the term 'ecopreneur'.

There were two entrepreneurs involved – myself and Brian Williams. My involvement arose out a dual motivation – to be involved in green entrepreneurial activity and to be part of an action research project in my 'other life' as an academic. Originally I studied for a degree in plant science at university, but upon graduation in 1979 I turned to a professional career in accounting, working for a medium-sized firm of chartered accountants in the West Midlands, UK while studying to qualify as an accountant myself.

The accountancy practice gave me experience of a range of accounting areas, including tax, audit, consultancy and accounts preparation for a variety of public and private enterprises. In 1990 I changed career direction again and began working as an academic at De Montfort University (originally Leicester Polytechnic). Hence I had been used to the business paradigm – profit-oriented enterprises with short- and long-term survival plans – but had also worked with not-for-profit and voluntary organizations (for instance, since 1996 I have been a trustee of Studentforce for Sustainability, a charity placing young people in environmentally-related work to enhance their employment prospects). I therefore had an interest and knowledge of how these types of non-profit organization could function alongside more 'traditional' business activities. I also had a long-standing interest in environmental issues, was a campaigner for various charities, such as Friends of the Earth, and was keen to explore how green principles could sit alongside business thinking. Finally, I brought all this together in a PhD based on the mechanisms of engagement with sustainability.

Brian had little formal education post-secondary school. His working background had been in the voluntary sector, working with disadvantaged young people and with women's refuges, before moving into local authority housing department, with responsibility for voluntary housing projects. From these experiences Brian developed a strong awareness of community development and social inclusion issues. In order to develop his commercial understanding, he then moved on to running his own business. In 1990 he set up the Williams Horse-Drawn Carriage Company, a firm that was created to provide horse-drawn vehicles using heavy (Shire) horses to a range of clients – organizational (for instance, community organizations) or individual (such as wedding parties). These have operated in a number of settings: historic trips, weddings, community outings and fetes and festivals, and as part of self-development projects for people with learning disabilities. Although the business was set up to run along commercial lines, there was often an emphasis on the community development aspects of the work. This reflected Brian's own thinking that small businesses could move away from their image of being economically driven, with profit maximization seen as their main rationale (see, for instance, Owen 1992; Holland 1999). Because of his background in non-commercial organizations, Brian understood the conflicts that could arise between meeting community needs and delivering financial benefits to the owners of a business. He wished to continue to operate his company because it had an identity in Leicester, but he also wanted to develop a more community-based organization that carried out environmental projects. As a result, he ran both organizations separately in terms of structure, but shared the livestock resources between the two.

Already well-known in the community for his activities with the horses (anyone who has seen two large horses 'pulling' a wedding carriage or a charabanc usually doesn't forget the scene), Brian felt that the promotional aspect of the proposed green collection scheme would be well supported by the use of such 'gentle giants'.

A good deal of research now exists on the motivational aspects of beginning such an enterprise, and this research indicates that the entrepreneur's ideological orientation and external influences (the existence of social capital in the form of networks, for example) are both important factors (Spear 2006). Both of these factors were evident in Mimosa. We were also typical of their genre in many ways. They were innovative, self-motivated, had vision and flair (Hemingway 2005), were good communicators and networkers (Dorado 2006), and were proactive and willing to take risks (Weerawardena and Mort 2005).

However, we were also less motivated by financial gain than by a desire to make a difference to the way in which society acted and to show their commitment to environmental concerns (Bennett 1991; Bolton and Thompson 2000; Dixon and Clifford 2007). This de-prioritizing of financial success is a source of some of the tensions in developing a green business, because the commitment to a greener future must be balanced against the need for some form of economic return in both the short and long term, in order for environmental measures to be delivered and maintained.

Creating the New Business Venture

Household waste collection and recycling activities in the United Kingdom are coordinated by local authorities but subcontracted to private-sector firms. Each local authority determines the service it will provide, and there are several variations on recycling activities. Many authorities are now providing a kerbside recycling scheme of some sort – for instance, Leicester in the East Midlands has a 'green box' scheme which recycles paper and plastics and is collected by the same firm that collects household waste. In other areas, such as Birmingham (the second largest city in England), a green waste scheme has been added to the other recycling services offered to residents. The UK central government has set targets of materials that it requires to be recycled, and each local authority must establish strategies to meet these targets.

We believed that there was a large potential for innovation in the recycling sector, particularly in domestic recycling. Innovative opportunity can arise from a variety of different sources: the unexpected, incongruities, a process need, demographics, industry and market structures, changes in perception and new knowledge (Drucker 1985). Certainly there was new knowledge to be tapped into with regard to domestic recycling – how recycled materials could be dealt with and how new systems were being developed around the United Kingdom in domestic collection services – which would lead to the need for new processes (Gliedt and Parker 2007). In addition, people were beginning to change their views about the acceptability of recycling activities, and we felt that this new perception could be turned into action if a service was provided that was attractive and easy to use. We believed that we could generate value by exploiting change (Walley and Taylor 2002; Dixon and Clifford 2007) – in this case, the change in the requirements imposed on local authorities to increase their recycling rates. If we could deliver this in a new way, we would enhance value in both economic and environmental terms.

The legal structure of the business was that of a company limited by guarantee, which required it to reinvest its surpluses into the organization. We chose this mechanism because we felt that it best reflected the ethos of the activities that would be carried out and would be better accepted by prospective local authority partners. It also enabled other people to become involved at a later date as members of the company, and it was anticipated that this would increase the democracy of the organization. This tends to conflict with the accepted view of entrepreneurs as driven by ego and as leaders, not group actors (Bolton and Thompson 2000). However, this challenge was recognized and was considered as part of a new approach to social business. Indeed, the term 'team entrepreneurship' (Gliedt and Parker 2007, p. 542) would apply here.

The company thus formed was called The Mimosa Project Ltd, named after a tree that is also known as 'the sensitive plant'; this title was chosen to reflect the fact that the company wished to be sensitive in its operations to both nature and to humans.

In order to assess the potential for success, we carried out a SWOT analysis (as suggested by Bolton and Thompson 2000) to examine both the personal qualities we brought to the project and the external factors we needed to consider. This acted as a focus for strategic development as well as a means of assessing the individual schemes we developed (see Figure 18.1).

The SWOT analysis enabled us to consider how to turn weaknesses and threats into strengths and opportunities. For instance, we produced a leaflet describing the business's activities to distribute in the communities, so that they could be reassured about horse welfare issues. We also formed alliances with private-sector organizations in the waste industry (such as the waste collection subcontractor in Leicester) with a view to working alongside them in the future and sought funding from appropriate funding bodies such as those under the Landfill Tax Credit Scheme. The Mimosa Project had good links with the local authorities in Leicester and Leicestershire and developed partnerships with both to facilitate new projects. This was helped by Brian's previous work in local government and his understanding of their structure.

We felt that our organization had a unique approach in that it was relatively small-scale and that other organizations working in the field were therefore not

Strengths	Weaknesses
• Commitment of individuals • Desire to demonstrate that an environmental business is possible • Innovation and vision • Knowledge of environmental issues • Business experience • Contacts with local authority • Experience of other non-profit organizations	• Lack of funding • Other time pressures • No track record in this area • Lack of acceptance of this type of business by other organizations • Negative perceptions of business activities – For example, horse welfare issues
Opportunities	**Threats**
• Recycling recognized as important by government • Partnerships encouraged via government and local authority sustainable development charters • Sustainable development recognized as important • Lack of facilities provided by the local authority • Potential to provide a different model of working • Increasing awareness of environmental issues	• Private-sector competition • Long-term survival • Conflicts of interest between entrepreneurs • Recycling may lose priority in society • Risks may be too great • Uncertain future with partners • Change in political outlook

Figure 18.1   SWOT analysis

in direct competition. For instance, Groundwork, a Leicester-based charitable consultancy and advocacy organization, ran recycling activities on a much broader scale, encouraging local people to deliver recyclable material to its facilities and advising businesses on waste minimization. This was similar in turn to the work of Leicestershire Waste Minimisation Association, which acted as a waste club for small companies in the area. Hence, whilst there was much innovative work being carried out, there was room for further development, especially where the approach combined education and awareness with practical environmental action. It was this approach that the Mimosa Project emphasized.

The business was set up to carry out a range of community recycling schemes and act in partnership with local authorities and private-sector firms, in line with the partnership principles of sustainable development. The proposed activities of Mimosa centred on two aspects – environmental issues as articulated by recycling activities and the use of horse-drawn vehicles as a means of 'being different' and of raising awareness of transport-derived environmental issues such as pollution. The schemes that began to be developed included:

- city-wide kerbside collection of recyclable materials, using the existing system but with horse-drawn collection;

- community gardening using an unused allotment space;

- environmental education using recycling activities to frame the issues;

- developing a multipurpose recycling centre with an arts theme;

- rural collection of green waste.

It is the last scheme which is described in detail in the following sections.

These activities were supported by a number of people who worked for the company on a subcontract basis – particularly a woman skilled in grooming and horse management, who was able to drive the transport and had an excellent understanding of horse welfare. Other people came on board to help with material collection and equipment maintenance when necessary; permanent employees were not recruited. Most supporters were sympathetic to the aims of the organization and held views similar to our own, which helped to develop a sense of common purpose.

The business operated from a site just outside Leicester, the United Kingdom's first Environment City which, as such, has a history of promoting environmental initiatives; the county of Leicestershire also encourages green practices and has supported a number of enterprises in the region. Within Leicestershire there are a number of borough councils, and the scheme described here was supported by the officers and councillors of Charnwood Borough Council which covers the area north of Leicester.

Environmental Management Practices within the Business

In order to 'practise what we preach' we felt that it was important to have sound environmental management practices in place, so that the communities in which we operated could see that our activities were sensitive to the environment and reflected the ethos of the organization. This not only added credibility to the business and its activities, but also reflected our own views and vision (see Figure 18.2).

The Green Waste Scheme in Detail

The first scheme carried out, which is used here to demonstrate the activities of the business, was the collection of garden and green kitchen waste from households in three villages, using horse-drawn trailers. A partnership was formed with the local authority. The collection service was designed to cover three rural villages in the East Midlands. Two of these villages (A and B) were arranged around a through road and were relatively compact; the third (C) was more extensively developed and had a more complex road structure. This village layout had an effect on the collection system and presented some difficulties in access. In addition, the third village had a central composting collection point which had been in situ for a number of years and was regularly used by the inhabitants.

Although the local authority already promoted home composting, it wished to provide further facilities by separately collecting green waste and thus avoiding disposal to landfill.

In a practical sense, the scheme involved drawing a trailer and hitch-cart around the residential areas of the three villages using Shire horses, collecting bags of green waste put out by householders and then delivering the collected

Because we see sustainability as integrating the economic, the environment and the social, we are committing ourselves to policies which help to address these issues. In each of these areas, we see the issues as being:

ECONOMIC

To make enough money fairly to:

- operate the company on a sound financial basis;
- generate profitable growth;
- increase the company's value so that its objectives are fulfilled;
- pay all employees a fair wage;
- have financially equitable dealings with our commercial partners;
- support local economic growth;
- provide funds for employees to set up and run community initiatives.

ENVIRONMENTAL

To work towards a healthier environment by:

- maximizing energy and waste efficiency procedures;
- having clean air practices;
- being sensible about resource use;
- being responsible and sensitive in its relationship with the communities in which it resides and operates;
- practising sound health and safety procedures;
- maintaining all land, buildings and vehicles in a way that such maintenance has little detrimental effect on the environment;
- respecting and understanding the ecosystems in which the company operates so that harm is reduced;
- raising the awareness of the environmental effects of doing business in the community;
- working towards continuous improvement in all aspects of this policy.

SOCIAL

To be fair to everyone who comes into contact with us by:

- ensuring that in all aspects of the company's work, discrimination in any form is recognized and mitigated;
- continually updating the skills of the workforce, so that their knowledge and understanding continues to develop;
- widening the scope of employment and employability;
- encouraging employees and the community to influence the development of the company and its policies;
- working towards greater understanding of the social effects of doing business in the community.
- the encouragement of recycling practices amongst the residents;
- the possibility of promoting other environmental schemes and ideas;
- more community partnership and a feeling of ownership of both problems and solutions; and
- encouraging alternative ways of working.

Figure 18.2   Company policies

material to a local authority composting facility. The environmental benefits of such a scheme involved:

- a reduction in air pollution;

- a reduction in landfill use and therefore volume.

The horses covered approximately 21 miles during each day of collection. The journeys round the villages were planned so that the most efficient routes were taken. Village A was quite compact with the heart of the village centred around its Parish Centre, although there was a large lane which was set apart. Village B was the smallest village and in many ways the easiest to collect from, as the houses were located in roads branching off the main street. Village C had many small roads and cul-de-sacs, and although the horses and hitch cart could easily manoeuvre in this setting, developing an efficient route was difficult. The horses, although generally fit, were tired by the distance they had to cover and suffered some discomfort because of the equipment used. An efficient use of the horses was important to remove the necessity of using fossil-fuel transport.

The business venture also suffered from a poor choice of pricing strategies. Whilst the business did cover its direct variable costs of providing the collection and delivering the material to the local authority composting facility, it failed to charge for all fixed costs and to generate a profit. With hindsight, there should have been an element of fixed costs built into the charge to cover the greater amount of management time needed to set up and operate the scheme, and further funding should have been sought for capital expenditure. This was important because a poor financial strategy endangered the organization's survival.

Participation by residents in the scheme was somewhat variable. This factor had not been anticipated, and there had been no prior market research undertaken to assess this in advance. It was therefore unclear whether the low participation rate was due to the public's unwillingness to get involved or simply reflected a lack of awareness about the recycling venture.

Benefits and Weaknesses of the Trial Venture

The participation rate was disappointing in some areas and would have benefited from further publicity. However, in other areas participation was encouraging, and in places it was linked to the use of very visible horses – people were keen to see the horses in their road and felt part of the scheme because they were contributing to the horses' work. This, however, needed to be linked to the activity of recycling and to general environmental issues so that contributors could begin to appreciate that this was part of a wider policy on environmental and social issues. This was where the partnership approach was fruitfully exploited – the business had a physical visibility in the community, and the local authority had the financial resources to follow up with leafleting and other forms of publicity.

Some of the environmental benefits of collection were offset by the need to transport the material a long distance to the composting facility. This demonstrated the need for 'joined-up' thinking in reviewing environmental projects: to benefit from the collection of composting material, the production of compost should have taken place as near to the site of production as possible.

The trial highlighted a number of developmental issues to be dealt with if the service was to be offered more widely:

1.   Greater publicity at the beginning of the scheme was needed.

2.   Greater awareness by the public about composting in particular, and environmental issues generally, should have been a more apparent objective.

3.   More capital investment in appropriate technology was required.

4.   More investment in operational requirements was needed. Additional horses and skilled staff would have allowed greater involvement of horses and less reliance on vehicles.

5.   A combined approach to composting to encourage home schemes was needed, which could be balanced against the local authority's need to increase its recycling rates.

6.   Distances needed to be feasible and practical, and a balance between promotion and collection should have been established.

7.   Vehicle transport should have been kept to a minimum, so consideration of the location of the composting facility is important.

8.   Further research was needed to tease out the reasons behind lack of participation.

In any scheme of this nature there are balances to be achieved between economic, environmental and social aspects, and this is always difficult to assess. The usefulness of a business venture of this nature is that it enabled the issues to be identified and the alternatives to what is regarded as 'normal commercial practice' to be considered.

Conclusion: What Lessons Have Been Learnt?

The business developed projects in partnership with other organizations to deliver recycling services, but there were inherent difficulties within the organization itself which became insurmountable, and Brian and I eventually parted company. We encountered two main areas of difficulty: one which affected our own relationship and one which affected the long-term plans of the business.

The first problem was a clash of principles between us. Our vision and priorities were not completely in alignment – one of us was more environmentally concerned and the other was more traditionally focused on the economic aspects – so that when compromises between environmental and economic issues were needed, there was friction between two strong-minded and determined people which in the end could not be resolved. Walley's and Taylor's (2002) suggested typology may be useful here. They suggest that there is a difference in ecopreneurial behaviour between the innovative opportunist and the visionary champion.

Although we both exhibited elements of each type of behaviour, each was closer to one or the other type (see Figure 18.3). Brian, for example, was more of an opportunistic innovator, whereas I could be regarded as a champion of environmental concerns.

Another potential for conflict was our prior knowledge. We both had substantial experience to bring to the new enterprise, and the sharing of different skills can be beneficial (Thompson 2002). Prior knowledge is recognized as a mechanism for exploiting new opportunities (Dorado 2006), but if experience has to be shared, rather than being common to both entrepreneurs, this has the capacity to cause friction.

Figure 18.3   The Mimosa Project founders on the spectrum of ecopreneurial behaviour

The second issue revolved around the associated need to find a balance between the environmental outcomes and economic ones (Gliedt and Parker 2007) and the need to obtain funding for these. Many businesses of this kind – those which attempt to provide social and environmental objectives – seek funding from outside agencies in order to run services at what is effectively a subsidized rate. There is a conflict between the provision of outside funding and the need to become self-sufficient financially – a strategy that allows ecopreneurs to develop more capacity (Dorado 2006). Such a strategy, though recognized as important by us both, was not successfully developed. Seeking external public funding is time-consuming and difficult – the success rate is often around one successful application in ten. Nevertheless, funding is essential to carry out such projects, especially in the initial stages of development. At the same time an emphasis on the financial aspects of a project could either detract from or compromise the possible environmental outcomes, so a constant review is needed to ensure that the most appropriate balance is obtained. This balance is likely to shift from project to project and over time, so it is essential that operational procedures are always related back to strategic objectives.

Other issues that emerged related to external influences. Because partnerships formed the basis of most of the work carried out, it was important to be aware of the objectives of outside organizations and the personnel within them. Relationships need to be established, and this can take time. There is also a need to build a range of external stakeholders and partners, and the most successful enterprises have a wide range of these (Alvord, Brown and Letts 2004). The Mimosa Project relied on local authority contacts and networks. However, particularly with local authorities, political changes may affect officers' work or priorities, and projects can change in nature before the operational stage. Another aspect is that of acceptance – even officers of similar environmental commitment may have difficulty accepting a business organization that does not prioritize economic or financial issues. The relationship has to be based on trust.

Finally an organization which is based on an innovation culture needs to maintain a level of multiple innovations to retain its identity and maintain a competitive advantage (Keinelger 2002). The types of project that we wished to engage in required enough radical ideas to encourage uptake, but not such radicalism as to make them unacceptable. Achieving a balance between environmental innovation and workable schemes sometimes proved very difficult, and our vision was often challenged by this need for balance. It is very easy for entrepreneurs to believe that everyone thinks as they do, and then later be shown to be too far ahead of their contemporaries. Acceptability may be as important as radicalism.

Hence the trial was successful in itself – the local authority now runs green collection schemes (but with motorized collection vehicles) within its area, but the Mimosa Project no longer operates, having lost its entrepreneurs to other organizations.

References

Alvord, S.H., Brown, L.D. and Letts, C.W. (2004) 'Social Entrepreneurship and Societal Transformation: An Exploratory Study', *Journal of Applied Behavioural Science*, Vol. 40, No. 3, pp. 260–282.

Austin, J., Stevenson, H. and Wei-Skillern, J. (2006) 'Social and Commercial Entrepreneurship: Same, Different or Both?', *Entrepreneurship Theory and Practice*, Vol. 30, No. 1 (January), pp. 1–22.

Bennett, S.J. (1991) *Ecopreneuring*, John Wiley, New York.

Bolton, B. and Thompson, J. (2000) *Entrepreneurs: Talent, Temperament, Technique*, Butterworth, Oxford.

Burns, P. (2001) *Entrepreneurship and Small Business*, Palgrave, Basingstoke.

Dart, R. (2004) 'The Legitimacy of Social Enterprise', *Nonprofit Management and Leadership*, Vol. 14, No. 4, pp. 411–424.

Dixon, S.E.A. and Clifford, A. (2007) 'Ecopreneurship – A New Approach to Managing the Triple Bottom Line', *Journal of Organizational Change*, Vol. 20, No. 3, pp. 326–345.

Dorado, S. (2006) 'Social Entrepreneurial Ventures: Different Values So Different Process of Creation, No?', *Journal of Developmental Entrepreneurship*, Vol. 11, No. 4, pp. 319–343.

Drucker, P. (1985) *Innovation in Entrepreneurship – Practice and Principles*, Heinemann, London.

Gliedt, T. and Parker, P. (2007) 'Green Community Entrepreneurship: Creative Destruction in the Social Economy', *International Journal of Social Economics*, Vol. 34, No. 8, pp. 538–553

Hemingway, C. (2005) 'Personal Values as a Catalyst for Corporate Social Entrepreneurship', *Journal of Business Ethics*, Vol. 60, pp. 233–249.

Holland, L. (1999) 'Horse-Power: Urban Domestic Recycling and the Development of Sustainable Local Community Structures', *Sustainable Development*, Vol. 7, No. 1, pp. 47–53.

Keinelger, B.H. (2002) 'A Comparative Analysis of Corporate Entrepreneurship Orientation between Selected Firms in the Netherlands and the USA', *Economic and Regional Development*, Vol. 14, No. 1, pp. 67–87.

Owen, D. (ed.) (1992) *Green Reporting: Accountancy and the Challenge of the Nineties*, Chapman and Hall, London.

Peredo, A.M. and McLean, M. (2006) 'Social Entrepreneurship: A Critical Review of the Concept', *Journal of World Business*, Vol. 41, pp. 56–65.

Schumacher, E.F. (1973) *Small is Beautiful*, Abacus, London.

Spear, R. (2006) 'Social Entrepreneurship: A Different Model?', *International Journal of Social Economics*, Vol. 33, Nos 5–6, pp. 399–410.

Thompson, J. (2002) 'The World of the Social Entrepreneur', *International Journal of Public Sector Management*, Vol. 15, No. 5, pp. 412–431.

Thompson, J. and Doherty, B. (2006) 'The Diverse World of Social Enterprise: A Collection of Social Enterprise Stories', *International Journal of Social Economics*, Vol. 33, Nos 5–6, pp. 361–375.

Vega, G. and Kidwell, R. (2007) 'Towards a Typology of New Venture Creators: Similarities and Contrasts between Business and Social Entrepreneurs', *New England Journal of Entrepreneurship*, Vol. 10, No. 2, pp. 15–28.

Walley, E.E. and Taylor, D.W. (2002) 'Opportunists, Champions, Mavericks …', *Greener Management International*, Vol. 38 (Summer), pp. 31–43.

Weerawardena, J. and Mort, G.S. (2005) 'Investigating Social Entrepreneurship: A Multidimensional Model' *Journal of World Business*, Vol. 41, pp. 21–35.

Index